## Praise for *Estate Planning (in Plain English)*®

"*Estate Planning (in Plain English)*® is an invaluable tool to help you collect the information your attorney needs to prepare your estate plan and to help your family put your plan into action. I strongly recommend that you add this book to your library."

—Michael Cragun, Utah State Tax Commissioner

"When the time for transitioning to the Great Beyond approaches, over one-half of all Americans follow in the shadows of actor James Dean, business mogul Howard Hughes, and President Abraham Lincoln and perish without a will, leaving a mess for others to sort. Better for your loved ones if you read DuBoff and Bryan's *Estate Planning (in Plain English)*® and organize your estate so that others don't have to. This treasure of a book, written in language for the lay audience, even explains how to dispose of your digital assets. Buy this book and start happily planning your estate!"

—Sherri Burr, Dickason Chair in Law Emerita, University of New Mexico School of Law, coauthor of *Wills and Trusts in a Nutshell*

"In my tradition, money is considered neither evil nor good. What matters is how one gets it and how one uses it. As always, we have an obligation to be responsible and thoughtful stewards of the resources with which we are entrusted. *Estate Planning (in Plain English)*® is an indispensable guide to doing just that. It will prove very useful to those of us who wish to put our affairs in order and thus spare those we love an unnecessary burden."

—Rabbi David Kosak

"Having an up-to-date estate plan is one of the greatest gifts you can give your loved ones. Without one, you leave unintended burdens and potentially divisive pain for those you love and have left behind. *Estate Planning (in Plain English)*® offers a practical road map for addressing all the issues in developing a solid estate plan, from the simplest estate with few assets to consideration of more complex matters that need to be addressed."

—Dan Schutte, composer-in-residence, University of San Francisco

T0003399

"Death is certain, and disability is likely. Unfortunately, the majority of individuals plan for neither. In *Estate Planning (in Plain English)*®, experienced practitioners Leonard D. DuBoff and Amanda Bryan provide expert guidance in layperson-friendly language on the multitude of reasons everyone needs an estate plan so that their wishes and desires are followed. Then, they succinctly explain the basic techniques available to carry out their intent. I am confident readers of this book will be motived to take action to make the inevitable transition more palatable for themselves, their family members, and their friends."

—Gerry Beyer, Governor Preston E. Smith Regents
Professor of Law, Texas Tech University School of Law

"There is no doubt that when one is caught up in the never-ending wave of a wide range of emotions upon the news and reality of a loved one's death, dealing with the practical parts of a loved one's passing is made more complicated and overwhelming. A sense of loss brings a family and gathering of friends into a strange new land, where there is no ready guide for understanding our next step on the journey of life. That's why it is incredibly helpful to have one part of the 'next step' of life's pilgrimage figured out before the loss of a loved one. *Estate Planning (in Plain English)*® does just that: it provides an incredibly helpful, easy-to-read road map for what to do, today, before a loved one's death."

—Brett Webb-Mitchell, ordained
Presbyterian Church (USA) pastor, Portland, Oregon

# Estate Planning

## (in Plain English)®

# Estate Planning

## (in Plain English)®

**Leonard D. DuBoff** *and* **Amanda Bryan**

### Attorneys-at-Law

**ALLWORTH PRESS**
NEW YORK

**Disclaimer:** This book is designed to provide accurate and authoritative information with respect to the subject matter covered. It is sold with the understanding that the authors and publisher are not engaged in rendering legal or other professional services. At the time of publication, this book is accurate regarding the legal and tax material discussed. However, both national and state laws change. If legal advice or other expert assistance is required, the services of a competent attorney, accountant, or other professional should be sought. While every attempt is made to provide accurate information, the author or publisher cannot be held accountable for errors or omissions.

Copyright © 2020 by The DuBoff Law Group, PC

All rights reserved. Copyright under Berne Copyright Convention, Universal Copyright Convention, and Pan American Copyright Convention. No part of this book may be reproduced, stored in a retrieval system, or transmitted in any form, or by any means, electronic, mechanical, photocopying, recording or otherwise, without the express written consent of the publisher, except in the case of brief excerpts in critical reviews or articles. All inquiries should be addressed to Allworth Press, 307 West 36th Street, 11th Floor, New York, NY 10018.

Allworth Press books may be purchased in bulk at special discounts for sales promotion, corporate gifts, fund-raising, or educational purposes. Special editions can also be created to specifications. For details, contact the Special Sales Department, Allworth Press, 307 West 36th Street, 11th Floor, New York, NY 10018 or info@skyhorsepublishing.com.

24 23 22 21 20    5 4 3 2 1

Published by Allworth Press, an imprint of Skyhorse Publishing, Inc. 307 West 36th Street, 11th Floor, New York, NY 10018. Allworth Press® is a registered trademark of Skyhorse Publishing, Inc.®, a Delaware corporation.

www.allworth.com

Cover design by Mary Belibasakis

Library of Congress Cataloging-in-Publication Data

Names: DuBoff, Leonard D, author. | Bryan, Amanda, author.
Title: Estate planning (in plain English) / Leonard D DuBoff and Amanda Bryan, attorneys-at- law.
Description: New York : Allworth Press, 2020. | Series: In plain english | Includes index.
Identifiers: LCCN 2019059403 (print) | LCCN 2019059404 (ebook) | ISBN 9781621537267 (trade paperback) | ISBN 9781621537274 (epub)
Subjects: LCSH: Estate planning--United States--Popular works.
Classification: LCC KF750.Z9 D83 2020 (print) | LCC KF750.Z9 (ebook) | DDC 332.024/016--dc23
LC record available at https://lccn.loc.gov/2019059403
LC ebook record available at https://lccn.loc.gov/2019059404

Print ISBN: 978-1-62153-726-7
eBook ISBN: 978-1-62153-727-4

Printed in the United States of America

# Dedication

To my mother, Millicent, and my father, Rubin, who provided me with the gift of life and the desire to use that gift effectively. To my mother-in-law, Cumi Elena Crawford, for her faith, trust, and inspiration, and to my wife, Mary Ann, for her enduring love and continuing support.

—Leonard D. DuBoff

To my children, Random, Grey, and Scout. You are as delightful, quirky, and compassionate as I could have wished for. Your love is my greatest treasure. And to my husband, Josh, for being my safe place and my other half.

—Amanda Bryan

# Table of Contents

# Acknowledgments

In order to assemble the vast quantity of statutes, cases, articles, and books that have become available on this topic, it was necessary to enlist the aid of numerous friends and colleagues. Their help is greatly appreciated, and some deserve special recognition.

Amanda and I would like to thank Greg Rogers of the accounting firm Rogers Financial Services and Tony H. Davidson of Tony H. Davidson CPA, PC for their time and expertise in reviewing the tax material in this book.

We are indebted to Gerry Beyer, Governor Preston E. Smith Regents Professor of Law at Texas Tech University School of Law, for allowing us to use portions of his material on cyber estate planning and administration in this book. We also appreciate the fact that he was kind enough to write a blurb.

We are honored to have a blurb written by Professor Sherri L. Burr, Dickason Chair in Law Emerita, at the University of New Mexico School of Law and coauthor of *Wills and Trusts in a Nutshell*.

We are also indebted to Dan Schutte, one of the St. Louis Jesuits and the composer of "Here I Am, Lord," one of the most popular pieces of Christian music available today and the creator of several works which help individuals with death and dying, for his review of the manuscript and useful recommendations. He was also kind enough to write a blurb for this book.

We are sincerely grateful to Michael Cragun, Tax Commissioner of the State of Utah, for the flattering blurb that he wrote and his helpful recommendations; and Rabbi Kosak, Senior Rabbi of one of the largest and most prestigious synagogues in the West, for the complimentary blurb he wrote.

We are also indebted to Tad Crawford, our editor Chamois Holschuh, and the entire Skyhorse Publishing staff for their help in publishing this volume. Not only were they instrumental in the publication of this work, they were also willing to review numerous copies of the manuscript and provide many valuable recommendations and suggestions.

Thanks also to our paralegals Francesca Hurd and Susana Fuentes for all of their assistance and recommendations.

We are indebted to Lynn Della, a long-standing friend, for her help in reviewing this manuscript, cleaning up numerous parts, and providing priceless recommendations.

Sherrey Meyer was kind enough to review this manuscript and recommend a number of helpful changes.

Tiffany Davidson, attorney at law, and Lauren Barnes, attorney at law, were gracious enough to review a draft of this manuscript and suggest numerous clarifications.

My brother, Michael H. DuBoff, attorney at law, was extremely helpful in reviewing several drafts of this manuscript and providing a number of useful recommendations.

I would also like to thank Colin Mackenzie, an attorney who worked for my law firm for a short time, for his assistance in reviewing the manuscript and providing recommendations. I would also like to thank Christopher Perea for his help in completing the final edit of this manuscript.

Amanda would like to thank her children, Random Gomm, Grey Gomm, and Scout Gomm, and her husband Josh Congdon for their patience and support during the writing process, giving up weekends and evenings with her and being okay with unfolded laundry and macaroni and cheese dinners during the initial writing of this book.

Leonard would like to thank his college English professor, Anne Lotham, for teaching him to write in plain English. He is also grateful for the support of his children and grandchildren. His son Robert and his daughter-in-law Bri Hunter have been very helpful with technology issues, and his daughter Colleen has been extremely creative with her graphic design skills. Her husband, Rudy, a lawyer who has recently joined our law firm, has been very helpful with research. Leonard is also grateful to his grandson Brian and Brian's fiancée Megan Randall for their personal assistance, and to the newest member of his family, his granddaughter Athena, for her cheerfulness. Leonard's late sister, Candise DuBoff Jones, JD, Northwestern School of Law, Lewis & Clark College, 1977; his late father, Rubin R. DuBoff; and his late mother, Millicent Barbara DuBoff, all provided him with the inspiration to create works such as this. Leonard valued his mother-in-law Cumi Elena Crawford's faith, trust, and inspiration, which helped him create this project.

Finally, Leonard would like to express his sincere gratitude and acknowledge the contribution to this project by his partner in law and in life, Mary Ann Crawford DuBoff. Without her, *Estate Planning (in Plain English)*® would never have become a reality.

# Introduction

When I first began writing the *Law (in Plain English)*® series more than four decades ago, my goal was to educate nonlawyers on the legal aspects of their businesses and professions. At the time, I was a full-time law professor and, as an educator, I felt that one of my missions was to provide educational tools. Later, as a full-time lawyer, I realized the importance of this series in educating my clients so that they could more effectively communicate with me. It became clear that the more knowledgeable my clients were about the myriad legal issues that they faced in their businesses and professions, the more effectively they could aid me in helping them. It is for this reason that I continue this series, and today there are *In Plain English*® books for writers, high-tech entrepreneurs, health-care professionals, craftspeople, gallery operators, photographers, small businesses, employers and employees, publishers, collectors, restaurants, nonprofit organizations, and now this universal volume for estate planning.

It is important to understand the genesis of this book. When Amanda Bryan was working for my law firm, assisting clients with estate planning problems, we realized how ill-prepared people were to discuss estate planning issues. We searched for a book to assist with this problem and were unable to find one that we believed would be useful for our clients. While there are many estate planning books available in the market, none provide the reader with clear, understandable explanations of the numerous complex issues that should be considered in estate planning. While there are numerous technical estate planning books, they are geared toward lawyers and not in plain English. The books available for nonlawyers are too limited. Further, none of the books we found are workbooks that allow the reader to collect all the necessary material to assist an estate planning lawyer when preparing an estate plan. In addition, none of the books contained material for the individuals who must deal with the estate after the person whose estate plan is involved has died. For these reasons, I began writing this book with Amanda's assistance. We spent numerous hours researching, revising, clarifying, and converting the manuscript into a clear and, hopefully, understandable book.

This book is not intended to be a substitute for the advice of estate planning professionals. Rather, it is designed to sensitize you to the issues that may require the aid of a qualified estate planning attorney or other expert. It is my sincere hope that this book will, like its predecessors in the series, be practical, useful, and readable. One of our goals in preparing this book is to enable the reader to identify potential problem areas and seek the aid of a skilled professional when necessary—or preferably before it becomes necessary—because it is quite common for individuals to postpone their estate plan for as long as possible (and far too often, too long).

Estate law is quite complex and rapidly evolving. The Internet has become a vehicle for communication and commerce, and the law has been scrambling to keep pace with technology. In writing this book, it was our intention to chronicle the law and restate it in a clear and understandable text that will aid the reader in understanding the current state of estate planning law. It is hoped that, by doing so, our readers will be able to more effectively communicate with their experts when developing and refining their estate plan, and provide a valuable resource for their survivors

—Leonard D. DuBoff
Portland, Oregon, July 2019

## PART I

# Building Your Estate Plan

# CHAPTER 1

# The Importance of Making an Estate Plan

When Aretha Franklin died in 2018, her family believed that she had died without a will. Without a will, her heirs were confused and conflicted, not knowing what the Queen of Soul's wishes were for her assets, her songs, or her memory. Over the course of the succeeding months, her family found two handwritten wills locked in a cabinet in her home. These wills were both dated from 2010. A short time later, a third will, also handwritten, but dated 2014, was found in the cushions of her couch. The wills were contradictory and difficult to decipher. Rather than resolving disputes between Franklin's friends and family, the documents raised new questions about who should represent the estate, as well as the validity and priority of the wills.

While most individuals will not die with a situation as complex as Aretha Franklin's, the lesson is clear—a comprehensive estate plan is important to reduce tension among your heirs, ease their grief at an already difficult time, and fulfill your wishes.

Like many people, you may be reluctant to think about planning for the disposition of your estate. The process brings up uncomfortable inevitabilities like death and, yes, as the saying goes—taxes. Thinking about *what* you will leave behind may bring up feelings of others' greed or your own inadequacy. Thinking about *who* you will leave behind may bring up feelings of fear and loss. You may have memories of deaths close to you and unresolved relationships. This book is designed to help you think through this process at your own pace. By the time you complete all of the reading and worksheets, you will be better able to meet with an estate planning attorney, explain your estate and your wishes in a clear and complete manner, and turn over the technical details to that attorney.

The unfortunate situation involving Terri Schiavo, who became a pawn in the battle between her family members, is a grim reminder of the importance of having an advance directive, also referred to as a living will or medical power of attorney. Schiavo was only twenty-six years old when she had a heart attack that ultimately left her in a persistent vegetative state. Her husband, Michael, who was her legal guardian, believed that his wife would not want her life to be prolonged artificially. Her parents disagreed and challenged the diagnosis and Michael's decision. A legal battle ensued. During that time, Schiavo's feeding was removed for a few days, only to be replaced, all pursuant to conflicting court orders. In the end, Michael ultimately prevailed and the feeding tube was removed. Schiavo died in 2005 at the age of forty-one.

An advance directive is a document that appoints an individual to make medical decisions on your behalf and states your wishes with respect to sustaining your life through artificial means. If Terri Schiavo had prepared such a document, her family would have been spared fifteen years of struggle. Federal law requires health-care facilities, such as hospitals receiving Medicare funds, to ask patients at the time they are admitted whether they have an advance directive; if they do, the facility must keep it on file.

While it is impossible to determine what specific situations might trigger an advance directive, it is vital for the representative identified in that document to determine whether you would wish to have your life sustained by artificial means, such as life-support systems or artificial feeding. The decision can be made by that individual by consulting with family, clergy, or an experienced attorney. Regardless, the person you identify to represent you in a medical emergency, usually a relative or very close friend, should already know your wishes.

Medical providers may also suggest to patients suffering from life-threatening conditions or who become seriously ill or frail and are toward the end of life that they complete a POLST form. A POLST form gives medical orders to emergency personnel based on your current medical situation. POLST forms and advance directives are both advance care plans but they are not the same. For more information, see https://polst.org. Be sure to check the POLST forms for your state since they vary depending upon location.

Your advance directive should be accessible so that it is available whenever it may be needed. You should make sure that your primary care physician, your named representative, and your attorney all have copies, and that a copy is kept with your other important papers. Bring a copy with you to the hospital if you ever undergo surgery and let your loved ones know where to find a copy if they need it. These documents can be updated, changed, or even revoked if desired.

An estate plan can be as simple or as complex as you need or want it to be. Completing the material in this book and then having a frank discussion with an experienced estate planning attorney about material you have gathered will aid you in evaluating what best serves your needs and objectives. A will (or will substitute) dictates what will happen to your property after your death and can reduce the cost of administering your estate. As mentioned before, another benefit of consciously and intentionally planning the disposition of your assets is that both income and estate taxes can be minimized or even eliminated. These subjects are discussed more fully in later chapters of this book.

Estate plans can also fill special needs. For instance, for a creative person, it is essential to identify an individual who will preserve the integrity of your creative works after death. This is especially important, since some individuals may be willing to exchange integrity for greed. A well-known cautionary tale is the story of the art critic Clement Greenberg. After artist David Smith's death, Greenberg was appointed executor of Smith's estate. During Smith's life, Greenberg had criticized the artist's use of color and praised his unpainted works. As executor of the estate, Greenberg was responsible for the care and maintenance of Smith's work. Greenberg deliberately stripped the paint off of some of Smith's painted sculptures to take advantage of Smith's popular polished works. Ironically, it was David Smith who had been quoted as saying that altering a work of art is akin to destroying it.

This underscores the importance of carefully selecting the individual to serve as the executor for your estate, even if you are not a world-famous sculptor. Once you have identified the person you believe has the patience, skill, and character to faithfully administer your estate, it is important to let that person know of your request. Your first choice may decline the opportunity, and it would be better for you to know in advance and have the opportunity to ask another to serve in that person's stead.

Estate planning may prevent your assets from being exhausted in stressful, costly, and time-consuming litigation. The plight encountered by Aretha Franklin's estate is by no means a unique situation, although, of course, she may have had more assets than most. Your belongings may, however, be greatly valued by those who survive you. A well-planned estate, with appropriate safeguards, will prevent the likelihood of a posthumous war among your heirs, the Internal Revenue Service, and others who may have some claim to your estate if you die without an estate plan. Of course, you could use up or dispose of your assets before you die. In this situation, you would not need a complex estate plan.

The expense associated with preparing an appropriate estate plan and implementing it is far less than the expense of having to legally sort through a variety of viable claims. The expense should also be weighed against the anguish that your heirs may experience if your property winds up being distributed in ways that are clearly inconsistent with your wishes.

There have been numerous prominent individuals who have regrettably died without having estate plans. The list includes: John Denver, Prince, Michael Jackson, Amy Winehouse, Bob Marley, Jimi Hendrix, Sonny Bono, and Kurt Cobain. In fact, this problem transcends fame and wealth. If you wish to avoid having your assets—both valuable and sentimental—wind up in the hands of individuals who you would not have selected or even worse, tied up in litigation, then it is essential for you to have an appropriate estate plan in place.

This book discusses wills, will alternatives, trusts, and the requirements for each of these documents. This book also contains worksheets that you can use to gather information to take to an estate planning lawyer. This will make the time spent with that lawyer more efficient and productive. Your lawyer will be able to use that information to prepare an estate plan for you to review. If you already understand the various options available to you, and know what kinds of items should be included in an estate plan, you will be able to gather that material at your leisure, be sure that your list of assets is complete and comprehensive, and complete this portion of the work without involving your estate planning attorney. This will save you a great deal of money and allow you to prepare the material at your own pace. You will then be able to review that plan with your attorney to be sure that it represents your wishes. By the time your estate plan is complete, using this book, you will have confidence that your assets will be distributed in accordance with your wishes, and the cost of the plan will be significantly less than if you had provided the material you put in this book directly to your estate planning lawyer.

This book also contains a section for your heirs so that they will have all of the necessary information regarding your estate after you pass. Your heirs will not have to worry that an unremembered asset is left unclaimed, a valuable document is in the cushions of the couch, or some account has been forgotten. Your heirs will have a complete portfolio of everything that is contained in your estate, instructions on how those assets should be distributed, and the documentation to efficiently carry out your estate plan.

You should devote the time necessary to review the material in this text, and then use the space provided to list the items, names, or other relevant information identified so that this book will be available for your estate planning lawyer to use when preparing your plan. By following the recommendations in this book and preparing a comprehensive list of the items discussed, you will improve the quality of your estate plan and allow your heirs to focus on your memory instead of worrying about what comes next.

# CHAPTER 2

# The Estate Plan

Developing your estate plan requires time, consideration, and attention to detail. In this chapter, we will take a step back and look at your estate plan as a whole and give you some things to keep in mind while you go through the remaining chapters.

## IN PLAIN ENGLISH

An *asset* is something of value, and is a financial or accounting term used to describe cash or property. Property can be tangible, which means you can touch it or see it, like buildings or jewelry. Property can also be intangible, which means it is invisible but still valuable, like copyrights, trademarks, or patents.

## ASSETS

Understanding all of the things you own or have an ownership interest in is a vital step in preparing a useful estate plan. As you complete the worksheet at the end of this section, consider all of your cash assets—bank accounts, treasuries and bonds, mutual funds, money market accounts, and the money under the mattress. Consider your land and buildings, also called *real property*—your personal home, vacation and rental properties, and land that you might share with a sibling or will likely inherit from a parent. Remember to include your intangible assets—an ownership interest in a company, your investment portfolio, life insurance policies, copyrights, trademarks, patents, licenses, and other legal rights. You most likely have personal property that may require special attention—fine art, jewelry, vehicles, or items locked away in a safety deposit box.

It is especially important to consider your digital assets—the hardware, software, files, photos, and documents that are stored on computers, flash drives, and in the cloud. Remember that many of your most valuable, sentimental assets may be locked behind passwords in digital accounts. You may have crypto-currency that requires personal verification to access. You might have a library of media—digital books, movies, and music—that may or may not be transferrable to others. You might even have email accounts that you wish deleted or archived. As you go throughout this book, add to your list of assets whenever you remember an old digital account or open a new one. We will discuss more about digital assets in Chapter 9 of this book.

## WILLS AND TRUSTS

Wills and trusts are the two things most people think of when considering an estate plan. A will is a written legal document that coordinates the distribution of your assets after your death. A trust is an arrangement where a third party, referred to as a *trustee*, holds property, including money, land, or tangible and intangible things for the benefit of other people or entities, called *beneficiaries*. Wills and trusts are powerful tools when used properly.

The most effective estate plans often use one or more trusts in combination with a valid will to not only distribute your assets, but also take care of children, pets, and loved ones with special needs, reduce or eliminate taxes, and manage all of the unique assets, relationships, and obligations that you will leave behind.

This book will discuss the basics of wills and trusts in Chapters 3–6; however, many other chapters will also discuss how to use wills and trusts to create guardianships, manage digital assets, and provide for your legacy.

## ADVANCE DIRECTIVES AND MEDICAL POWERS OF ATTORNEY

One reason that encourages many people to finally sit down and make an estate plan is going through the process for a loved one who has not planned well. It is difficult for surviving loved ones to make focused and deliberate decisions when grappling with grief. This is no truer than when faced with medical decisions when a loved one is incapacitated or going through end-of-life treatment. You can relieve some of this burden by making decisions ahead of time and making your wishes known regarding lifesaving measures, organ donation, and permanent unconsciousness.

An *advance directive* or *living will* is a document that will communicate your wishes concerning medical treatments and end-of-life care. A *medical power of attorney*, also called a healthcare proxy or healthcare power of attorney, is a document that appoints a person to be a surrogate decision maker who is authorized to make medical decisions on your behalf.

### IN PLAIN ENGLISH

Before an advance directive or medical power of attorney goes into effect, your physician must conclude that you are unable to make your own medical decisions. If you regain the ability to make decisions, your agent cannot continue to act on your behalf.

Neither advance directives nor medical powers of attorney expire, but one state's document may not always work the way it was intended in another state. If you spend significant amounts of time in multiple states, it will be important to discuss this with your estate planning attorney to determine whether you must prepare multiple advance directives or medical powers of attorney in order to have your objectives followed no matter where you are.

You may already have one or both of these documents. If so, it would be appropriate to review them to make sure they still reflect your wishes. It is also important to discuss your wishes with the person appointed as your health-care agent. Not only will this ensure that your wishes are followed, it is also a kindness that will allow the individual to cope ahead of time with the decisions they may need to make and find peace knowing that they are helping you live as you intended. We will discuss more about advance directives and other powers of attorney in Chapter 7 of this book.

## GIFTING

When most people begin making an estate plan, they think mostly of the gifts that will be given through a will after death. However, gifting is an important part of any estate plan because once a gift is given away, it is no longer part of your estate. Reducing the value of your estate with gifts will help you avoid paying extra taxes and let you share wealth while you are still living. Giving a gift while you are still alive also gives you the added enjoyment of seeing the recipient use and enjoy the gift. Gifts can be made to family members, friends, organizations, and charities. Establish a gift-giving budget as part of your estate plan and keep a list of individuals and organizations that you would like to give to—and remember that gifts can include not only cash but all kinds of property. See Chapter 13 for a more in-depth discussion of this subject.

### IN PLAIN ENGLISH

A gift can be cash or other property, and can be given during your lifetime or after your death. Gifts given after death are also called *bequests* and can be distributed through a will or trust. If you sell property to a friend or family member at a price below the fair market value of the property, it might be classified as part-sale/part-gift.

## DIVIDING PROPERTY

There are many ways to divide property. Real property—land and buildings— can be co-owned, sold with the proceeds divided among the inheritors, or sub-divided and deeded as separate plats of land. The right answer to how to divide real property will depend on the property itself and the individuals inheriting it. The same can be true of most other property, although the mechanism for co-ownership will change depending on whether you're talking about a roy-alty agreement for a copyright or a diamond necklace. If you want property to be divided, note what the property is and among whom you would like it divided. Be prepared to discuss the various options with your estate plan-ning lawyer by deciding what the purpose of the division is—is it to force co-ownership, provide equally for your beneficiaries, or some other purpose? For a more in-depth discussion on co-ownership, see Chapter 14.

### IN PLAIN ENGLISH

*Real Property* is a term used to describe land and buildings. It may also include leases for land if the lease is for a period of time described in the state law where the lease is used. Many states say that if the lease is for three years or more, it is considered real property and the lease can be filed where deeds to property are recorded.

## PROTECTING THE INHERITANCE

We will discuss several ways to protect the inheritance in the second part of this book, including how to protect the inheritance from gift and estate taxes. However, in addition to the government, you may have debts and obligations that should be addressed in your estate plan to protect the inheritance from creditors. Further, you may need to protect the inheritance from the inheritors themselves. This is especially true for minors who need assistance managing wealth or property, or for individuals who are incapacitated, disabled, or otherwise incapable of wisely managing an unexpected gift. Note who these individuals are and the particular concerns you have. Throughout the book, we will discuss trusts and other devices that can protect the inheritance from creditors, immature beneficiaries, and beneficiaries who are unable to manage their own funds.

### IN PLAIN ENGLISH

A *special needs trust* is a trust established to provide for an incapacitated or disabled person. It is specially formed so that it will not interfere with Medicaid or other government benefits the individual may already receive. Special needs trusts are discussed in more detail in Chapter 6.

## BENEFICIARIES

*Beneficiaries* are all of the individuals that will inherit—or benefit—from your estate plan. As you read this book, you may be reminded of family members, friends, organizations, and others that have brought you comfort and joy throughout your life and to whom you wish to return some portion of your estate. As you remember these people, make a note of who they are and track down contact information for each of them. In the case of organizations, there may be a contact person or office within the organization that would be most appropriate to handle gifts and bequests. It is also important to note why this organization is receiving the gift. That way, your estate plan can adapt in the event that the organization no longer exists and give the intended gift to a different organization with the same charitable purpose.

## Children and Grandchildren

Families are complicated. Your estate plan will need to reflect the state of your family and all of its relationships. In some cases, even people who are left out of your estate plan may receive an inheritance if you do not clearly specify that they were left out on purpose. It is important, therefore, as you go through the worksheets, you list not only the children and grandchildren you wish to include in your estate plan but, also the children and grandchildren you wish to exclude.

## Pets

Do not forget your pets. This does not mean that you need to leave an outlandish inheritance to Fido. It does mean, however, that it would be helpful to your family if you leave instructions about how the pet is to be cared for and address who should receive the pet or what to do if there is a dispute over who will get the pet. Your pet likely also has belongings—a doghouse, a habitat, food, etc.—that should go with the pet to its new home. Some states allow pet trusts to provide for the care of the animal that is managed by the new owner.

## YOUR LEGACY

No estate plan would be complete without pausing to consider who you are leaving behind and how you would like them to remember you. To some, it is important to leave a monument or protect a generational family home. For others, it is enough to know they are remembered for how they lived. Consider the legacy you would like to leave behind. Chapter 11 of this book will help you address the questions of final thoughts, parting messages, and missives of love or encouragement that you may want to leave behind.

---

In the chapters that follow, we will provide places where you should list the individuals to whom you wish to leave property, their contact information, property, its location, value when acquired, as well as current fair market value (if possible), the person or organization you wish to receive that property, and the myriad of other items which you feel would be important for your estate planning attorney to assist you in preparing the best possible plan for your estate. By completing these lists thoughtfully and revisiting them when you remember a sentimental item or open a new account, you will be more likely to address the significant issues your survivors will face after your death. In addition, your attorney will be able to assist you in the best way possible and prepare your estate plan quickly and for significantly less cost than if you had to meet with your attorney and have that attorney continuously contact you for the information until your plan is complete.

# CHAPTER 3

# Wills

A will is a written legal document that coordinates the distribution of your assets after your death. A will typically names an *executor* or *personal representative*—the person who will oversee the execution of the will and ensure that your wishes are fulfilled. A will also names *beneficiaries*—the people or organizations that will benefit or receive assets through the will. A will can also create trusts, transfer property to preexisting trusts, provide guardians for minor children, waive bonds for your executor, and make legal elections that may arise when your estate is distributed. In this chapter, we will discuss points to consider and introduce you to a variety of provisions that you will be able to discuss with your estate planning attorney so your attorney can draft an effective will.

### IN PLAIN ENGLISH

Estate planning is notorious for its use of legal jargon and acronyms. Often, the terms used in wills and trusts are archaic and, even worse, they vary from state to state and attorney to attorney. Be sure to check in with the glossary and list of common acronyms at the end of this book whenever you run into a term you do not recognize.

## GENERAL OVERVIEW

All people, their wishes for the future, their families, and their assets are different. Because of this, there is no single prototype for a will. However, no matter how complicated your will may ultimately become, it can be defined simply as a statement of what you want to happen with your property and obligations after you die.

Some estimates say that one out of every three wills is contested. You probably know someone who was involved in a dispute over a loved one's belongings. Because of this, strict laws governing wills, their construction, and the procedure to validate them have been passed in every state. Most states require wills to be in writing and signed in front of one or more witnesses. Oral wills (also called a *nuncupative wills*) and handwritten wills (also called *holographic wills*) are only allowed in limited circumstances by a small number of states. Even in those states, it is recommended that you not rely on oral or handwritten wills since there is a possibility that the laws could change before you die or that your survivors would contest them.

### IN PLAIN ENGLISH

*Testator* is the legal term for the person who makes a will. You will be the *testator* for your own will—also called your "last will and *testament*." A person who dies with a will is said to have died *testate*. A person who dies without a will is said to have died *intestate*.

Witnesses to a will must be *competent*—meaning they must be over the age of eighteen and mentally capable of understanding the process. Some states prohibit an individual from being a witness if they are also a beneficiary under the will or a creditor of the estate. Your spouse should not be a witness to your will. Witnesses do not have to read the will but they do need to know you or the testator. Often your estate planning attorney will have staff members available to witness the will signing. It is important to not only have the name of the witnesses but their contact information as well.

Many states have adopted self-proving will procedures that make it easier to validate the will after the testator dies. These procedures usually require you to execute, or sign, the will in the presence of a notary and sign an affidavit stating that you and the witnesses have complied with all of the required formalities to create a valid will. Some states allow testators to record the will with the appropriate state or county agency. Keep in mind recording the will with the state or county creates a public record, and your will can be viewed by anyone. You should therefore determine whether this is acceptable to you. Even in those states that do not have laws that allow you to establish that your will is valid ahead of time, it is a good idea to follow this procedure since it strengthens the validity of your will and is more likely to deter individuals from contesting it on the grounds that it was not properly signed.

A video of a person reciting her will is generally considered to be a supplement to the will. It can be comforting to the family and useful in determining intent but it should be accompanied by a written, signed, and witnessed document. In most states, if the person leaves only a video, and not a formal will, the court will find the person died *intestate* or without a will.

## IN PLAIN ENGLISH

*Aleatory* is an adjective that describes any contract that is contingent, or dependent, on a certain event happening before the provisions are triggered. A will is said to be aleatory because it is contingent upon the death of the person who made the will. In other words, the assets cannot be distributed under the will unless and until the testator has died.

A will is *aleatory* because it is contingent upon the death of the testator. A will is also *revocable*—meaning it can be voided or modified at any time during your lifetime. In order to avoid confusion when a new will is drafted, the will should contain a *revocation clause* that cancels all prior wills and amendments. Written amendments to wills are also called *codicils*.

In states where a spouse has a legal claim to a portion of the marital property, often called an *elective share*, a spouse cannot be *disinherited* (left out) of the will. However, a spouse can be disinherited if the spouse signed a prenuptial agreement promising not to receive anything from the will. Most states, even those without community property laws, have some protection for spouses that are disinherited or receive less of the estate than the law allows. In this event, the surviving spouse is permitted to claim the higher statutory amount. Your estate planning attorney can help you determine what your state laws are and how to avoid these problems.

In most states, an ex-spouse will be treated as if he or she died before you and will not inherit from your will. It is also the rule in most states, for the purposes of distributing an estate, a spouse becomes an ex-spouse on the day the legal separation or divorce papers were filed, regardless of whether that divorce had been finalized on the day of death.

A will can distribute property in equal or unequal shares and does not have to comply with any guidelines or laws that would otherwise govern the distribution of property if the individual died without a will.

You do not need to give gifts to all of your children or grandchildren in your will. Some people mistakenly believe that in order to disinherit a child they must leave them at least $1 in their will. This is not true. In reality, a minimum gift might be useful to prove that a child was not inadvertently left out of the will—as sometimes happens when a child is born after the will has been drafted. The same result can be accomplished by including a statement identifying any children that were intentionally disinherited.

Wills often direct transfers of property to trusts. We will discuss trusts in more detail in later chapters, but trusts can be used in conjunction with wills to provide gifts to minors or incapacitated beneficiaries. Trusts may also be a useful tool if you believe your will is likely to be contested, as trusts are more difficult for a court to void. Trusts are also commonly used to achieve tax benefits.

Generally, the person you choose to administer your estate, called the executor, administrator, or personal representative, must be a resident of the United States but does not need to be a resident of the state where the will was drafted or of the state in which you die. While it is not a requirement for the executor to be a resident of the state where the will is probated, it is much more convenient. The executor should be eighteen years of age or older, and be competent to wrap up your business affairs and exercise the powers required to execute the will.

## COMMON MISTAKES

The biggest mistake individuals make in regard to their estate plan is not to make an estate plan in the first place. It is true in the context of wills and estates that if you fail to plan, you plan to fail. Other common mistakes include assuming that owning everything jointly with a spouse or a child will be sufficient to take care of the entire estate.

Failing to plan for disability or divorce, choosing the wrong executor, mishandling insurance or retirement benefits, leaving money outright to minor children, forgetting about digital assets or pets, and failing to review and update your estate plan are some of the common mistakes that this book and a careful estate planning attorney can help you avoid.

As individuals live longer and end-of-life health-care options improve, the chance of becoming disabled or mentally incompetent during your lifetime grows. Before assigning all of your assets through a will or trust, consider long term–care insurance to preserve the assets of your estate.

Divorce is a reality of life that is sometimes out of our control—especially when the divorce is that of a child or grandchild. Without proper planning, an ex-spouse of a child could wind up inheriting under the will. If this is not your intention, it will be important to discuss how to prevent this with your estate planning attorney.

As we will discuss in a later chapter, designating the proper beneficiaries of your life insurance policy and retirement benefits is essential to ensure the money goes to your beneficiaries rather than to the Internal Revenue Service in gift and estate taxes.

You and your family are unique and the assets, the value—both monetary and sentimental—of those assets are unique as well. There is no such thing as a one-size-fits-all will. The most common mistakes can often be avoided by asking the right questions and having a frank discussion with your estate planning attorney about your hopes and plans for the future.

## CAPACITY

You have likely heard the phrase "of sound mind and body" in reference to wills. In order to create a valid will, the testator must have *testamentary capacity*. This means you must know the nature and extent of your property, know who the people are who would inherit your estate if there was no will, and you must understand the distribution plan you have created under the will. If a testator had limited mental capacity around the time that the will was drafted, the will might be challenged and could be voided if the court determines the testator did not have *testamentary capacity* at the time the will was signed.

Determining mental capacity is very difficult for the court. If the issue arises, the court will look at whether the circumstances suggest undue influence—if an elderly person suddenly rewrites a will to leave everything to a caregiver, there is a possibility that the caregiver unduly influenced the person in their care. If the court determines that the person was unduly influenced, the will is void *ab initio*, or from the beginning. This means the will is ignored as if it were never created and a prior will may be revived.

If you are concerned that your mental capacity may be subject to a challenge, have a doctor provide an opinion as to your mental capacity or write a letter in your own handwriting validating the will.

If you are physically unable to sign a will, then it would be appropriate to have you orally confirm the accuracy of the will in a video with the required witnesses present. This will likely satisfy the signing requirements in most states. Here too, you should discuss your situation with your estate planning attorney.

## REVOCATION AND REVIVAL

A will can be revoked, or voided, by physically destroying the original: tearing it up, burning it, crossing it out, etc. A will can also be revoked by executing a new will that includes an express phrase that revokes all prior wills and amendments, known as codicils. Sometimes a will can be voided by the court during probate. This can happen if the facts show that the will was drafted under duress or through some sort of fraud or deceit. If an entire will is voided, including the language revoking all prior wills, sometimes an older will—one that was revoked by the newer, then void will—can be revived. This happens very rarely and will depend on the surrounding circumstances and the law of the state that is probating the estate. The safest way to ensure that a prior will is not used is to tear up or destroy the original and all copies of that will.

### IN PLAIN ENGLISH

There are steps you can take to reduce the likelihood that your survivors will dig up an old will and contest a newer one. However, the best way to make sure this does not happen is to keep track of each and every copy of a will and completely destroy it once you have made a replacement will.

As mentioned in an earlier chapter, in the recent case involving the estate of Aretha Franklin, a number of handwritten wills by Ms. Franklin were in dispute. Ms. Franklin handwrote and signed several possible wills identifying different beneficiaries in each. Those beneficiaries each claimed to be entitled to the proceeds of Aretha Franklin's estate. Unfortunately, the dispute between beneficiaries was not resolved, and it wound up in a very expensive legal battle, one which continues as of the date of this publication. If Ms. Franklin had worked with an experienced estate planning attorney, that attorney would likely have created a final will that provided that all preexisting estate planning documents were revoked by and superseded by the final will. In addition, the attorney would be sure that the final will was signed in front of at least two witnesses, since many states do not allow wills which are not properly witnessed to be enforced. Only a handful of states permit handwritten, hand-signed wills to be considered valid. See Appendix E for a list of those states.

The cost of litigating this dispute will likely be significant and the result may not be what Aretha Franklin actually intended. If she had worked with an experienced estate planning lawyer, the cost of hiring that attorney would probably be insignificant compared to the cost of this ongoing litigation and her wishes would clearly be established. The takeaway from this regrettable case is that it is far better to plan ahead and work with an experienced estate planning lawyer rather than to try to save a little bit initially and wind up having your estate pay a much larger price.

## PARTIAL INVALIDITY OF A WILL

Courts take their job to determine and follow the wishes of a person who has died—referred to as a *decedent*—very seriously. Sometimes finding out what the decedent's intentions are can be difficult. This is especially true when a will has multiple versions and codicils (amendments) that contradict one another or invalidate other parts of the will. If only a part of a will or codicil is invalid, the court can strike only the invalid part and enforce the remainder. In the case of a more recent codicil that does not revoke a previous codicil but is inconsistent with it, the newer codicil will be treated as though it did revoke the previous one. You can see that it is very important for your estate planning attorney to have all of the documents that you want to be in effect upon your death to ensure they do not inadvertently contradict or invalidate each other. It would also be helpful for you to provide earlier versions of those documents even though you would not want them to be used since they may be helpful to the attorney in understanding the latest version of that document.

## SIMULTANEOUS DEATH

Most states have statutes that deal with how to divide property in the case that both the testator and the beneficiary of a will die simultaneously. If it is impossible to determine who died first, such as if both individuals died in a plane crash, and the ownership of the property depends on the priority of death, the property is distributed as if each survived the other.

Example: Bob and his daughter, Carol, both die in a plane crash. In Bob's will he left his property to his daughter Carol, unless she predeceased (died before) him, and if so, the property will pass to his brother, David. In Carol's will she left all of her property to a charity. Because Bob and Carol died simultaneously, Bob's will is interpreted as though Carol survived him. Bob's property passes to Carol, rather than to his brother, David. The property transfers to Carol's estate, which then passes the property to the charity.

If your will includes a provision that addresses simultaneous death, it will override any default rules provided by state statute. Your will should, therefore, have a contingency clause for this situation. Many wills use a clause that states a spouse (or other beneficiary) must survive the decedent by thirty days in order to receive property through the will. If Bob had used such a provision in the example above, the property would have gone to his brother, David, instead of to Carol's charity.

## WILL PROVISIONS

A will usually begins with an *exordium*, or introductory, clause which declares that this is the "Last Will and Testament" of the testator and often states where the person lived when the will was made. This can be useful for the court to determine what state's law the testator was relying on when writing the document.

The next paragraph typically names an executor, personal representative, or administrator (we will refer to each of these as *executor* throughout this book), waives the requirement of a surety bond, and lays out the rights and responsibilities of the executor. This paragraph will also usually name one or more successor executors.

A surety bond is generally required for all probated estates and can cost a significant amount. It is used to bond the honesty of the executor—if the executor acts negligently or dishonestly, the bond will be used to cover any resulting damages or loss. Since you obviously trust the individual you have identified as the executor, and since that individual will likely be working with an estate planning attorney during the probate, having the estate pay for an expensive bond is likely a waste of the estate's money and can be waived.

The following paragraphs of the will may name guardians for minor children and trustees for trusts created in the will. The next section of the will usually lays out trust provisions and specific bequests. The will typically ends with a residuary provision that disposes of any property not previously distributed.

Wills must give bequests or gifts to people or legal entities. Gifts cannot be made to pets or to property. For example, you cannot leave $500 to your cat or your truck—as much as you may love your cat or your truck. If you do wish to leave such a gift, it will have to be made to a trustee to care for the pet or the property.

You can give conditional gifts through a will. As long as the condition is legal, specific, and not against public policy, it will be enforced. Conditions that are discriminatory or against marriage and religion, are considered to be against public policy. Gifts can, and should, be left with survivorship clauses to explain what you wish to happen if the named beneficiary dies before you, or rejects the gift, or the entity to which the gift is given is unable to accept it.

Taxes will be due from the residuary of the estate unless the will has a tax apportionment clause. Without a tax apportionment clause, the will may have the unintended result of having one beneficiary pay all of the estate taxes and fees while the other beneficiaries pay nothing. For a more complete explanation of this subject, see Chapter 10.

## EXECUTOR'S DUTIES

The executor must administer the estate. If an executor is not named in the will, the court will appoint one. In this case, the person administering the estate is called an administrator. The executor or administrator may hire an attorney to assist in the process, but the ultimate responsibility for obligations of the estate and decisions for its distribution cannot be delegated.

The executor must protect the estate from loss or waste, follow funeral and burial instructions, read and follow the instructions in the will, collect all of the decedent's property, pursue all claims the estate may be entitled to, pay all claims, debts, and taxes, file federal and state taxes, keep detailed records, pay spouse and minor awards, provide an accounting to the court, and distribute property to the beneficiaries. We will discuss these important duties more fully in Chapter 17.

## CREATIVE AND PROFESSIONAL EXECUTORS

For creative people, the will should identify an individual who will be appointed to handle the creative assets of the estate. For writers, a Literary Executor should be appointed so that the literary property can be handled by an experienced individual and maximize its value for the beneficiaries. Artists should have Artistic Executors to maximize the assets in the deceased artist's estate. In fact, every creative person should consider the most appropriate person to handle the creative assets in order to achieve the maximum benefits for the estate and its beneficiaries. Here too, if you fail to identify the right person to handle creative assets and they are administered through the residuary clause, then the individual who handles those assets may not recognize their value or be able to achieve their true benefits for the estate. Similarly, professionals such as doctors, lawyers, accountants, engineers, architects, and other professionals are customarily licensed by regulatory boards. Those organizations have rules that define requirements for the disposition of the professional's interest and obligations when the professional dies. These rules must be followed and the estate planning attorney must assist in appropriately complying with the professional association's rules.

---

Throughout this chapter, we have discussed individuals who play important roles in your estate plan such as administrators, executors, personal representatives, and creative executors. We strongly recommend that you identify at least three individuals who can serve in the particular role, determine the order in which you would prefer to have the individuals serve, and provide that if the person you have identified for that role dies before you you or is unable or unwilling to serve, then the second individual will be identified as that person's replacement. You should do the same for that second individual as well. In this way, you will have identified backup individuals for each required position. It is also very important for you to work with an experienced attorney throughout the estate planning and probate process. In this way, you will have the aid of a trusted, experienced lawyer so that you can be assured that your estate will be handled in the best way possible.

# CHAPTER 4

# Testamentary Trusts

A *trust* is defined as an arrangement whereby someone referred to as a *trustee* holds property, including money, land, or tangible and intangible things in that person's name for the benefit of other people or entities, identified as *beneficiaries*. There can be one or more trustee and there can be one or more beneficiary. We will discuss a variety of different types of trusts that have specific objectives in the next few chapters.

There are many ways to set up and use a trust. Every trust must have a *trustor*—the person who creates and funds the trust. This person can also be called a *grantor* or *settlor*. Every trust also has one or more *trustees*—the person(s) who oversees the maintenance and distribution of the trust assets. The property that is put into the trust, whether it is cash, real estate, or other property, is called the *trust property, corpus*, or *res*. Finally, every trust has instructions to the trustee and beneficiaries. A trust made during your lifetime is called an *inter vivos* trust. A trust created at death using a will or some other instrument is called a *testamentary trust*. Trusts can be drafted so the trustor can modify the trust—called a *revocable* or living trust. Trusts can also be drafted to be permanent, or *irrevocable*.

## GENERAL OVERVIEW

Most trusts are *express trusts* that were created intentionally by the trustor or settlor. Some trusts are created to fulfill the legal intentions of the parties when their intention could not be fulfilled directly. These are called *constructive trusts* and will arise when, for example, an individual leaves money to a pet. Since an animal cannot own property or manage cash, the court will create a constructive trust with the purpose of caring for the pet. This may also happen when someone acquired property through fraud or if a beneficiary is responsible for the death of the trustor. The court will create a constructive trust to hold the property until it can be returned to the lawful owner.

Trusts can be used instead of a will to transfer property at death without going through a probate proceeding. Like wills, trusts can have complicated split-interest beneficiaries where one group of beneficiaries receives the trust proceeds until some event—often the death of the beneficiary—and the benefits of the trust then go to a different person. For example, the proceeds of the trust can go to pay for the college tuition of a child, and when the child finishes college, the remainder can create a scholarship fund for other students. While trusts are an important part of an estate plan, a trust cannot perform all of the functions of a will, such as nominating guardians for minor children.

Trust agreements are generally private, although certain parts of the trust may need to be disclosed when transferring property or dealing with financial institutions.

A trustee can be a person or an organization. Banks often provide professional trustee services that are paid for out of the trust assets. If there is to be more than one trustee, then care should be taken to not have an even number of trustees or, if there is to be an even number of trustees, then some provision must be made to resolve disputes between cotrustees. Under the federal tax laws, most irrevocable trusts cannot have a family member as a trustee. Certain types of trusts allow the trustor to act as the initial trustee.

Trusts have complicated tax implications that can be a benefit to the trustor and the estate that are beyond the purview of this book. Your estate planning attorney will be able to walk you through the basics of these tax implications and a qualified accountant or tax attorney can help you maximize your benefits while minimizing your tax burden.

## TRUST AGREEMENTS

Trust agreements must be in writing, signed by the trustor and trustee(s), and be notarized. If the trust is *revocable*, the agreement must state that the trustor retains the right to amend or revoke the trust agreement, and explain how those amendments will be made. If the trust is *irrevocable*, the trust should expressly state that as well.

The trust agreement must contain the term, or duration, of the trust. This can be a specific time period or can be based on the life of an individual. Your estate planning attorney may ask you additional questions in order to make sure the term complies with the state law against perpetuities—which prohibits trusts that have no reasonable end or effectively allow the trustor to control property from the grave.

## IN PLAIN ENGLISH

The Rule Against Perpetuities is one of the most complex rules in American law. It essentially provides that a provision that is not limited by a certain period of time defined in the law is invalid and will not be enforced.

The trust agreement must contain instructions for the disposition of income generated by the trust and the trust property. Distributions can be mandatory with the amount and time of the distribution outlined in the trust agreement, or distributions can be made at the discretion of the trustee. Thus, the agreement must identify all of the rights and responsibilities of the trustee.

The trust agreement must identify all of the beneficiaries and provide for all of the present and future interests of the trust property. Trust agreements should contain simple boilerplate language identifying what state's law should control its interpretation and a severability clause that allows a court to strike any provision that violates the law without destroying the entire trust. That is, the trust should be enforced in such a way as to achieve the identified intent of the trustor even if the trust is modified by the court.

## ABUSIVE TRUST ARRANGEMENTS

As mentioned above, the laws governing trusts are complex. Unscrupulous promoters have taken advantage of this complexity to prey on unsuspecting individuals by claiming they can help the person avoid tax liability and personal liability by putting the money into a specific kind of trust. The promoter promises benefits under federal tax laws that are misinterpreted or nonexistent. The claim that a trust can insulate you from personal liability is also misstated. The promoter then takes a fee to establish the trust and may even name the promoter's organization as professional trustee and take monthly fees for that service. The IRS has identified these as *abusive trust arrangements* and actively looks to stop this kind of behavior. However, if a salesman calls to entice you with the benefits of a trust—even a foreign trust in another country—check with your accountant or attorney before signing a contract. While the promoter may be liable for fraud, you may also be liable for the large penalties associated with abuse of the tax laws.

## SUCCESSOR TRUSTEES

If your selected trustee cannot or will not perform the duties of the trustee, you should have a second and even a third alternate trustee named in your documents. Your trust should also include language that provides a mechanism for choosing an alternative trustee if there is none named who is able to do the job, though it is best for you to identify successor trustees at the beginning so that you can be assured of having the individual you select serve if the primary individual is not available.

## TRUSTEE'S DUTIES

Trustees are subject to state laws and fiduciary duties common in all states. In general, a trustee must use the care, skill, prudence, and diligence of an ordinary person engaged in a similar business. A trustee must act in good faith and will not be held responsible for errors in judgment made in good faith. A professional trustee will be held to a higher standard. In most states, the trust agreement cannot relieve the trustee of the responsibility to be fair to all beneficiaries, but it may be able to reduce the standard of care.

The trustee has a duty of good faith and loyalty to the trust, and cannot have a conflict of interest with the trust estate. The trustee must follow the trust agreement. If the trustee deviates from the instructions, a court may find that the trustee acted negligently and assess penalties against the trustee. The trustee has a duty to exercise reasonable care in dealings with all of the beneficiaries and to protect the trust property from waste. The trustee has the duty to perform the work personally and not delegate responsibility unless the trust agreement provides otherwise. The trustee has a duty to pay trust income and principal to the beneficiaries in accordance with the terms of the trust agreement, and to deal impartially with the trust. This means that the trustee cannot self-deal, that is, personally deal with the trust for the trustee's benefit, or profit from the trust.

## IN PLAIN ENGLISH

Waste is defined the abuse, destruction, or permanent change to property by someone who is merely in possession of that property. This means that the trustee cannot allow the property to fall into disrepair, make permanent changes to the property, or otherwise destroy the property in the trust.

# ESTATE PLANNING TRUSTS

There are several common types of irrevocable trusts that are used by estate planners to reduce the estate's overall tax burden. The estate tax is assessed on the property that you own or control at death. If the property is transferred out of your control through an irrevocable trust, the property is not included in your estate, thus the estate's taxes are reduced.

## Grave Maintenance Trusts

A grave maintenance trust is one that is created for the purpose of maintaining the grave site after you die. This could either be a stand-alone trust or created as part of another ongoing trust if another trust is created that is intended to continue operating eternally. This is discussed more fully in Chapter 20.

## Irrevocable Life-Insurance Trusts

Life-insurance proceeds will be included in your taxable estate if there is evidence of ownership or control of the policy at your death. You can give away a life insurance policy to take it out of your estate, but there is no guarantee that the recipient will pay the premiums or distribute the proceeds according to your wishes. This can be avoided by creating an irrevocable life-insurance trust. You must do this at least three years prior to your death in order to avoid having the policy included in your estate. You cannot be the trustee of the trust, nor retain ownership of the policy. There are additional considerations that your estate planning attorney can help you navigate to ensure the trust is sufficiently funded to pay for the life-insurance premiums. This type of trust is often used as part of a business arrangement, and you should also discuss life insurance trusts with your business attorney. We will discuss life insurance policies further in Chapter 10.

---

In this chapter, we have introduced the basic structure and rules for trusts. We have also identified some types of trusts that are of particular importance to estate planning. In the next three chapters, we will discuss some other important types of trusts which you should consider.

# CHAPTER 5

# Living (Inter Vivos) Trusts

A living or *inter vivos* trust is an estate planning device that you can use during your lifetime to control property that is placed into a trust. If you become unable to manage your affairs, a trustee is already selected to handle the affairs of the property. There are many advantages to living trusts; however, there are strict rules that must be followed to take advantage of the benefits and avoid the pitfalls that can occur, such as losing Medicaid benefits, loss of control of the property, costly maintenance fees, and unanticipated probate costs. If you have a durable power of attorney, you can add specific language granting that person the power to add property to a living trust. The trustee is the only one with power over the property in the trust. The power of attorney does not perform the same function. In this chapter, we will explain the general requirements and advantages of a living trust and explain the basics of properly funding a living trust.

### IN PLAIN ENGLISH

A *trustor* is the person who creates and funds the trust. This person can also be called a *grantor* or *settlor.* A *trustee* is the person or persons who oversees the maintenance and distribution of the trust assets. The property that is put into the trust, whether it is cash, real estate, or other property, is called the *trust property, corpus,* or *res.*

## GENERAL OVERVIEW

The living trust is a very old legal concept that has its roots in English common law. Originally, a living trust was used by English nobility to transfer landholdings without interference from the government. All states now allow living trusts. While this estate planning technique has been used by wealthy families for centuries, living trusts have come into favor with ordinary citizens because of the many benefits they may provide. For example, a living trust can be created by a person for the person's own benefit. A living trust can be revoked or amended any time prior to the death or incapacity of the person who created the trust. This allows for changes to estate plans. Property held in the living trust does not go through probate; rather, it goes to the named beneficiaries upon the death of the person who created the trust.

Because a trustee has a duty to preserve and protect the trust assets and abide by the detailed instructions included in the agreement, a living trust can be very helpful for long-term care of the beneficiary.

If you have a living trust, you may also have a provision in your will that transfers some or all of your assets to the trust after you die. This is known as a *pour-over* provision. Typically, after all of your specific gifts have been distributed and the claims against the estate have been paid, a pour-over provision transfers the remaining property into the living trust.

Living trusts are contested less frequently than wills. Wills are often contested based on undue influence, duress, menace, or fraud. Since the creator of the trust will meet with an attorney to discuss the living trust agreement and usually act as the initial trustee, trusts are less frequently challenged based on the capacity of that person to execute a valid trust or because the trustor was under undue influence.

A single document can create any number of trusts. While the trustor will commonly be the initial trustee of an inter vivos trust, typically they will name successor trustees to step in upon the incapacity of the trustor. The trustor can also name cotrustees, although an instruction should be included to resolve any disputes that may arise between cotrustees and provide that the trustor or the trustor's identified representative will have the final say in any dispute. Spouses can execute a joint living trust agreement for any shared property. A significant advantage of a living trust is that it can be used for the care of the trustor in case of incapacity, whereas a will would have no effect until the person died.

## ADVANTAGES AND DISADVANTAGES

A living trust is a useful vehicle for long-term financial care of a disabled person's affairs. Trusts are more private than a will as they do not need to be filed with the clerk's office and typically do not go through probate. However, there are situations where the trust will have to be disclosed. A living trust can help avoid probate and is also contested less frequently than transfers performed under a will. A living trust can help shield property from creditors and may prevent a spousal claim for inheritance.

---

### IN PLAIN ENGLISH

A power of attorney gives one or more persons the power to act on your behalf as your agent (also known as an attorney-in-fact). The power may be limited to a particular activity, such as making medical decisions, or be general and give broad powers to the agent to act on your behalf in any capacity.

---

A trust has some advantages over a mere power of attorney, which is discussed in more detail in Chapter 7. The trustee has a duty to act for the benefit of the beneficiary or beneficiaries of the trust, whereas the individual identified in the power of attorney to act on behalf of the grantor of that power does not have a duty to act on behalf of the person granting that power. The agent for a power of attorney can resign, whereas a trustee has a duty to continue in office until replaced.

Living trusts have higher initial and annual expenses than a will. A poorly drafted trust may be open to multiple interpretations, which can lead to far more complications and expenses than if it had never existed. In general, a trust cannot make tax-deductible gifts. If property that you intend to give as a gift is in a trust, you must transfer property from the trust to yourself and then to the person to whom you're making a gift in order to obtain tax benefits.

Property transferred into a trust may have some consequences with respect to Medicaid. This is quite technical and should be discussed with your estate planning attorney.

When a person dies and the estate is opened, creditors have a specified period of time to file claims against the estate. This cutoff period is typically shorter for wills than for trusts—typically six months for a will and two years for a trust. This means that creditors have a longer period to pursue claims when a trust is involved.

If you execute a living trust and fail to fund it, your estate may end up going through probate anyway, and these general rules will not apply. A living trust will also not remove property from the estate for purposes of pending lawsuits. Some state laws will not allow you to place your residence in a living trust without affecting the homestead exemption for taxes or bankruptcy. A living trust can also have tax implications for your beneficiaries if your living trust is funded by an IRA account. Most trusts cannot own subchapter S stock for more than sixty days.

As you can see from the above, this is a very complex situation and you should discuss the benefits of creating a living trust with your estate planning attorney.

## SPENDTHRIFT TRUSTS AND MARITAL LIVING TRUSTS

Assets can be protected from the claims of future creditors by transferring them to a spendthrift trust established for third party—for example, a spouse. Such a trust, however, is usually irrevocable and includes a spendthrift clause. The purpose of a spendthrift clause is to protect the beneficiary's interests from being assigned to or attached by creditors. The law governing the trust will determine the rights of the parties. In all situations in which there is a transfer without paying fair value, the question of fraudulent transfers always exists. Transferring assets to a trust for the purpose of evading a creditor is likely a fraudulent transfer and the creditor can still likely go after those assets.

### IN PLAIN ENGLISH

Historically, spendthrift trusts were used to protect an individual who wastes the individual's financial resources, in order to avoid having the individual deplete all of the individual's assets. The trustee would have control of the assets in order to protect the spendthrift.

Since a living trust is revocable, it can be amended at any time by a written document. A joint marital living trust created by both spouses can only be amended by both spouses. This is to safeguard each spouse against any wrongdoing by the other. In a joint spousal living trust, when one spouse dies, the deceased spouse's portion becomes irrevocable, while the surviving spouse's portion of the trust remains revocable, and the surviving spouse can amend that person's share as if it were a single person's trust.

A marital joint living trust can be revoked by either spouse at any time. Revocation restores both spouses to the same position they were in prior to the creation of the trust.

Separate trusts for children who are beneficiaries of a living trust can be created as part of the living trust document. In doing so, you can designate when the child will receive the trust property, who will manage it for the child, and what benefits the child will receive during the trust's term. In such an instance, the trustee should have broad powers to use the assets of the trust for the support, maintenance, and welfare of the child.

## PROFESSIONAL ASSET MANAGEMENT

A living trust can be managed by a professional, such as a bank or other professional fiduciary, although a professional trustee is not required. If the beneficiaries are young or financially naïve, professional management is very attractive, because after your death, the trustee will be able to protect the assets until the beneficiaries are able to exercise responsible judgment on their own. Designating a professional trustee to manage a living trust will also give you the opportunity to see how they will manage the living trust after your death. If you do not like how it is being managed, you can make changes. There is, of course, a higher cost in having a professional trustee.

## FUNDING A LIVING TRUST

Placing cash, real property (land and buildings), and personal property (tangible goods such as furniture or jewelry) and intangible goods (such as copyrights and trademarks) into the trust is referred to as *funding* the trust. Prior to funding the trust, check with your attorney, accountant, and financial planner. These professionals will be able to alert you to any potential tax implications, issues such as triggering an acceleration clause in a mortgage, or other restrictions on transferring legal ownership such as may be present with some types of stock. In some states, placing real property into a trust changes the character of the property to personal property with potential loss of creditor protection rights.

_____

As you can see, there are a number of complex legal and practical issues that must be considered when determining whether to create a living trust. It is very important for you to discuss these issues with an estate planning attorney in order to be sure that your wishes are complied with and your estate achieves the maximum benefit available.

# CHAPTER 6

# Special Needs Trusts

Families that have a child, spouse, parent, or other member with special needs must consider the emotional, physical, and financial issues that are unique to their situation. Not only must you consider the individual with special needs but also the other family members who will continue to care for them. A special needs trust is created for the benefit of a surviving spouse or disabled individual who is unable to care for himself or herself. If the special needs trust is set up as a supplemental security income trust ("SSI trust"), the trust can supplement any government assistance the individual receives. In this chapter, we will discuss this and other important considerations that make the special needs trust an invaluable tool for anyone with special needs.

## IDENTIFYING A CARETAKER

One of the most important things you must consider when you are a caretaker of someone with special needs is who will assume those responsibilities once you are no longer able or willing to perform that function. In some cases, there will be family members able and willing to assume the responsibility. In other cases, hiring a professional caregiver is the only real option. In either case, you may wish to establish a trust to help pay for the care of your loved one. The special needs trust document can identify a caretaker who is also a trustee or identify a separate caretaker and trustee. The document should identify at least one successor caretaker and trustee, and more if possible, in the event that your first choice is unavailable. Identifying a professional caregiving agency as a final option if all other caregivers cannot accept the responsibility can be a good way to prevent your loved one from receiving care from an individual without the strength, skill, knowledge, or good intentions you desire.

Using a professional caretaker is likely to be more expensive, but if the situation requires that form of assistance, then the added cost is justifiable. In addition, identifying the individual or agency will provide you and the other members of your family with an opportunity to determine the best possible individual or group for your special-needs person.

## GUARDIANSHIP

When the individual with special needs is unable to make decisions regarding personal affairs, legal, or civil rights without assistance, it may be necessary to appoint a guardian. Guardianship can affect the rights and decision-making power of the individual, so you should take great care to consider all of the options available to you and your family when deciding whether to appoint a guardian. We will discuss guardianship in more detail in the next chapter.

## GOVERNMENT ASSISTANCE AND INCOME LIMITATIONS

If your loved one is receiving government assistance, there are federal and state laws that control whether a special-needs person can reject an inheritance, whether the principal or income from a trust will be included as income in a benefit determination, and many other situations. These laws are complex and always changing. In order to enable your estate planning attorney to help you navigate these treacherous waters, you should identify individuals that can be trusted to accept gifts on behalf of the special-needs individual, identify others who may have claims over the property of a special-needs individual (such as a spouse), and all businesses and creditors with which the individual might have dealings. The worksheet at the end of this section will guide you through the identification process.

## ADDITIONAL CONSIDERATIONS FOR THE TRUSTEE

Whenever possible, appoint a trustee that understands the individual's particular needs. This will help ensure the trustee has the information needed to invest and manage the trust assets well. If there is a significant amount of money in the trust, a professional trust management company can be named to act as the financial cotrustee and a trusted friend or relative can be appointed as the personal cotrustee. It may be preferable to have a family member who is financially savvy serve as the financial cotrustee and a family member who will be the caregiver serve as the personal cotrustee. Sometimes, family members who serve as trustees may eventually be recipients of the principal of the trust, so care must be given to avoid a conflict of interest when appointing trustees. In addition, disputes between cotrustees must be considered and a satisfactory tiebreaker should be built into the trust documents. There can be many pitfalls with how cotrustees are appointed, so be sure to discuss the risks and benefits with your estate planning attorney.

### IN PLAIN ENGLISH

A conflict of interest would exist, for example, where the same individual is both the trustee and one of the beneficiaries. In this type of situation the individual could, as trustee, use the position of trustee to benefit him or her self as beneficiary and reduce the share other beneficiaries receive.

A special needs trust should contain a provision reciting your intention. The trust document must also provide that the trustees have absolute and uncontrolled discretion with regard to paying from the income or principal for the benefit of the beneficiary to fulfill your stated intention. This will create a true discretionary trust and is an important part of establishing what is and is not "income" for various assistance programs and taxes.

## ADDITIONAL INSTRUCTIONS TO INCLUDE

While each special needs trust must be prepared by the attorney for the unique considerations of the special-needs individual, there are some instructions which are likely to be included. These clauses are commonly found in special needs trusts, and you should discuss them with your estate planning attorney.

### Escape Clause

Each special needs trust should include an escape or "fail-safe" clause that will terminate the trust if any creditors attempt to reach the trust fund. The principal would then be distributed to the remainder beneficiaries—the individuals who will receive the principal of the trust once the trust is no longer needed by the special-needs individual. Such a clause can also preserve the trust principal if the federal or state law governing the trust changes.

### Predeath Termination Clause

An individual with special needs may overcome a disability later in life. In this case, they may no longer need someone else to manage their financial affairs. A predeath termination clause can distribute the principal to the individual or make some other arrangement to give the individual more control over the funds. There are many potential triggers that can be written into a trust including a period of continuous gainful employment, a certain medical diagnosis, or other event specific to the disability of the individual. Special care should be given in circumstances where a disability may recur to allow the trust to be reinstated to care for the individual.

### Spendthrift Clause

The special needs trust should contain a provision that prevents the beneficiary from encumbering the trust assets. This will prevent creditors, including the state, from acquiring the trust principal to satisfy a debt. This is called a spendthrift clause.

### Sprinkling Benefit Clause

A sprinkling benefit clause allows the trustee to sprinkle or spray the benefits of the trust, whether income or principal, to other members of the family or organizations who are providing services to the individual. This can be helpful to pay for a family member to take unpaid time off work to care for an individual on a temporary basis and a host of other situations where additional costs should be paid from the trust.

### Housing Clause

Some nonprofit organizations provide housing for disabled adults. The laws governing Medicaid and related programs prevent certain funds from being used to "create" housing. This means that it may be difficult for organizations to find funds for capital purchases of housing facilities. For this reason, a clause allowing a trust to gift money to the organization that provided appropriate housing to the individual can be included in a special needs trust.

### Remaining Assets Clause

Finally, a clause should be included in the trust that disposes of the principal and remaining income in the event that the trust is terminated or the beneficiary passes away. The remaining assets can be used to cover burial expenses and then be distributed in a variety of ways to family, friends, or organizations.

## IRREVOCABLE INTER VIVOS TRUSTS

Rather than waiting to establish a special needs trust in your will, it is worth considering creating a special needs trust during your lifetime as an irrevocable inter vivos trust. A minimal amount can initially be put into the trust, with additional assets added to it upon your death. This will allow you to establish, test, and fine-tune the trust, and establish a receptacle for the gifts of other family members who wish to contribute to the welfare of the special-needs individual.

### IN PLAIN ENGLISH

*Inter vivos* means that the trust is created during the individual's lifetime.

## INSURANCE

Many individuals who are caring for a loved one with special needs do not have a large estate to devote to the care of their loved one. In this situation, a special needs trust can be made the beneficiary of a life insurance policy. The right policy can provide adequate principal to care for the individual, and the structure of the special needs trust can ensure that money is used for the proper purpose. We will discuss life insurance more thoroughly in Chapter 13.

---

A special needs trust is very important for individuals and families when special needs are involved. Your estate planning attorney will be able to assist in creating a special needs trust when appropriate. These may be created before you die as a standalone trust if appropriate, or in your living trust or will.

CHAPTER 7

# Guardians, Powers of Attorney, Advance Directives, and Other Essential Documents

In addition to considering creating a trust and preparing a will, you should also consider a number of other important estate planning documents. In this chapter, we will discuss many of them and provide some recommendations. As pointed out throughout this book, it is essential for you to discuss all of the suggestions we have provided with your estate planning attorney in order to be sure your plan provides you with the best possible arrangement.

## GUARDIANS

When a person is unable to manage money, care for themselves, or make appropriate decisions, you should consider whether a guardian should be appointed to care for that person. In this section, we will discuss the methods by which you can identify and appoint a guardian.

### Guardianship of Children

All states allow parents to nominate the guardian who will take over raising children upon the death of the custodial parent. If you are divorced, the surviving parent will typically become the custodian automatically, but it is always best to name a guardian in the event that the other parent is unable or unwilling to act as guardian. In some states, for example Oregon, the custodial parent may nominate someone other than the noncustodial parent in the event that the custodial parent has good justification (i.e. the non-custodial parent has a history domestic violence or drug addiction). This situation, however, does trigger potential issues with parental Constitutional rights, so you should enlist the help of an attorney well versed in this area of law if you are hoping to nominate someone other than the noncustodial parent.

The guardian will take the place of a parent in raising the child and will also be the Social Security recipient for the child's survivor benefits. A conservator can also be designated to handle the child's money. The guardian and conservator can be the same individual, but that is not required. Children may also have a trustee managing the assets of a trust if a trust was established for their welfare. A guardian can be identified in a will. Some states also allow a guardian to be appointed using an affidavit, but a trust document cannot establish guardianship.

## Guardianship of Adults

Adults who are mentally or physically disabled, whether by accident or illness, and have become unable to care for themselves must have a guardian. If the court establishes that the adult is incompetent and no guardian is identified, a guardian will be appointed by the court. Court-supervised guardianship is difficult for the family and has reporting requirements that involve court appearances, attorney fees, and other expenses. Your estate planning attorney can help you prepare for your own guardianship in the case of your incapacity and the guardianship of other adults in your care, such as a parent, spouse, sibling, or child.

### IN PLAIN ENGLISH

There difference between a *guardian* and a *conservator* depends on what state you are in. In many states, a *guardian* is the person with control over the personal, day-to-day decisions of a ward, while a *conservator* is the person with the authority to control the ward's financial decisions. In some states, the term *guardian* is used when the ward is a minor, while a *conservator* is the person who takes care of an incompetent or incapacitated adult.

## *Defining Disability*

It is not unheard of for disagreements to arise among family members over whether an individual is actually incapacitated. Children often disagree as to the extent of a parent's disability. Estate planning documents should contain a definition of "disability" for the purposes of establishing a guardianship. As an alternative to defining disability, you and your estate planning attorney can describe a method by which disability can be established. For example, requiring a licensed medical practitioner to examine the individual in order to determine whether that individual is disabled for purposes of triggering the appointment of a guardian. The procedure could go on to say that if the individual is unhappy with the characterization, then the individual may have a second opinion from a qualified medical practitioner and, if that opinion is inconsistent, the two professionals must identify another qualified medical practitioner and that third person will determine the characterization.

## POWER OF ATTORNEY

A power of attorney is accepted in all states, but the rules and requirements differ from state to state. A power of attorney gives one or more persons the power to act on your behalf as your agent (also known as an attorney-in-fact). The power may be limited to a particular activity, such as closing the sale of your home, or be general and give broad powers to the agent to act on your behalf in any capacity. These powers include handling financial and business transactions, buying life insurance, settling claims, operating business interests, making gifts, and employing professional help.

The power may be given temporarily or permanently, and may take effect immediately or only upon the occurrence of a future event, usually upon a determination that you are unable to act for yourself due to mental or physical disability. The latter is called a "springing" power of attorney. A general power of attorney is an effective tool if you will be out of the country and need someone to handle certain matters, and is often included in an estate plan to make sure someone can handle financial matters.

You can specify exactly what powers an agent may exercise by signing a special power of attorney. This is often used when one cannot handle certain affairs due to other commitments or health reasons. Selling property (personal and real), managing real estate, collecting debts, and handling business transactions are some of the common matters specified in a special power of attorney document.

A power of attorney is only valid if you are mentally competent when you sign it and, in some cases, incompetent when it goes into effect. If you think your mental capability may be questioned, have a doctor verify it in writing. It may also be prudent to have two unrelated doctors verify your competency if you anticipate that it may be challenged in court.

You must sign and notarize the original power of attorney document, and certify several copies. Banks and other businesses will not allow your agent to act on your behalf unless they receive a certified copy of the power of attorney. In some states you can record the power of attorney and make it a matter of public record. The place where the recording is to occur varies from state to state. Your estate planning attorney will be able to assist in determining whether recordation is available in your state and, if so, where the recording must take place. Your estate planning attorney can ensure you comply with all of the formalities required by your state's law.

## Choosing an Agent

There are no special qualifications for someone to act as an agent except that the person cannot be a minor or otherwise incapacitated. You should be sure the individual selected to serve as your attorney-in-fact is the right person for that position. The best choice is someone you trust. Integrity, rather than financial experience, is often the most important trait of an agent.

You may wish to choose a family member to act on your behalf. Many people name their spouses or one or more children. Naming more than one person to act as agent at the same time can present problems if the co-agents disagree. You should indicate whether you wish to have the majority act in the absence of full agreement and what to do in case of an unresolvable tie. You should always name one or more successor agents in case the person named as your agent is unavailable, unable, or unwilling to act when the time comes.

## Durable Power of Attorney

A durable power of attorney is simply a general, special, or health-care power of attorney that has a durability provision to keep the current power of attorney in effect if you become mentally incompetent due to illness or accident while it is in effect.

If you wish for your power of attorney to go into effect only upon your mental or physical incapacity, specify in the power of attorney that it cannot go into effect until a doctor certifies you as incompetent. You may name a specific doctor whom you wish to determine your competency, or require that more than one licensed physician agree on your mental state.

A durable power of attorney is only effective while you are alive. When you die, it ends, and the agent no longer has the power to act on your behalf.

## Medical Power of Attorney

A medical power of attorney (sometimes referred to as a health-care power of attorney or health-care proxy) allows you to appoint a person you trust as your health-care agent (or surrogate decision maker), who is authorized to make medical decisions on your behalf.

Before a medical power of attorney goes into effect, a person's physician must conclude that he or she is unable to make his or her own medical decisions. In addition, if a person regains the ability to make decisions, the agent cannot continue to act on the person's behalf.

Many states have additional requirements that apply only to decisions about life-sustaining medical treatments. For example, before your agent can refuse a life-sustaining treatment on your behalf, a second physician may have to confirm your doctor's assessment that you are incapable of making treatment decisions. If the two physicians are unable to agree, a third physician may be appointed by the two physicians, and that physician's decision will be final.

## Duration

A power of attorney does not expire but it can be revoked. Simply notify your agent in writing and destroy all copies of the document. Notify any financial institutions and the recording office, if it has been recorded, that your agent's power of attorney has been revoked.

### IN PLAIN ENGLISH

An *advance directive* or *living will* is a document that will communicate your wishes concerning medical treatments and end-of-life care. A *medical power of attorney*, also called a health-care power of attorney or health-care proxy, is a document that appoints a person to be a surrogate decision maker who is authorized to make medical decisions on your behalf.

## ADVANCE DIRECTIVES

Advance directives, also called living wills, document your wishes concerning medical treatments at the end of life. Advance directives are governed by state law. In most states, before an advance directive can guide medical decision making, two physicians must certify that (1) you are unable to make medical decisions, and (2) you are in the medical condition specified in the state's living will or advance directive law (such as "terminal illness" or "permanent unconsciousness"). Other requirements may also apply depending upon your state.

Advance directives are legally valid throughout the United States. Your advance directive becomes legally valid as soon as you sign it in front of the required witnesses. Your estate planning attorney can ensure that you comply with the formalities of your state's law.

Emergency medical technicians and paramedics *cannot* honor advance directives, living wills, or medical powers of attorney. Once emergency personnel have been called, they must do what is necessary to stabilize a person for transfer to a hospital. Only after a physician fully evaluates the person's condition and determines that the requirements have been met can the advance directive be implemented.

One state's advance directive does not always work in another state. Some states honor advance directives from another state; others will honor out-of-state advance directives as long as they are similar to the state's own law; and some states do not have an answer to this question. The best solution, if you spend a significant amount of time in more than one state, is to complete the advance directives for all the states you spend a significant amount of time in.

Advance directives do not expire. An advance directive remains in effect until you change it. If you complete a new advance directive, it invalidates the previous one.

You should review your advance directives periodically to ensure that they still reflect your wishes. If you want to change anything in an advance directive once you have completed it, you should complete a whole new document. In many states, medical practitioners will require you to provide a copy of your advance directive before you receive any treatment from that professional. For this reason, it is essential for you to have a current advance directive.

## OTHER ESSENTIAL DOCUMENTS

In addition to wills, trusts, powers of attorney, and advance directives, there may also be other essential documents that you and your estate planning attorney may wish to create. Below, we have identified two of the most common. Your estate planning attorney may have some other recommendations based on your unique situation.

### Personal Property Designation

A personal property designation or personal property memorandum is a list of items that you want people to inherit. To make the designation legally binding, you sign it and refer to it in your will. Not all states recognize a personal property designation. Your estate planning attorney can ensure that you properly dispose of your personal property.

You can use a personal property designation with your will for items classified as tangible personal property, which includes furniture, art, jewelry, collections, vehicles (in some states), and household items such as china and silverware. You cannot use it for real estate or for intangible property such as money, including bank accounts, stocks, or bonds, and copyrights, patents, trademarks, or licenses. In most states, personal property designations cannot be used to leave tangible business property.

### Trust Certificate

A trust certificate is a document that summarizes certain parts of your trust. It can also be called a *certificate of trust existence*, an *abstract of trust*, or other titles. Institutions will require this document to prove that the trustee has the authority and the trust has the power to conduct certain transactions. Title companies and banks will not accept the original trust certificate if it is more than thirty days old. Often the institutions will have a form that includes the exact language they require. The estate planning attorney that prepared your trust can also prepare a trust certificate for you.

---

Your estate planning attorney will suggest that you prepare a number of important documents that can help you prepare for end-of-life care and other unforeseen circumstances. It is essential for you to discuss all of the suggestions we have provided with your estate planning attorney in order to be sure that your plan provides you with the best possible arrangement.

# CHAPTER 8

# Life Insurance

In this chapter we will first explain some things to consider when determining whether life insurance is appropriate for you and what possible alternatives may be available. We will then define some of the different types of life insurance and the methods by which the life insurance can be held in order to give the maximum benefit to your heirs. We will also recommend methods by which you may be able to reduce or eliminate tax liability for your estate and the beneficiary of the insurance policy.

## ALTERNATIVES TO LIFE INSURANCE

Life insurance is a gamble where you are essentially betting the insurance company that you will die early and therefore that the premiums it receives will be less than what it pays out. The insurance company is gambling that you will live longer than anticipated so that it can earn significantly more premiums than will be necessary to pay the proceeds of the insurance. The life insurance company uses an actuarial table to make sure it makes its money. It may be financially better to put the premium investment into a high-yield money market account, real estate, or another stable investment. In this way, your money will be available to your heirs through the proceeds of those investments and there will not be any deduction for the agent's or broker's commission in selling the insurance. Nor will the insurance company receive any portion of those investments. Essentially, all of the money, plus interest or enhanced value, will be available for your heirs. If you do live longer than the actuarial tables predict, the amount available will definitely be higher than it would be if you purchased insurance. If, on the other hand, you die before the actuarial tables predict, then less money will be available than if you had purchased life insurance. For this reason, deciding whether to purchase insurance or establish your own after-death account is a gamble, and you will need to decide which option you would prefer.

## COMMON TYPES OF LIFE INSURANCE POLICIES

If you decide that you do not want to establish your own after-life fund and instead wish to purchase life insurance, then there are a host of insurance policies to choose from that go far beyond the basic term life insurance policies that most people think of. Below are brief descriptions of eleven of the most prevalent types of insurance policies available on the market today. Of course, insurance companies continue to come up with new varieties of life insurance in order to expand their offerings, appeal to new customers, address new situations, and earn more money. For this reason, you should ask the insurance agent or broker that you deal with what other kinds of life insurance may be available for you given your age, health, gender, income, and the payout you would like to obtain for your heirs.

### 1. Term

Term life insurance is the most basic type of life insurance. Term life insurance is purchased for a certain length of time (a term) which can be as short as five years or ten, twenty, thirty years, or even longer. Most term life insurance policies have an option to renew for an addition one or more years. If the insured dies during the term of protection, the premiums are paid-to-date, and all of the other terms and conditions have been met, the beneficiary of the policy will receive the death benefits.

Term life insurance offers pure death benefit protection only without any cash value buildup in the policy. This means if you stop paying the premium, you and your heirs will receive nothing. It also means that you cannot borrow against this kind of policy.

Term life insurance is often very affordable—especially for individuals who are young and in good health when they apply for coverage. The premiums for term life insurance generally remain the same throughout the entire term of the policy.

Once the term, and any renewal, has expired, the policyholder must requalify for a new policy at the age and health that they are at that time. Policyholders often reevaluate the type of insurance they have and opt for different coverage at the end of a term—especially if many years have passed or their health has deteriorated. Many companies will allow an insured to purchase a term policy for a fixed premium that will remain the same for a number of years. The benefit of having this arrangement is that the premium is locked in so that it will not increase, even if your health significantly declines. Customarily, there is a charge for this kind of arrangement. The lock in period can be five, ten, or more years.

## 2. Increasing and Decreasing Term

For decreasing term life insurance policies, the death benefit—or amount paid out on the death of the insured—decreases over time while the premium remains fixed. When the death benefit reaches zero, the policy terminates. This kind of policy may be useful for homeowners with an unpaid mortgage to provide a guarantee to the survivor that the mortgage will be paid if the other owner dies before the mortgage is fully satisfied. A policy designed to pay off a mortgage could have a term equal to the remaining years on the mortgage. As the mortgage balance decreases, the insurance benefits decrease accordingly. Decreasing term life insurance is often less expensive than policies with a fixed death benefit. This type of insurance would be available for significant loans where the loan principal decreases as it is paid off.

With increasing term life insurance policies, the death benefit increases over time. This is typically accomplished using an additional provision that is added to a typical term life insurance policy called a cost of living rider. This kind of policy may be useful for young individuals who anticipate additional expenses that come with larger homes and growing families. Increasing term life insurance is often more expensive than policies with a fixed benefit. With this type of insurance, fixed premium arrangements may also be available in the same way as they are for regular term life insurance discussed above.

## 3. Permanent

Permanent life insurance, as the name suggests, does not have a time limit like term life insurance. The policy is intended to last for the remainder of the insured's lifetime, or until the premiums are no longer paid. Permanent life insurance is an umbrella term for life insurance plans that do not expire, but typically offer both a death benefit and a savings component. The savings portion allows the policy to build cash value with the policy. The policy owner can then borrow from the policy or withdraw funds for specified uses—such as a child's college education or medical expenses. The cash value of the policy typically grows on a tax-deferred basis, which means the policyholder will not pay taxes on that money as long as the policy is active. Loans on the policy are not taxable; however, withdrawals may be if they exceed the amount of premiums paid into the policy. Note: If money is withdrawn or loans are taken against the policy, the proceeds paid on death will be reduced by the amount of all outstanding loans and withdrawals.

Permanent life insurance policies are useful for individuals whose term life insurance policies have expired but they wish to continue coverage. Many term life insurance policies will offer the option to convert to a permanent policy without the need to requalify by having another medical exam. For individuals in failing health or who may have developed a chronic medical condition that make other insurance options cost prohibitive, this can be an attractive solution. Permanent life insurance policies are typically much more expensive than term life insurance policies.

## 4. Whole

The simplest type of permanent life insurance coverage is whole life. With this type of coverage, the premium amount is locked in and will remain the same throughout the entire lifetime of the policy. This can be helpful for those who need to stick to a budget. It also means that if a person purchases a whole life policy at a very young age, they will still pay the same amount of premium when they get older—regardless of advancing age, or even an adverse health issue. In some cases, where a person's preexisting conditions require the individual to buy high-risk life insurance, whole life policies are the only feasible option.

Like other permanent life insurance policies, whole life coverage offers both a death benefit and a savings component. The cash that is in the cash value component of a whole life insurance policy is allowed to grow on a tax-deferred basis. This means that the gain on these funds will not be taxed until or unless they are withdrawn. This means the savings portion can compound exponentially over time. Some whole life insurance policies pay dividends to their policyholders. Because these dividends are considered to be a return of the premium to the policyholder, they are also not taxed. Dividends can also help the cash value in a policy grow significantly—although they cannot be guaranteed. If money is withdrawn from the policy or a loan is taken against it, the proceeds of the death benefit will be reduced when the insured dies. Individuals may believe that the investment aspect of whole life policies is extremely beneficial. Unfortunately, that is not generally the case, and neither whole life or permanent life insurance should be considered investment vehicles. They are both life insurance.

## 5. Universal

Another form of permanent coverage is universal life insurance. This type of life insurance also provides a death benefit and a cash value component where the funds are allowed to grow tax-deferred. Universal life insurance is more flexible than whole life coverage because the policyholder is allowed— within certain guidelines—to choose how much of his or her premium dollars will go towards the policy's death benefit, and how much will go toward the policy's cash value.

Because universal life is a permanent life insurance policy, the policyholder will have access to the cash value account. So, just as with a whole life plan, the cash can be borrowed or withdrawn for any reason—including paying off debt, supplementing retirement income, or even going on a vacation.

There is also an indexed universal life insurance policy available that can aggressively grow your cash value in the policy over time, but the aggressive investment strategies that could result in greater returns also brings greater risk.

Here too, any money withdrawn, or if the policy is borrowed against, reduces the death benefit by that amount. In addition, these policies may not be considered the best investment vehicle.

## 6. Variable

Variable life insurance is also a form of permanent life insurance coverage. These types of life insurance policies offer a death benefit as well as a cash component. However, with variable life insurance, the policyholder can take part in a variety of different investment options such as equities.

This means that the funds have the opportunity to grow a great deal more than the funds in a whole life policy can. It also means that there can be more risk as funds are exposed to the ups and downs of the equities market.

It is important to note that while the policyholder can increase their funds based on market movements, their cash is not invested directly in the market. Rather, it is invested in "sub-accounts" by the insurance company.

With a variable life insurance policy, the death benefit may go up or down—however; it will not go below the set guaranteed amount. This is usually the original amount of death benefit that is purchased at the time of policy application.

Here too, if any money is withdrawn, or if the policy is borrowed against, then the death benefit is reduced by that amount. In addition, these policies may not be considered the best investment vehicle.

## 7. Variable Universal

Variable universal life insurance is similar to regular universal life insurance coverage, except in this case, the policyholder is allowed to invest the cash in their policy into different types of investments such as mutual funds. Also, there will be no guaranteed minimum cash value in this type of policy.

## 8. Survivorship

With a survivorship life insurance policy, more than one person is covered. This is customarily used for spouses, partners, or in other situations in which two or more individuals wish to acquire life insurance and are interested in only having a single payoff when the first or last of them dies.

These policies can be set up in a couple of different ways. One way is called *first to die*. With this type of policy, the coverage is designed to pay out when the first person passes away.

In most instances, the premium that is charged for this type of policy can be higher than for a policy on just one insured. However, it can often be less than purchasing two separate life insurance policies.

There are also joint and survivor, or last to die life insurance policies. With these policies, the coverage pays out when the second person on the coverage passes away. These can either be term or permanent coverage.

These policies can also have other advantages, too, in that they typically will cost less than two separate life insurance policies, and they may have less strict underwriting criteria—especially if one of the individuals is in very good health.

## 9. Final Expense

Final expense life insurance coverage is often called burial insurance and is purchased by those who are considered "seniors," or persons between the ages of fifty and eighty-five—although there are some insurance companies who will sell policies to applicants who are older.

This type of coverage is typically geared toward those who want to ensure that their loved ones will not be saddled with the high cost of a funeral and other related expenses, such as a headstone, burial, flowers, and memorial service.

Today, the average cost of such items nationwide can be in the range of $10,000—an amount that many families just simply do not have readily available. So, a final expense life insurance policy can help. It should be noted, however, that a final expense insurance policy does not cover expenses related to end-of-life care, such as ambulance fees and hospital costs. You should speak with your estate planning attorney and financial advisors about the feasibility of establishing an "end of life" or "final expense" account to cover these potential expenses.

## 10. No Medical Exam

As its name implies, no exam life insurance coverage does not require an applicant to undergo a medical examination. In most cases, when applying for life insurance, individuals must meet with a paramedical professional who will ask them in-depth health questions, perform a medical exam, and take a blood and a urine sample.

Because of this, those who have certain types of adverse health conditions may be denied for the life insurance that they need. But, with no medical exam coverage, they could be approved for the coverage that they need—and, because there are no medical requirements to contend with, these policies are often approved within just a day or two after application.

While no medical exam life insurance is the best option for some, they are much more expensive, so if you feel you could pass the medical exam, you should try that first to get lower premium rates.

## 11. Key Person Life Insurance Coverage

Key person life insurance, or corporate-owned life insurance, protects a company in the event of the loss of an employee who plays a significant role in the business.

Employees covered by this type of life insurance might include executive officers, specialized skill players, and highly effective members of the sales force.

Key person policies are unique in that the beneficiary and the policy-holder are one in the same. The company simply informs the employee it will be purchasing a policy to insure them. With the employee's signature in hand, it can purchase a policy. Key person insurance can provide companies with a solid source of protection for their businesses. This is frequently used in partnerships, corporations, and LLCs.

## LIFE INSURANCE ANNUITIES

If you have life insurance and you've been keeping up with your premiums, when you die the life insurance company will pay out a death benefit to your beneficiaries. The amount of the death benefit is called coverage, and the amount of coverage you need depends on your financial situation and the amount the recipients of the payout (known as the beneficiaries) need to survive without you.

How the death benefit gets disbursed is usually up to the beneficiaries. Most people choose a lump-sum disbursement—meaning they get the entire amount at once, tax-free, divided between the number of beneficiaries.

Another option is to receive the death benefit as an annuity. An annuity works like a periodic income in that the death benefit is divided up over a number of years into equivalent amounts that the beneficiary receives each year.

If there are two or more beneficiaries, and each desires a different form of payout, the policy must be reviewed in order to determine whether different forms of payout will be permitted. If it is not, then an arrangement between them will be required. It might be best for the insured to make this determination initially.

## INSURANCE TRUSTS

An insurance trust is an irrevocable trust set up with a life insurance policy as the asset, allowing the grantor of the trust to remove the life insurance policy as an asset from the estate. Once the life insurance policy is placed in the trust, the insured person no longer owns the policy, which will be managed by the trustee on behalf of the policy beneficiaries when the insured person dies.

The insurance trust, typically called an irrevocable life insurance trust (ILIT), is often used to set aside cash proceeds that can be used to pay estate taxes, as the life insurance policy should be exempt from the taxable estate of the decedent. It is also customarily used to fund business buy-sell agreements, which will be discussed in the next section.

One catch of an insurance trust is that the life insurance policy must be transferred to the trust at least three years before the death of the insured. To get around this rule, a new policy can be taken out with a spouse as owner, then placed in the trust. Alternatively, the trust can be established, and then the trustee of the ILIT can purchase the policy.

Your estate planning attorney or business attorney may have other recommendations to set up ownership in the insurance policy to avoid estate taxes and make sure the proper beneficiaries receive the benefit of the policy.

## BUY-SELL AGREEMENTS

A buy-sell agreement is a legally binding agreement between the co-owners of a business. It is sometimes referred to as a buyout agreement. A buy-sell agreement governs the situation if a co-owner dies, is forced to leave the business, or simply chooses to leave the business. It serves as a kind of prenuptial agreement between the business partners and/or shareholders of a company—sometimes called a "business will."

With a buy-sell agreement that is funded by life insurance, the company or the individual co-owners buy life insurance policies on the lives of each co-owner. Thus, if you die, the company or the co-owners receive the death benefits from the insurance policies on your life. Plus, your family would get a sum of cash as payment for your interest in the business. This provides financial support for them after your death and it also provides stability for the company.

The kind of insurance used in this situation is key person insurance, discussed above.

Buy-sell agreements can take different forms, but the two typical structures are cross-purchase plans and entity redemption plans, with a hybrid version also available as a third possible option.

Cross-Purchase Plan—In a cross-purchase plan, each owner purchases a life insurance policy on the other owner or owners. Each owner pays the annual premiums on the policy they own and each is the beneficiary of the policy. When an owner dies, the surviving owners use the death benefit to purchase the deceased owner's share of the business. If there are a large number of owners of the business, multiple policies must be purchased by each owner. These policies can be key person insurance policies, which are discussed above.

**Entity Redemption Plan**—In an entity redemption plan, each owner has an arrangement with the business for the sale of their respective interests to the business. The business purchases separate life insurance policies on the lives of the owners. The business pays the premiums. And the business is the owner and beneficiary of the policy. When an owner dies, his or her share of company stock will pass to his or her heirs or estate, and the company may purchase them with the proceeds from the life insurance policy.

**Hybrid Plan**—A hybrid plan, as you might have guessed, combines the first two types of buy-sell agreements: cross-purchase and entity redemption. Typically, the owner is required to offer his or her interest to the entity. If the entity declines or cannot make the purchase, however, other co-owners or partners can purchase the shares. This type of arrangement may also allow certain employees, like longtime company officials, to purchase the interest. This can also be used by groups of employees.

## TAX IMPLICATIONS

Generally speaking, when the beneficiary of a life insurance policy receives the death benefit, this money is not counted as taxable income, and the beneficiary does not have to pay taxes on it. However, a few situations exist in which the beneficiary is taxed on some or all of a policy's proceeds. If the policyholder elects not to have the benefit paid out immediately upon death but instead held by the insurance company for a given period of time, the beneficiary may have to pay taxes on the interest generated during that period. When a death benefit is paid to an estate, the person or persons inheriting the estate may have to pay estate taxes on it.

Income earned in the form of interest is almost always taxable at some point. Life insurance is no exception. This means when a beneficiary receives life insurance proceeds after a period of interest accumulation rather than immediately upon the policyholder's death, the beneficiary must pay taxes, not on the entire benefit, but on the interest. For example, if the death benefit is $500,000, but it earned 10 percent interest for one year before being paid out, the beneficiary owes taxes on the $50,000 growth. Though, that interest is passive income, which is taxed at a lower rate than ordinary income. However, cash-value policies that are comprised of dividends, rather than interest, are typically not taxable, unless the dividends exceed the exceed the total premium payments of the policy.

In some cases, life insurance proceeds are paid to the estate of the deceased. This often happens when the policy's beneficiary dies first and no contingent beneficiary is named. The death benefit adds to the value of the estate, which may be subject to estate taxes or inheritance taxes. The easiest way to avoid this situation is to name a primary and contingent beneficiary to a life insurance policy or establish a life insurance trust.

For business-related insurance policies, if structured properly, the payment for the premium may be tax deductible as a business expense. In this event, the insurance proceeds may wind up being taxable. You should discuss the best way to handle this type of arrangement with your business or estate planning attorney.

---

Life insurance policies and methods by which they can be used have been presented in this chapter. As noted above, insurance companies continue to expand their programs, so you should find out from your life insurance agent or broker whether other, newer options may be available for you. Life insurance is a complex and technical area and should be discussed with your estate planning attorney, accountant, or tax attorney. Additionally, you should also discuss life insurance strategies with a financial professional specializing in life insurance because of its complexity.

# CHAPTER 9

# Digital Assets

Digital assets are a relatively new asset class. As such, the best practices with how to manage and plan for digital assets upon death is a work in progress. In fact, even defining what a digital asset is can be a challenge. Generally, digital assets are electronic records in which you have a right or an interest, or the hardware that stores those electronic records. Digital assets may have sentimental value (such as Facebook photos) or financial value (such as a PayPal account). Digital assets may even be currency themselves, as is the case with Bitcoin and other cryptocurrencies. As a result of the growing value and prevalence of digital assets, it is important to plan for your digital assets in case of your incapacity or death.

## THE IMPORTANCE OF PLANNING FOR YOUR DIGITAL ASSETS

At present, most US states, including Arizona, Florida, Illinois, Indiana, Kansas, Minnesota, and Wisconsin, have adopted some form of the Revised Uniform Fiduciary Access to Digital Assets Act (referred to as "RUFADAA"). When adopted, this state law allows you to name an individual in your estate plan (such as an agent under a power of attorney, an executor or personal representative under your will, or a trustee under your living trust) to act as a digital agent and access your digital assets. In order to access electronic communications, such as email, RUFADAA requires that you, as the account owner, specifically state your wish that your digital agent have access to such communications. If you've already designated someone to access an online account through a particular service provider's online tool, let your attorney know, because an online tool designation takes priority over any persons you've named in your estate plan—and the designation you made in the online tool might conflict with the estate plan you discuss with your attorney.

## DESIGNATING A DIGITAL AGENT

Your digital agent, sometimes called a *digital fiduciary*, should be someone you trust and who has the knowledge to manage digital information. If your executor does not have enough digital savvy to manage your online presence, you can designate a separate agent for digital assets.

Make sure your digital agent knows where to find your digital asset inventory and login information. Remind your agent that this list must be kept in a safe place. The information may also be stored digitally, but it may then be subject to hacking attacks.

## IDENTIFYING YOUR DIGITAL ASSETS

The first step to properly planning for your digital assets is to identify what they are. This may be one of the most dynamic parts of your estate plan, as all of us are constantly creating and deleting accounts, transferring digital assets, and trying out new technology. In order to make a useful tool for your friends and family, it is vital that you not only complete the worksheet at the end of this section, but that you update it frequently. Examples of digital assets include email; social media networks such as Facebook, Instagram, and Twitter; Internet "cloud" accounts like Dropbox or iCloud; payments accounts like PayPal and Venmo; frequent flier accounts; online retailer accounts such as Amazon.com; online bill-paying accounts; blogs; photo-sharing accounts like Flickr or Shutterfly; and electronic devices, such as smartphones, tablets, and laptops.

## DIGITAL ASSET INVENTORY

Begin by making a list of your hardware, data, accounts, and related login information including the answers to security questions. Close old and unused accounts to reduce the number of active accounts that you no longer need or use. Update your preferences on your online accounts for any sites that allow you to make decisions about what will happen to the account in the case of your death or disability. Update your information regularly to keep your list of accounts, usernames, and passwords up-to-date. Some accounts may allow access to multiple users such as Flickr or Google Docs. Consider giving access to a trusted friend or family member immediately. Create back-ups of tangible media like photos and videos that are not locked behind user-names and passwords. Include a digital asset provision in your will and power of attorney. It is vital that you store a repository of all of your login credentials in a secure location. While your digital agent will need this information to access your accounts, most states will allow your digital agent to have your accounts closed. However, the laws typically do not give your digital agent the authority to retrieve login information from the online sites directly.

Be very sure to keep your digital asset inventory, which includes user-names and passwords, stored in a secure location so unauthorized users can't easily access your accounts. Depending on your circumstances, a secure location might be a lockbox, your safety deposit box, or with a trusted profes-sional or loved one. You may also use a password manager service to help cre-ate and securely store passwords on your computer. Password management systems require a master password to gain access to your data. A copy of that main password should be kept in a secure location as well.

We recommend setting a reminder on your calendar or smartphone to update your digital asset inventory at least as often as once per quarter.

### Hardware

Begin by taking an inventory of your hardware such as computers (laptops and desktops), external hard drives, flash drives, tablets, phones, e-readers, digital cameras, digital music players, gaming consoles, and handheld gam-ing devices. Some of these devices may be password protected. Others may contain sensitive information that you want only a designated individual to manage. There may be flash drives or SD cards in unexpected or hidden loca-tions. All of these devices should be identified and located with instructions on how to access each.

### Data

After all of your hardware has been inventoried, take an inventory of all of your data. Data can be stored on hardware you own, a third party's servers, or in the cloud. Data can generally be divided into two categories. The first is data with monetary value. This will include any e-commerce accounts, income-generating websites, online payment systems like PayPal, accounts with points programs like hotel or airline programs, and other digital assets that generate income or can be sold for value. The financial value of Bitcoin or a PayPal account can be easily determined, whereas online photo albums are likely to hold only sentimental value. But it can be more challenging to value other types of digital assets, such as a popular blog. If the blog creates revenue, that revenue can be tracked, but if you plan to sell the blog, you may need to work with a web appraisal expert to estimate the blog's "digital finance" value.

The second category is data that have no monetary value. These data may have sentimental value or may be nontransferable digital content. This category of data includes personal photographs, music, ebooks and other documents stored digitally, content posted on social media, data in email accounts, social media and gaming accounts, and accounts with shopping, media, or utility companies.

## Online Accounts

You likely have online access to bank accounts, credit card accounts, brokerage accounts, and other financial accounts. The underlying accounts are the real assets for estate purposes. However, access to these accounts will be important for the person you identify to manage your digital assets and should be recorded and kept confidential.

Each email and social media company has its own requirements for how an account may be closed in the event of the death of the account holder. This is typically a time-consuming effort that involves sending legal documents, such as a death certificate and court documents. The terms of service usually prohibit the transfer of an email or social media account or allowing someone else to use your login information. However, many states have passed or are in the process of passing laws that allow you to identify a person to act as your digital agent to access and manage the account. Some social media platforms and email service providers may automatically delete an account after a certain period of inactivity, so it will be important for your digital agent to act quickly to recover online data.

Review your account options. Determine whether each of your providers offers an online tool for you to name another person to access your accounts. Two common online tools are Google's Inactive Account Manager and Facebook's Memorialization settings. If an existing online tool provides the access you want or need, you may decide to use the tool.

# ROADBLOCKS TO ACCESS

Planning for digital assets is particularly tricky. Not only are we constantly creating and deleting accounts, but each account will have unique restrictions and the law is still evolving. Below, we have outlined a few roadblocks that may stand in the way of your digital agent accessing your accounts after your death. It is important for you and your estate planning attorney to be aware of the particulars of each account and plan accordingly.

## User Agreements

When you sign up for a new online account or service, you typically agree to its terms of service. Sometimes the terms of service will include a provision that explains what will happen on the death of the account holder. Often, there is a term that expressly states that the account cannot be transferred. In its terms of services, Yahoo! states that the account cannot be transferred and upon receipt of a death certificate, your account will be terminated and the contents permanently deleted. This kind of policy protects the privacy of users and may be exactly what you intend. If it is not your intention to have the content of your account permanently deleted, you must take steps to ensure your digital agent knows how to access and archive the account. Keep in mind that state law may allow your digital agent to access the account without breaking the law, but it will not prevent the company from deleting an account pursuant to its terms of service if it learns about your death before the account has been dealt with.

## Nontransferable assets

Unlike physical books, CDs, DVDs, or vinyl records, purchasing digital works online usually does not grant you ownership rights in the digital work. Most companies simply sell you a license or subscription to access and use the song or video. This is obvious with a streaming service like Netflix or Pandora, but it is also true of other services like iTunes or Amazon where you store a copy of music files, movies, or ebooks on your local device. You likely do not "own" these assets in a traditional sense and are merely borrowing them under the terms of a license agreement. This often means that you cannot transfer these assets to another person, user, or account.

For example, if you read Amazon's Conditions of Use, you'll find that "Amazon or its content providers grant you a limited, nonexclusive, non-transferable, non-sublicensable license to access and make personal and noncommercial use of the Amazon Services." In Amazon's Music Terms of Use, it also notes that your account cannot be shared or transferred, stating, "You may not share your Amazon.com username and password with others or use anyone else's Amazon.com username and password."

Every company treats digital assets differently. For example, Air Miles Canada allows you to transfer ownership of air miles at no charge when an account holder passes away. American Airlines' AAdvantage program states that mileage credit is not transferable, even to heirs upon the death of the account holder. However, American Airlines may make exemptions in its sole discretion. The Delta SkyMiles policy states that miles are not the property of any member and may not be transferred under any circumstances, including death.

### Federal Laws

Two federal laws, the Stored Communications Act and the Computer Fraud and Abuse Act, were both passed into law in 1986. The purpose of these laws was to prevent computer hacking and fraud and were passed in a time long before the era of social media and online purchasing. The laws have been updated slowly but are still not in line with how most individuals understand and use their online accounts. For example, sharing your Netflix password with another person likely violates both of these laws. Neither law was intended to address a digital agent acting on behalf of someone who has died. However, because of the laws' age and the way they are worded, they shape the policies of online companies with respect to releasing accounts to others. While the Department of Justice has made it clear that it does not intend to prosecute "minor violations" of these laws, it is still an important concern when dealing with digital assets. Because of these laws and the constantly shifting legal landscape, it is vital to discuss your digital asset plan with your estate planning attorney.

## WILLS

Your will should include specific powers to handle digital assets and contain either a digital asset inventory or reference to a separate digital asset inventory. Your estate planning attorney can help make sure the language in the will conforms to your state's digital access laws, and may have additional language to address specific terms in end-user agreements.

## DURABLE POWERS OF ATTORNEY

Because a will only comes into play after your death, a durable power of attorney that identifies your digital agent in the case of your incapacity is a wise document to prepare. Your estate planning attorney can help you draft a document that defines when the agent's powers will be triggered, identify who your digital agent will be, and outline the agent's powers. Like a will, the digital power of attorney will likely need to contain specific language to make sure it complies with state digital access laws. Without specific language, an online service provider may refuse to accept the document. Your estate planning attorney can help you draft this language so that your digital agent will have access to all of the hardware, accounts, and data that the agent will need to manage your digital affairs while you are unable to.

## TRUSTS

Creating a living trust to own digital assets has the potential to avoid many of the problems that arise upon death. First, many of the state digital asset laws allow for trusts to create online accounts. If the trust creates the account, the trustee will have access to the digital account throughout the life of the trust. As we discussed more fully in Chapter 4, you can be the trustee of a living trust. Once you pass away, a new trustee will be appointed. In this circumstance, that new trustee will still have the same access to the account that you had when you were alive.

Transferring your digital accounts into a trust may also allow the trust to continue to access digital books, music, and movies that you would not be able to transfer to your heirs because of the user agreements. This method is not available for accounts that are not transferable, so you should work with an estate planning attorney who has access to all of the relevant user agreements in order to ensure your plans will work properly.

## MAKE YOUR INTENTIONS KNOWN

If you've named someone to access your digital assets on your behalf in an online tool or in your estate plan, give them some guidelines in advance. For instance, do you want family members to leave your Facebook page in place as a memorial after your death, or take it down after a certain period of time?

Do you want your children to sell your blog, leave up archived posts, or delete it entirely? Explaining your wishes in advance can make it less stressful for family members to manage your digital affairs in your absence. These conversations also make it more likely that your representatives will understand and follow your specific requests.

## ONLINE AFTERLIFE MANAGEMENT COMPANIES

In recent years, a number of companies have begun offering services to manage the digital affairs of their users after death. There are a number of problems with this kind of arrangement. Most notably, many of these companies fail within a few years. If you are in reasonably good health, you have a pretty good chance of outliving the company. The company may transfer its accounts to another group that can do the job or it may simply vanish. Another problem is that most of these companies cannot legally perform the duties that they market. This creates a number of problems for the companies, but for your estate, it means the assets must all still be transferred through your will and not much time or effort will be saved. That is not to say the companies are all bad. The services these companies offer can help you create a digital asset inventory and can help make the transfer of assets to your digital agent go more smoothly. However, before signing up for a service, do your homework and speak with your estate planning attorney for more information about how they operate in conjunction with your state's laws.

---

Regardless of your digital prowess, the number of social media followers, or the size of your online footprint, you probably have a number of digital assets that contain sensitive information or have sentimental or monetary value. Planning ahead with an experienced estate planning attorney can be a tremendous gift to your friends and family. Even a step as small as listing all of your digital accounts can cut down on months of frustration for those who are trying to settle your affairs. Be sure to keep your digital asset inventory up-to-date, store it in a secure location, and discuss your wishes with the person you identify to be your digital agent.

CHAPTER 10

# Tax Considerations

Older taxpayers have issues which are generally different from those of younger individuals. For example, older individuals will likely have significant retirement accounts and may have reached the age where they are making distributions. Choosing the right beneficiary in distribution elections can decrease the amount of taxes paid and increase the opportunity for tax-deferred growth in the account over your beneficiaries' lifetime. In addition, the decisions you make when you retire from a company will affect the amount of taxes you or your beneficiaries ultimately pay. You may have deferred compensation plans; vacation homes or time-shares you would like to remain in the family; you may be considering relocating to another state for personal reasons, or have higher medical expenses. It is always best to check with a estate planning attorney when a significant event occurs in your life, such as retirement or a change of your permanent residence. In this chapter, we will explain some of the tax considerations you may wish to take under advisement when preparing your estate plan.

## PRINCIPAL POINTS TO CONSIDER

First, federal tax law requires that you start taking withdrawals from your retirement accounts such as IRAs and 401(k)s by April 1 of the year after you turn 70½. You are permitted to withdraw funds without a penalty when you reach 59½.

Second, if you wish to reduce the size of your estate through gifts, it is important to know that gifts of different types of property will have different tax consequences for you and the person to whom you give the property.

Third, the form by which you withdraw money or property from your company's retirement plan will affect the income taxes that you may have to pay.

There are likely to be other items you should consider, but these are the three that apply to virtually everyone. Other considerations may apply to your unique circumstances.

## PRIMARY RESIDENCES

The exclusion for capital gains on the sale of your home is currently $250,000 ($500,000 for couple filing a joint return), provided you meet the use and ownership tests. You must have owned the home for at least two years and lived in the home as your primary residence for two years. Temporary absences from the home, like extended vacations, will not disqualify you from the exclusion.

You may still qualify for the exclusion if you do not meet the use and ownership tests but sold the home due to a change in employment, health, or unforeseen circumstances. This exclusion may be used more than once and a person's age does not matter.

When an administrator or executor is reviewing land and buildings you owned, they should establish how you acquired the property. If you did not pay for the property—for example, your spouse, partner, or friend simply put your name on the title—the executor will have to determine whether you actually owned that property, whether the property will be included in the estate, and the taxable value of the property.

## INDIVIDUAL RETIREMENT ACCOUNTS

An individual retirement account ("IRA") may be your single largest asset. If you made the correct designations and elections, you could take advantage of the minimum distribution rules to extend the life of your IRA over not only your own life, but over the life expectancy of your beneficiary as well. For example, you can designate your child as the beneficiary of the IRA and elect to have the distributions calculated over both of your joint life expectancies. This allows your account to grow tax-deferred for a longer period and increases the benefit of the account. However, if you designate a charity, your estate, or a nonqualifying trust as the beneficiary, only your life expectancy can be used to estimate the life of the IRA in calculating the distribution amount.

In addition, if your spouse is named as beneficiary of the IRA, the account will not be subject to federal estate taxes upon your death since gifts to a spouse are tax-exempt. Note, this does not apply to unmarried couples, and the gift will increase the size of the surviving spouse's estate when the spouse dies.

Distributions may be made from an IRA account prior to age 59½ without penalty for the following reasons:

- The distribution was to a beneficiary (or to the estate of the person) on or after the death of the person.
- The person becomes permanently and totally disabled.
- The distribution is made as part of a series made for the life (or life expectancy) of the person or the joint lives (or joint life expectancies) of the person and the person's designated beneficiary.
- Distributions made to pay qualified medical expenses.
- To pay health insurance premiums if the person is unemployed for at least twelve weeks.
- To pay for qualified higher education expenses of the person and their spouse, child, or grandchild.
- Distribution of up to $10,000 for first-time home purchases.
- The distribution is due to tax charges on the qualified plan.
- The distribution is to a qualified member of the military reserves who is called to active duty.

In some cases, a beneficiary may want to refuse to accept an IRA payment to save federal estate taxes. This is a very complex concept and it is important for you to discuss the possibility of having you, your spouse, or your beneficiaries refuse an IRA distribution with your tax advisor and estate planning attorney.

## GIFTS AND GIFT TAXES

One method of decreasing the size of any estate is simply to give away some of the estate's property during your life. While gifting is discussed in other chapters of this book, it is important enough to consider it in this chapter as well. When making gifts there are a number of issues that need to be considered.

First, property interest transfers need to be a present interest, not a future interest, in order to qualify for the annual exclusion. For example, if you give stock to a grandchild, you must actually transfer the stock, not merely make a promise to transfer the stock in the future.

Second, in general, gifts made within three years of the date of death are brought back into the estate for estate tax purposes. Try to start a gifting program to your beneficiaries early to decrease the overall estate tax burden.

Third, if you are transferring passive activity property (such as rental property), check with your tax accountant prior to making the gift because the rules are very complex.

Fourth, if possible, do not give away stock that has decreased in value, because you will be losing the benefit of having a capital loss that you can use to settle capital gains, and the recipient of that stock will not receive a beneficial tax basis. It is far better for you to sell the stock, realize the capital loss, and make a gift of the proceeds of the sale.

Fifth, consider giving away life insurance policies. If you retain ownership or control of the policies, the death benefits of that policy will be included in your estate. Also, the current value of a term policy may be almost nothing, which means it will be within the annual exclusion amount for gift purposes.

For a more detailed look at gifts as they relate to the estate plan, please see Chapter 13 of this book.

## DECEDENT TAX FORMS

There are a number of IRS forms that need to be filled out and federal taxes that may need to be paid on behalf of the estate. Below are the most common forms that must be prepared and filed:

- **Form 1040 (for the person who died).** The person who died must have a final US Individual Income Tax Return Form 1040 filed for that person by April 15 of the year after that person died. The final income tax return will be for the period of January 1 through the date of the person's death. Also, if the person died before filing taxes for the year before death, those taxes must be prepared and filed as well.

- **Form 1040 (of the beneficiary).** The beneficiary must report any income the beneficiary received from the estate on the beneficiary's Form 1040.
- **Form 706.** The Estate Tax Return Form 706 must be filed nine months after the date of death if the estate's gross assets plus gifts exceed the unified federal tax credit amount—that is, if there is a taxable estate. This form is more than thirty pages long and very complex. We strongly recommend that you enlist the aid of your tax and legal advisor when preparing this form.
- **Form 1041 (filed by the estate fiduciary).** Form 1041 must be filed if the estate's gross income exceeds $600. It is due on April 15 of the year after death.

All of the tax forms mentioned are available at the official IRS website, www.irs.gov.

## INCOME AND DEDUCTIONS IN RESPECT OF A DECEDENT

All income, including wages, commissions, royalties, interest, and deferred compensation that you would have included on your income taxes if you had not died is called *income in respect of a decedent* ("IRD"). There are situations in which IRD will appear on both tax Form 706 and 1040. In this situation, the estate will wind up being taxed twice, and the estate will be able to deduct one of those taxes in order to avoid double taxation. This is a very complex area of tax law and we strongly recommend that the estate's administrator work with an experienced tax advisor and estate planning attorney in situations where there is a taxable estate.

## GENERATION-SKIPPING TAX

A generation-skipping tax ("GST"), also sometimes called the generation-skipping transfer tax, may be incurred when grandparents directly transfer money or property to their grandchildren without first leaving it to their children (the grandchildren's parents). The GST doesn't just apply to grandchildren. It also addresses gifts or transfers made to other family members and to unrelated individuals who are at least 37½ years younger than the person making the gift. Often the middle generation is skipped to avoid inheritance being subject to taxes twice—once when it moves from the grandparents to their children, then from those children to the grandchildren. The Internal Revenue Service has therefore created an additional tax to these inheritances to compensate for estate taxes that might otherwise have been avoided.

Every person may transfer up to $11,400,000 (2019 amount) to beneficiaries two generations below—for example, a grandparent to a grandchild—without the imposition of additional generation-skipping transfer taxes.

There is an exception for grandchildren whose parents have died before the grandparent. In this case, the children effectively move up to their parents' place in line so the GST no longer applies to them because the gift isn't skipping a generation.

---

It should be clear from the material in this chapter that dealing with an experienced estate planning lawyer and accountant is essential not only when preparing your estate plan but also when implementing it. The worksheet that appears at the end of this section should contain the information your estate planning team will need when preparing your estate plan. You should also identify any documents which you believe might be helpful for those individuals when you prepare your plan. When in doubt as to the relevance of a document, it would be best for you to provide it to your estate planning attorney so that the lawyer can evaluate it and have it available if necessary.

# CHAPTER 11

# Your Legacy

Your will, trust, tax forms, and other estate planning documents are required to comply with state and federal laws. In this chapter, we are recommending that you consider preparing material that you believe would be beneficial and appreciated by those you leave behind so that they can remember you. That is, what would you like to say to your family and friends that will remain after you die.

Recording the thoughts and words that you wish to comprise your legacy is sometimes called recording your ethical or spiritual will. This can be an important part of your own process of dealing with death and a great comfort to those you leave behind. In this chapter, we will provide prompts that may inspire you to reflect on your values and document what you have loved about your life and learned along the way. We strongly recommend that you consider leaving lasting memories by which those who survive you will be able to remember you. In addition to the material you leave for your friends and family, you should also consider the possibility of establishing a lasting memorial such as a scholarship fund, endowed positions at a university, a monument, or some significant donation for the purpose of perpetuating your memory.

## HELPFUL TIPS

It can be difficult to sit down and attempt to summarize everything you have learned and enjoyed throughout your life. To make that easier, consider the following tips:

- When you get stuck, consider beginning a sentence with: "What I love about my life is . . ." or "What I will miss when I die . . ."

- Write only one thing in each sentence. Be specific.
- Write things that only you know about, things that you care deeply about, that will die with you if you don't record them.
- Think through your life many times, focusing on a different theme each time. Consider the passions that drove you as well as your values.
- Take time to focus your attention on your senses: smelling, touching, hearing, seeing, tasting. For example, "I love the sound of a canoe paddle dipping into a calm lake."
- Consider relationships, social, family, communal and private moments that you value.
- Move gently from memory to meaning and allow yourself to be carried away. You will not regret writing too much, only too little.
- Date your writing and return often.
- If writing isn't your thing, consider recording yourself or ask someone to interview you.
- Focus on the positive.

Your legacy should only focus on the positive aspects of your life and your relationships with those who survive you. Any problems or negative issues should disappear after you die. Remember that the letter, recording, or other legacy will remain forever, and you should decide how you would like the individuals who survive you to remember you.

## PARTING THOUGHTS

Since nobody knows when they will actually die, it is important for you to begin working on this portion of your legacy as soon as possible. Begin taking notes, arrange for recordings or interviews, and start collecting the material that you would like to include in your legacy.

In the worksheet that appears at the end of this section, you should list the positive things you would like to have the individuals who survive you remember about you, your relationships with them, and positive experiences you have had during your life and when interacting with them. Think about vacations, parties, celebrations, holiday events, and everything that you would like to have the individuals who you leave behind remember when they think about you.

The time you spend in preparing the letters, recordings, posts, tweets, stories, and videos will be time well spent since it will help you recall those positive memories and provide those who survive you with a permanent reminder of them as well.

## LAST POSTS, TWEETS, ETC.

Many social media sites have a mechanism for users to either draft a final message or have a designated person post a final message on your behalf. This message will likely remain the first post others will see when they visit your account, so consider what tone you would like to take and how you would like others, some of whom may have never met you, to remember you. For more information about social media accounts, see Chapter 9 of this book.

## STORIES AND VIDEOS

In the worksheet that follows this chapter you should list the people you would like to receive copies of your legacy, including their names and other contact information; a list of positive events that you would like to discuss including vacations, parties, holiday events, and other celebrations; how you overcame challenges including physical, emotional, and spiritual challenges; and significant historical events that may have influenced you.

Since there have been numerous significant events that likely occurred during your lifetime, you may wish to list some or all of the events you can remember and identify your thoughts and experiences when those events occurred. For example, if you recall the day President John Kennedy was assassinated or when the planes hit the World Trade Center on 9/11, where were you at that time, what did you experience when you learned of the tragedy, and how did it affect you?

## IN MEMORIAM

For some individuals, having their name identified on all or a portion of a building, in connection with a scholarship or some other prestigious project, is an important part of their legacy. If you desire this, then it can be established as part of your estate plan in your trust or your will. It is important for you to determine the identity of the project and the amount of money you are willing to make available for that project. If your objective may be overly optimistic—for example, you decide that you would like to donate enough money to have a new wing added to a museum and have that wing bear your name—you should specify that in the event that the funds identified for this project are insufficient, a significant remodel that bears your name would also be acceptable. By providing the less-expensive alternative, you are assisting the individuals who are responsible for carrying out your request if a problem arises, and saving the estate from having to enlist the aid of a court to deal with the change. Examples of projects that you might consider are: scholarship funds, which can be established at colleges, universities, through professional associations such as bar associations for lawyers, medical associations for doctors, accounting associations for accountants, and engineering associations for engineers. A scholarship fund can be structured to have the institution hosting the fund create the requirements for obtaining the scholarship, or the scholarship fund can have its own rules for providing the benefits. Working with your estate planning attorney and the institution you intend to benefit when creating this type of fund is important.

You may desire to have a building, portion of a building, or room in a building bear your name. Customarily, these types of arrangements are for government buildings, hospitals, educational institutions, libraries, public auditoriums, and other structures that are highly visible and benefit a large portion of the community. Here, too, it is important for you to work with your estate planning attorney and the institution if having your name associated with this kind of project is important.

Many communities have public art such as sculptures and murals. Arranging for your name to be associated with public art may also be important to you. If this is your objective, then you should decide whether to merely identify a person to obtain the art and arrange for the installation, or whether you would prefer to be involved with that before you die. If you prefer the latter, then you should identify the art, its ultimate location, and have as much of the project completed as possible so it will be available when you die. Estate planning lawyers should certainly be involved in this type of project as well.

The possibilities of having your name associated with scholarships, buildings, public art, and other public benefits are endless and only limited by your creativity and your resources. You should discuss these ideas with your estate planning attorney and anyone else you feel might be helpful in assisting you with your legacy.

In some situations, creating a legacy such as those described in this section may not have been planned before death, and survivors may feel that it is important to create one. If the estate does not have the resources or if its money is not available for this type of project, then other methods for accomplishing the project can be employed. When a young lawyer was killed in the late 1970s, her friends and family wished to have a scholarship created in her name. In order to fund that scholarship, they requested that her friends, family, and others who wished to honor her memory donate money to a scholarship fund bearing her name. The fund was created and it has provided an annual scholarship since it started. The scholarship will be available indefinitely. See www.cdjmemorialscholarship.org.

In another example, a prominent judge had a courthouse named for him even though his estate did not pay for that courthouse. This was because his colleagues and the legislators who knew him felt that it was important to honor his legacy.

As noted above, the possibilities of having your legacy memorialized in some prominent way is only limited by your creativity and the imagination of your friends, family, and the others who survive you. You should determine whether any of these projects are important to you or whether some other public benefit would be appealing. If so, you should begin to plan. Your trust or will can describe the project and either fund it or request that your executor or personal representative solicit donations for the project.

## WORKSHEET 1

In addition to the fillable pages included in this section, you should add supplemental pages whenever necessary and fasten them to this part of the book.

## GENERAL INFORMATION ABOUT YOU

| General Information |
| --- |
| Name: |
| Birth date: |
| Location of birth: |
| Address: |
|  |
| Alternative addresses: |
|  |
| Phone number: |
| Alternative phone number: |
| Email address: |
| Alternative email address: |
| Estate planning documents I already have: |
|  |
|  |
|  |
|  |
|  |
|  |
|  |

# EXECUTOR OR PERSONAL REPRESENTATIVE

This is the person who will manage your estate and distribute assets under your will. You should include at least one backup individual. For more information, see Chapter 3.

- **Executor**
  - Name: _____
    - Address: _____
    - Phone number: _____
    - Email address: _____
- **Contingency Executor**
  - Name: _____
    - Address: _____
    - Phone number: _____
    - Email address: _____
- **Second Contingency Exectuor**
  - Name: _____
    - Address: _____
    - Phone number: _____
    - Email address: _____

## Specialized Executors

This is the person who will manage any special property you may have. This is important for people with creative assets, professionals who must comply with licensing board requirements, and to identify digital agents. For more information, see Chapters 3 and 9.

Specialty (Digital Agent, Literary Executor, etc.): _____

1. Specialty Executor: _____
   - Name: _____
     - Address: _____
     - Phone number: _____
     - Email address: _____
2. Contingency Specialty Executor: _____
   - Name: _____
     - Address: _____
     - Phone number: _____
     - Email address:_____

3. Second Contingency Specialty Exectuor: _____
   - Name: _____
     - Address:_____
     - Phone number: _____
     - Email address:_____

**Specialty (Digital Agent, Literary Executor, etc.):** _____

1. Specialty Executor: _____
   - Name: _____
     - Address:_____
     - Phone number: _____
     - Email address:_____
2. Contingency Specialty Executor: _____
   - Name: _____
     - Address: _____
     - Phone number: _____
     - Email address:_____
3. Second Contingency Specialty Executor: _____
   - Name: _____
     - Address: _____
     - Phone number: _____
     - Email address:_____

**Specialty (Digital Agent, Literary Executor, etc.):** _____

1. Specialty Executor: _____
   - Name: _____
     - Address: _____
     - Phone number: _____
     - Email address:_____
2. Contingency Specialty Executor: _____
   - Name: _____
     - Address: _____
     - Phone number: _____
     - Email address:_____
3. Second Contingency Specialty Executor: _____
   - Name: _____
     - Address: _____
     - Phone number: _____
     - Email address:_____

## WITNESSES

These are the individuals who will witness your will. It is common for these to be staff members of your estate planning attorney, but it is still important for you to record the witnesses' contact information. For more information, see Chapter 3.

**1. Witness**
- Name: _____
  - Address: _____
  - Phone number: _____
  - Email address: _____

**2. Witness**
- Name: _____
  - Address: _____
  - Phone number: _____
  - Email address: _____

## BENEFICIARIES

List all of the individuals who you would like to receive gifts under your will. Include any specific gifts you would like to give to that individual. A separate list will be included below for those who you wish to leave out of your will. For more information, see Chapter 3.

**1. Spouse**
- Name: _____
  - Address: _____
  - Phone number: _____
  - Email address: _____
  - Specific gifts: _____

**2. Children**
- Name: _____
  - Address: _____
  - Phone number: _____
  - Email address: _____
  - Specific gifts: _____

- Name: _____
  - Address: _____
  - Phone number: _____
  - Email address: _____
  - Specific gifts: _____

- Name: _____
  - Address: _____
  - Phone number: _____
  - Email address: _____
  - Specific gifts: _____

### 3. Grandchildren

- Name: _____
  - Address: _____
  - Phone number: _____
  - Email address: _____
  - Specific gifts: _____

- Name: _____
  - Address: _____
  - Phone number: _____
  - Email address: _____
  - Specific gifts: _____

- Name: _____
  - Address: _____
  - Phone number: _____
  - Email address: _____
  - Specific gifts: _____

- Name: _____
  - Address: _____
  - Phone number: _____
  - Email address: _____
  - Specific gifts: _____

## 4. Other Family

- Name: _____
  - Address: _____
  - Phone number: _____
  - Email address: _____
  - Specific gifts: _____

- Name: _____
  - Address: _____
  - Phone number: _____
  - Email address: _____
  - Specific gifts: _____

- Name: _____
  - Address: _____
  - Phone number: _____
  - Email address: _____
  - Specific gifts: _____

## 5. Friends

- Name: _____
  - Address: _____
  - Phone number: _____
  - Email address: _____
  - Specific gifts: _____

- Name: _____
  - Address: _____
  - Phone number: _____
  - Email address: _____
  - Specific gifts: _____

- Name: _____
  - Address: _____
  - Phone number: _____
  - Email address: _____
  - Specific gifts: _____

- Name: _____
  - Address: _____
  - Phone number: _____
  - Email address: _____
  - Specific gifts: _____

## 6. Charities

- Name: _____
  - Address: _____
  - Phone number: _____
  - Email address: _____
  - Specific gifts: _____

- Name: _____
  - Address: _____
  - Phone number: _____
  - Email address: _____
  - Specific gifts: _____

- Name: _____
  - Address: _____
  - Phone number: _____
  - Email address: _____
  - Specific gifts: _____

## 7. Other Organizations

- Name: _____
  - Address: _____
  - Phone number: _____
  - Email address: _____
  - Specific gifts: _____

- Name: _____
  - Address: _____
  - Phone number: _____
  - Email address: _____
  - Specific gifts: _____

- Name: _____
  - Address: _____
  - Phone number: _____
  - Email address: _____
  - Specific gifts: _____

- Name: _____
  - Address: _____
  - Phone number: _____
  - Email address: _____
  - Specific gifts: _____

## 8. Other Family

- Name: _____
  - Address: _____
  - Phone number: _____
  - Email address: _____
  - Specific gifts: _____

- Name: _____
  - Address: _____
  - Phone number: _____
  - Email address: _____
  - Specific gifts: _____

- Name: _____
  - Address: _____
  - Phone number: _____
  - Email address: _____
  - Specific gifts: _____

## Disinherited Individuals

Please list all individuals you want to specifically leave out of your will.

- Name: _____
  - Relationship: _____
  - Address: _____
  - Phone number: _____
  - Email address: _____

- Name: _____
  - Relationship: _____
  - Address: _____
  - Phone number: _____
  - Email address: _____

- Name: _____
  - Relationship: _____
  - Address: _____
  - Phone number: _____
  - Email address: _____

## PROFESSIONAL ASSOCIATIONS

List any professional associations or licensing boards that should be notified about your death or who may have specific requirements about what must be done to inform your clients, secure patient records, etc.

- Association: _____
  - Contact person: _____
  - Phone number: _____
  - Email address: _____
  - Address: _____

- Association: _____
  - Contact person: _____
  - Phone number: _____
  - Email address: _____
  - Address: _____

- Association: _____
  - Contact person: _____
  - Phone number: _____
  - Email address: _____
  - Address: _____

## ASSETS

List all of your assets below.

### Real Property

List all of your real property—land and buildings—below. Include as much of the requested information as possible. Include property that you are currently leasing.

| Residence (your home) | |
|---|---|
| Type of property (house, condo, apartment, etc.) | |
| Ownership (own, co-own, lease, etc.) | |
| Address | |
| Cohabitants | |
| If a deed (or lease) is recorded, where? | |
| Who has copies of the keys? | |
| Housekeeping services, if any | |
| Landscaping services, if any | |

Information about additional residences is located: _____

| Vacation Property | |
|---|---|
| Type of property (house, condo, apartment, etc.) | |
| Ownership (own, co-own, lease, etc.) | |
| Address | |
| Caretaker, if any? | |
| If a deed is recorded, where? | |
| Who has copies of the keys? | |

Information about additional vacation property is located: _____

| Rental Property | |
|---|---|
| **(residential property you own and rent to others)** | |
| Type of property<br>(house, condo, apartment, etc.) | |
| Ownership<br>(own, co-own, lease, etc.) | |
| Address | |
| Tenant(s) | |
| Leases are located where? | |
| Property Management Information | |
| If a deed is recorded, where? | |
| Who has copies of the keys? | |

Information about additional rental property is located: _____

| Commercial Property | |
|---|---|
| **(commercial property you own and/or rent to others)** | |
| Type of property | |
| Ownership<br>(own, co-own, lease, etc.) | |
| Address | |
| Tenant(s) | |
| Leases are located where? | |
| Property Management Information | |
| If a deed is recorded, where? | |
| Who has copies of the keys? | |

Information about additional commercial property that I own is located:

_____

| Commercial Property (commercial property you use and rent from others) | |
|---|---|
| Type of property | |
| Ownership (own, co-own, lease, etc.) | |
| Address | |
| Lease is located where? | |
| Property Management Information | |
| If a lease is recorded, where? | |
| Who has copies of the keys? | |

Information about additional commercial property that I use or rent is located: _____

| Other Property | |
|---|---|
| Type of property (house, timeshare, commercial building, etc.) | |
| Ownership (own, co-own, lease, etc.) | |
| Address | |
| Tenant(s) | |
| Leases are located where? | |
| Property Management Information | |
| If a deed is recorded, where? | |
| Who has copies of the keys? | |
| Housekeeping services, if any | |
| Landscaping services, if any | |

Information about additional property is located: _____

## Personal Property

| Vehicle 1 | |
|---|---|
| Year, Make, Model | |
| VIN | |
| License | |
| Keys are located where? | |
| Title is located where? | |
| Insurance Information | |
| Loan Information | |
| Preferred mechanic, if any | |
| Other information | |

| Vehicle 2 | |
|---|---|
| Year, Make, Model | |
| VIN | |
| License | |
| Keys are located where? | |
| Title is located where? | |
| Insurance Information | |
| Loan Information | |
| Preferred mechanic, if any | |
| Other information | |

Information about additional vehicles is located: _____

| Jewelry | | | |
|---|---|---|---|
| Item | Location | Value (if known) | Leave to (if anyone) |
| | | | |
| | | | |
| | | | |
| | | | |
| | | | |
| | | | |
| | | | |
| | | | |

Information about additional jewelry is located: _____

| Furniture | | | |
|---|---|---|---|
| Item | Location | Value (if known) | Leave to (if anyone) |
| | | | |
| | | | |
| | | | |
| | | | |
| | | | |
| | | | |
| | | | |
| | | | |

Information about additional furniture is located: _____

| Firearms | | | |
|---|---|---|---|
| Item | Location | Value (if known) | Leave to (if anyone) |
| | | | |
| | | | |
| | | | |
| | | | |
| | | | |
| | | | |
| | | | |
| | | | |

Information about additional firearms is located: _____

| Antiques | | | |
|---|---|---|---|
| Item | Location | Value (if known) | Leave to (if anyone) |
| | | | |
| | | | |
| | | | |
| | | | |
| | | | |
| | | | |
| | | | |
| | | | |

Information about additional antiques is located: _____

| Creative Assets | | | |
|---|---|---|---|
| Item | Location | Value (if known) | Leave to (if anyone) |
| | | | |
| | | | |
| | | | |
| | | | |
| | | | |
| | | | |
| | | | |
| | | | |

Information about additional creative assets is located: _____

| Other Tangible Property | | | |
|---|---|---|---|
| Item | Location | Value (if known) | Leave to (if anyone) |
| | | | |
| | | | |
| | | | |
| | | | |
| | | | |
| | | | |
| | | | |
| | | | |

Information about additional tangible property is located: _____

| Intangible Assets (include licenses, copyrights, patents, trademarks, and other rights) | | | |
|---|---|---|---|
| Item | Location | Value (if known) | Leave to (if anyone) |
| | | | |
| | | | |
| | | | |
| | | | |
| | | | |
| | | | |
| | | | |
| | | | |

Information about additional intangible assets is located: _____

| Stocks and Bonds | | | |
|---|---|---|---|
| Item | Brokerage or account | Value (at time of purchase) | Leave to (if anyone) |
|  |  |  |  |
|  |  |  |  |
|  |  |  |  |
|  |  |  |  |
|  |  |  |  |
|  |  |  |  |
|  |  |  |  |
|  |  |  |  |

## TRUSTS

Types of trusts include life insurance, college funds, guardianship, pets, grave maintenance, endowments, scholarships, Special Needs trusts, and other trusts. Trust property, or assets to be held in trust, could be land, buildings, money, life insurance policies, and other types of tangible (things that you can touch, feel, and see) property and intangible property such as copyrights, trademarks, patents, licenses, and other rights. If you do not know the type of trust or what specific property or amount of money will go into trust, leave the columns blank and discuss it with your estate planning attorney. Contact information for the trustees and beneficiaries will be listed below the table. For more information about trusts, see Chapters 4, 5, and 6.

| Trusts | | | |
|---|---|---|---|
| Type of trust | Trust Property | Trustee | Beneficiaries |
|  |  |  |  |
|  |  |  |  |
|  |  |  |  |
|  |  |  |  |
|  |  |  |  |
|  |  |  |  |
|  |  |  |  |
|  |  |  |  |

| Trustee(s) and Contact Information | |
|---|---|
| **Name** | |
| Address | |
| Telephone Number | |
| Email Address | |
| **Name** | |
| Address | |
| Telephone Number | |
| Email Address | |
| **Name** | |
| Address | |
| Telephone Number | |
| Email Address | |
| **Name** | |
| Address | |
| Telephone Number | |
| Email Address | |
| **Name** | |
| Address | |
| Telephone Number | |
| Email Address | |

| Beneficiaries and Contact Information (Individuals, pets, charities, organizations, etc.) | |
|---|---|
| **Name** | |
| Relationship to you | |
| Address | |
| Telephone number | |
| Email address | |
| **Name** | |
| Relationship to you | |
| Address | |
| Telephone number | |
| Email address | |

| Beneficiaries and Contact Information, *continued* (Individuals, pets, charities, organizations, etc.) | |
|---|---|
| **Name** | |
| Relationship to you | |
| Address | |
| Telephone number | |
| Email address | |
| **Name** | |
| Relationship to you | |
| Address | |
| Telephone number | |
| Email address | |
| **Name** | |
| Relationship to you | |
| Address | |
| Telephone number | |
| Email address | |

| Individuals with Special Needs and Contact Information | |
|---|---|
| **Name** | |
| Relationship to you | |
| Nature of the special need | |
| Address | |
| Telephone number | |
| Email address | |
| Current caretaker | |
| Physician | |
| Physician's contact information | |
| Insurance information | |
| **Name** | |
| Relationship to you | |
| Nature of the special need | |
| Address | |
| Telephone number | |
| Email address | |
| Current caretaker | |
| Physician | |
| Physician's contact information | |
| Insurance information | |

## PENSION AND RETIREMENT ACCOUNTS

| | |
|---|---|
| **Type of Account** | |
| Name on the account | |
| Account number | |
| Beneficiaries named (if any) | |
| Brokerage or account location | |
| Secure location of account access information | |
| Current value | |
| Location of plan documents | |
| **Type of Account** | |
| Name on the account | |
| Account number | |
| Beneficiaries named (if any) | |
| Brokerage or account location | |
| Secure location of account access information | |
| Current value | |
| Location of plan documents | |

## TAXES

| | |
|---|---|
| **Last year's taxes** | |
| Prepared by: | |
| Contact information for tax preparer (if any) | |
| Location of tax returns | |
| **Taxes from two years ago** | |
| Prepared by: | |
| Contact information for tax preparer (if any) | |
| Location of tax returns | |
| **Taxes from three years ago** | |
| Prepared by: | |
| Contact information for tax preparer (if any) | |
| Location of tax returns | |

# LIFE INSURANCE

List all life insurance policies and as much information as you know about them. This information will be used by the estate planning attorney to make sure your beneficiaries receive as much of the death benefit with as little of the tax burden as possible. More insurance information should be listed in the final section of this book for use by your survivors.

| Insurance You Currently Have | |
|---|---|
| **Type of policy** | |
| Term (if applicable) | |
| Policyholder | |
| Company | |
| Account number | |
| Beneficiary(s) | |
| Death benefit | |
| Other information | |
| Location of policy documents | |
| **Type of policy** | |
| Term (if applicable) | |
| Policyholder | |
| Company | |
| Account number | |
| Beneficiary(s) | |
| Death Benefit | |
| Other information | |
| Location of policy documents | |

| Information Regarding Insurance You May Need | |
|---|---|
| Monthly Financial Obligations | |
| Dependent (Name and age) | |
| Dependent (Name and age) | |
| Dependent (Name and age) | |
| Dependent (Name and age) | |
| Your age | |
| Your medical condition | |
| Amount available to pay monthly premiums | |
| Insurance available through an employer | |
| Other information | |

# GUARDIANSHIP OF MINOR CHILDREN

| Name of Minor Child | Birthday | Guardian |
|---|---|---|
| | | |
| | | |
| | | |
| | | |
| | | |

| Minor Child Information | |
|---|---|
| **Name** | |
| Relationship to you | |
| Shared custody (if applicable) | |
| School information | |
| Location of birth certificate and other legal documents | |
| Day care or babysitter information | |
| Physician | |
| Special instructions | |
| Contact information if the child does not live with you | |
| **Name** | |
| Relationship to you | |
| Shared custody (if applicable) | |
| School information | |
| Location of birth certificate and other legal documents | |
| Day care or babysitter information | |
| Physician | |
| Special instructions | |
| Contact information if the child does not live with you | |

| Minor Child Information, *continued* | |
|---|---|
| **Name** | |
| Relationship to you | |
| Shared custody (if applicable) | |
| School information | |
| Location of birth certificate and other legal documents | |
| Day care or babysitter information | |
| Physician | |
| Special instructions | |
| Contact information if the child does not live with you | |
| **Name** | |
| Relationship to you | |
| Shared custody (if applicable) | |
| School information | |
| Location of birth certificate and other legal documents | |
| Day care or babysitter information | |
| Physician | |
| Special instructions | |
| Contact information if the child does not live with you | |
| **Name** | |
| Relationship to you | |
| Shared custody (if applicable) | |
| School information | |
| Location of birth certificate and other legal documents | |
| Day care or babysitter information | |
| Physician | |
| Special instructions | |
| Contact information if the child does not live with you | |

| Guardian of Minor Child's Contact Information | |
|---|---|
| **Name** | |
| Address | |
| Telephone number | |
| Email address | |
| **Name** | |
| Address | |
| Telephone number | |
| Email address | |
| **Name** | |
| Address | |
| Telephone number | |
| Email address | |
| **Name** | |
| Address | |
| Telephone number | |
| Email address | |
| **Name** | |
| Address | |
| Telephone number | |
| Email address | |

## GUARDIANSHIP/CONSERVATORSHIP FOR ADULTS

| Name of Adult | Nature of Special Need | Guardian/Conservator |
|---|---|---|
|  |  |  |
|  |  |  |
|  |  |  |

| Individuals with Special Needs | |
|---|---|
| Name |  |
| Relationship to you |  |
| Nature of the special need |  |
| Address |  |
| Telephone number |  |
| Email address |  |
| Current caretaker |  |
| Physician |  |
| Physician's contact information |  |
| Insurance information |  |
| Name |  |
| Relationship to you |  |
| Nature of the special need |  |
| Address |  |
| Telephone number |  |
| Email address |  |
| Current caretaker |  |
| Physician |  |
| Physician's contact information |  |
| Insurance information |  |

| Guardian/Conservator of Adult Contact Information | |
|---|---|
| **Name** | |
| Address | |
| Telephone number | |
| Email address | |
| **Name** | |
| Address | |
| Telephone number | |
| Email address | |
| **Name** | |
| Address | |
| Telephone number | |
| Email address | |
| **Name** | |
| Address | |
| Telephone number | |
| Email address | |
| **Name** | |
| Address | |
| Telephone number | |
| Email address | |

# POWER OF ATTORNEY

| Digital Power of Attorney | |
|---|---|
| Designated Agent's Name | |
| Address | |
| Telephone number | |
| Email address | |
| Restrictions on authority or special instructions | |
| Location of digital asset inventory | |
| Alternate Agent's Name | |
| Address | |
| Telephone number | |
| Email address | |
| Second Alternate Agent's Name | |
| Address | |
| Telephone number | |
| Email address | |

| Medical Power of Attorney | |
|---|---|
| Designated Agent's Name | |
| Address | |
| Telephone number | |
| Email address | |
| Restrictions on authority or special instructions | |
| Do you want your representative making life-support decisions for you? | Yes/No |
| Do you want your representative making tube feeding decisions for you? | Yes/No |
| Alternate Agent's Name | |
| Address | |
| Telephone number | |
| Email address | |
| Second Alternate Agent's Name | |
| Address | |
| Telephone number | |
| Email address | |

| General Power of Attorney ||
|---|---|
| Designated Agent's Name | |
| Address | |
| Telephone number | |
| Email address | |
| Special instructions or triggering events | |
| Alternate Agent's Name | |
| Address | |
| Telephone number | |
| Email address | |
| Second Alternate Agent's Name | |
| Address | |
| Telephone number | |
| Email address | |

## ADVANCE DIRECTIVES

Fill out the chart below to the best of your ability. Your estate planning attorney may need additional information depending on your state law.

| Information Needed to Prepare an Advance Directive ||
|---|---|
| Name of Healthcare Representative or Medical Power of Attorney | |
| Address | |
| Telephone number | |
| Email address | |
| Alternate Agent's Name | |
| Address | |
| Telephone number | |
| Email address | |
| Second Alternate Agent's Name | |
| Address | |
| Telephone number | |
| Email address | |

| **Information Needed to Prepare an Advance Directive,** *continued* | |
|---|---|
| Limitations or special instructions | |
| Do you want your representative making life-support decisions for you? | Yes/No |
| Do you want your representative making tube feeding decisions for you? | Yes/No |
| **When you are CLOSE TO DEATH** | |
| Do you want to receive tube feeding? | Yes/No/As my physician recommends |
| Do you want to receive life support? | Yes/No/As my physician recommends |
| **If you are PERMANENTLY UNCONSCIOUS** | |
| Do you want to receive tube feeding? | Yes/No/As my physician recommends |
| Do you want to receive life support? | Yes/No/As my physician recommends |
| **If you are diagnosed with an ADVANCED PROGRESSIVE ILLNESS** | |
| Do you want to receive tube feeding? | Yes/No/As my physician recommends |
| Do you want to receive life support? | Yes/No/As my physician recommends |
| **If you are experiencing EXTRAORDINARY SUFFERING** | |
| Do you want to receive tube feeding? | Yes/No/As my physician recommends |
| Do you want to receive life support? | Yes/No/As my physician recommends |
| **Generally** | |
| Do you want to receive tube feeding? | Yes/No/As my physician recommends |
| Do you want to receive life support? | Yes/No/As my physician recommends |
| Do you want to be allowed to die naturally if you are close to death, permanently unconscious, diagnosed with an advanced progressive illness or suffering extraordinary pain? | Yes/No |
| Additional instructions | |

## ORGAN DONATIONS

More information about organ donation and more instructions that you can leave for your survivors are located in Chapter 20.

☐ I want to donate all of my usable organs.
☐ I **do not** want to donate my organs.

☐ I want to donate my eyes and tissue.
☐ I **do not** want to donate my eyes and tissue.

☐ I want to donate my body for anatomical study.
☐ I **do not** want to donate my body for anatomical study.

☐ I want to donate the above for any legally authorized purpose.
☐ I want to donate the above for transplant or therapeutic purposes only.

Limitations or special wishes:

_____

_____

_____

## DIGITAL ASSETS

### Hardware

| Device | Username | Password/PIN | Recovery email/phone number |
|--------|----------|--------------|----------------------------|
|        |          |              |                            |
|        |          |              |                            |
|        |          |              |                            |
|        |          |              |                            |
|        |          |              |                            |
|        |          |              |                            |

## Email Accounts

| Account | Username | Password | Recovery email/phone number |
|---|---|---|---|
| | | | |
| | | | |
| | | | |
| | | | |
| | | | |
| | | | |
| | | | |

## Social Media Accounts

| Account | Username | Password | Recovery email/phone number |
|---|---|---|---|
| | | | |
| | | | |
| | | | |
| | | | |
| | | | |
| | | | |
| | | | |

## Data Storage Accounts

| Account | Username | Password | Recovery email/phone number |
|---|---|---|---|
| | | | |
| | | | |
| | | | |
| | | | |
| | | | |
| | | | |
| | | | |

## Shopping Accounts

| Account | Username | Password | Recovery email/phone number |
|---------|----------|----------|-----------------------------|
|         |          |          |                             |
|         |          |          |                             |
|         |          |          |                             |
|         |          |          |                             |
|         |          |          |                             |
|         |          |          |                             |
|         |          |          |                             |

## Photo- and Video-Sharing Accounts

| Account | Username | Password | Recovery email/phone number |
|---------|----------|----------|-----------------------------|
|         |          |          |                             |
|         |          |          |                             |
|         |          |          |                             |
|         |          |          |                             |
|         |          |          |                             |
|         |          |          |                             |
|         |          |          |                             |

## Gaming Accounts

| Account | Username | Password | Recovery email/phone number |
|---------|----------|----------|-----------------------------|
|         |          |          |                             |
|         |          |          |                             |
|         |          |          |                             |
|         |          |          |                             |
|         |          |          |                             |
|         |          |          |                             |
|         |          |          |                             |

## Websites, Blogs, and Domain Names

| Account | Username | Password | Recovery email/phone number |
|---------|----------|----------|------------------------------|
|         |          |          |                              |
|         |          |          |                              |
|         |          |          |                              |
|         |          |          |                              |
|         |          |          |                              |
|         |          |          |                              |
|         |          |          |                              |

## Financial Accounts

| Account | Username | Password | Recovery email/phone number |
|---------|----------|----------|------------------------------|
|         |          |          |                              |
|         |          |          |                              |
|         |          |          |                              |
|         |          |          |                              |
|         |          |          |                              |
|         |          |          |                              |
|         |          |          |                              |
|         |          |          |                              |
|         |          |          |                              |
|         |          |          |                              |

## Subscription Accounts

| Account | Username | Password | Recovery email/phone number |
|---------|----------|----------|------------------------------|
|         |          |          |                              |
|         |          |          |                              |
|         |          |          |                              |
|         |          |          |                              |
|         |          |          |                              |
|         |          |          |                              |

## Security Questions

| Question | Answer |
|----------|--------|
|          |        |
|          |        |
|          |        |
|          |        |
|          |        |
|          |        |

## YOUR LEGACY

### Parting Thoughts

See Chapter 11 for tips for writing parting thoughts.

_____

_____

_____

_____

_____

_____

_____

_____

_____

_____

_____

_____

_____

Recordings of my final thoughts are located: _____

Additional parting thoughts are located: _____

| Please send my parting thoughts to the following people | |
| --- | --- |
| **Name** | |
| Address | |
| Telephone number | |
| Email address | |
| **Name** | |
| Address | |
| Telephone number | |
| Email address | |
| **Name** | |
| Address | |
| Telephone number | |
| Email address | |
| **Name** | |
| Address | |
| Telephone number | |
| Email address | |
| **Name** | |
| Address | |
| Telephone number | |
| Email address | |
| **Name** | |
| Address | |
| Telephone number | |
| Email address | |
| **Name** | |
| Address | |
| Telephone number | |
| Email address | |
| **Name** | |
| Address | |
| Telephone number | |
| Email address | |
| **Name** | |
| Address | |
| Telephone number | |
| Email address | |

| Please send my parting thoughts to the following people, *continued* | |
|---|---|
| **Name** | |
| Address | |
| Telephone number | |
| Email address | |
| **Name** | |
| Address | |
| Telephone number | |
| Email address | |
| **Name** | |
| Address | |
| Telephone number | |
| Email address | |
| **Name** | |
| Address | |
| Telephone number | |
| Email address | |
| **Name** | |
| Address | |
| Telephone number | |
| Email address | |
| **Name** | |
| Address | |
| Telephone number | |
| Email address | |
| **Name** | |
| Address | |
| Telephone number | |
| Email address | |

| Notes or Recordings for Specific Individuals | |
| --- | --- |
| Name | |
| Location of recording or note | |
| Address | |
| Telephone number | |
| Email address | |
| Name | |
| Location of recording or note | |
| Address | |
| Telephone number | |
| Email address | |
| Name | |
| Location of recording or note | |
| Address | |
| Telephone number | |
| Email address | |
| Name | |
| Location of recording or note | |
| Address | |
| Telephone number | |
| Email address | |
| Name | |
| Location of recording or note | |
| Address | |
| Telephone number | |
| Email address | |

## Final Social Media Messages

| Final Social Media Messages | |
|---|---|
| Social Media login information is securely located here: | |
| Platform (Facebook, Twitter, etc.) | |
| Final message: | |
| Platform (Facebook, Twitter, etc.) | |
| Final message: | |
| Platform (Facebook, Twitter, etc.) | |
| Final message: | |
| Platform (Facebook, Twitter, etc.) | |
| Final message: | |
| Platform (Facebook, Twitter, etc.) | |
| Final message: | |

## In Memoriam

I would like the following projects to be funded in my name:

| Project | Trust information or how the project will be funded | Trustee or individual named to have responsibility for the project | Acceptable alternatives |
|---|---|---|---|
| | | | |
| | | | |
| | | | |
| | | | |
| | | | |
| | | | |

# PART II
# Avoiding Probate

# CHAPTER 12

# What Is Probate?

In Chapter 1, we described the numerous problems that occur when an appropriate estate plan has not been prepared. It is likely that you do not want that situation to occur for your heirs. Throughout this section, we will provide you with information that will aid in creating an estate plan to help you avoid some of the more common problems.

When an individual dies, that individual's assets must be distributed to others through a process called *probate*. Probate is the legal process to transfer property from a person who is no longer living to that person's survivors. The probate process is supervised by the court. A judge determines who owns property, appoints a person to legally transfer the property, facilitates an orderly transfer of the property, and eliminates much of the temptation for survivors to commit fraud or prolong disputes unnecessarily. Probate is necessary in order to take possession of the decedent's property, protect the estate, pay all of the debts, claims, and outstanding taxes owed by the estate, determine who is entitled to the estate assets, and distribute them accordingly.

If you have a will, your heirs will have to petition the court to admit the will to probate. After the petition is filed, the court will determine ownership of your property, address all debts, claims, and taxes, and eventually determine who, including your creditors and taxing agencies, is entitled to your property. If anything is left, the assets will be distributed according to the will. The entire proceeding is paid for by your estate and open to the public.

If you die without a will or an appropriate substitute, then you will be said to have died *intestate*. In most cases, a probate case will have to be filed to determine who will receive your assets. The determination of who is entitled to your assets will be made in accordance with the laws of the state where you died. Dying intestate can have results that you never intended if you had planned while you were alive. Divorce, remarriage, stepchildren, unmarried partners, and all manner of relationships that are not contemplated by a state's intestate laws may leave your loved ones without any inheritance, while other undesirable individuals inherit everything.

Regardless of whether you have a will or not, the probate process may last for a very long time. A simple probate process may last between six and ninth months while complicated, or contentious proceedings may last for years.

Probate proceedings are not required for all estates. The size of the estate, the types of assets, the type of estate planning that was done, and the relationship of the decedent to the survivors all help determine whether probate is needed. In Part II: Avoiding Probate, we will discuss numerous methods by which certain assets can be dealt with for your heirs and beneficiaries without having to go through the probate process or having a trust. In later chapters of this book, we will discuss wills, trusts, and the entire probate process.

## IN PLAIN ENGLISH

Many people have a misconception that having a will means you will not have to probate the estate. This is incorrect. All property that does not pass automatically upon the death of an individual must go through the probate process in order to legally pass title to the beneficiary. If you do not have a will, the probate process can be much more difficult, costly, and stressful.

# CHAPTER 13

# Gifts

Every estate plan should include a gifting program for the purpose of reducing estate taxes and providing benefits to individuals and organizations that you wish to benefit. A *gift* is legally defined as a transfer of money, property, or anything of value without compensation.

There are many things to consider when setting up a gifting plan. The first consideration is taxes—both state and federal. You should also consider the form of the intended gift and whether to give the gift now or after death, and whether to give the gift outright or in trust. Of course, selecting which property is transferred during your life and which property will be distributed after death is another very important consideration.

This chapter outlines allowable gifts and when they can be given tax-free. Charitable gifts and gifts between spouses have important tax benefits. Gifts to noncitizen resident spouses require special planning in order to be effective.

## GIFT TAXES

A gift tax is a federal or state tax that is applied to a person who gives anything of value to another person. That's right—when you give a gift of value to someone else, YOU are taxed on it. Of course, you do not have to pay taxes whenever you give your niece a $20 gift card or spend $50 on your brother's engagement present. This is because there is an exemption for gifts below a certain amount. You will only pay taxes on gifts that exceed this amount.

Under federal law in 2019, each individual is allowed an annual gift tax exemption of $15,000 per person per year and, if a spouse joins in the gift, $30,000. The annual gift tax exemption will vary, though the change will not occur annually. This means that if you give a gift of less than $15,000 to one, two, twenty, or even a thousand individuals, you will not be required to pay federal taxes on those gifts. This annual gift tax exemption is not counted toward the federal lifetime exemption—called a *unified credit*.

## IN PLAIN ENGLISH

If the value of a gift you give is over $15,000, you will have to pay taxes on that gift as part of your income taxes for the year the gift was given.

## FEDERAL LIFETIME EXEMPTION OR UNIFIED CREDIT

The current federal lifetime exemption in 2019, or unified credit, allows each person to give away $11.4 million before you need to begin paying taxes on that amount. That is to say, if the value of all of the gifts that you have made during your lifetime (excluding gifts made under the annual gift tax exemption) plus the value of your estate upon your death exceeds $11.4 million, then the amount that exceeds that exemption will be taxed. That tax is quite aggressive. A married couple can combine their exemptions to get a total federal lifetime exemption of $22.8 million. To complicate matters, the annual gift exemption noted above does *not* count toward that $11.4 million lifetime exemption. Each state has its own tax rules and exemptions for gifts. See Appendix E.

While this is very complicated, the important thing to keep in mind is that there are advantages to giving away property up to the federal lifetime exemption during your life. One advantage is that if you transfer an appreciating asset (an asset that is gaining value over time), such as rental real estate, the appreciation on the gifted real estate will not be part of your estate at death because the value of the real estate is applied against your uniform credit when the gift is made. If you wait to transfer the real estate to the date of death, the fully appreciated value will be applied against the lifetime exemption. For example, let's say you purchased a building in 1980 for $100,000 and transferred it now for $500,000. You live a long and happy life and die years from now. At the time of your death, the building is worth $50 million. If you had waited to transfer the property through your will, it would have used up all of the unified credit (assuming for this purpose, that the unified credit did not increase in those years). Your estate would have to pay the aggressive estate tax on the gift. But because you transferred it now, you only used $500,000 of the unified credit and you will not need to pay taxes on the gift.

Keep in mind that by transferring assets while you are alive, the recipient will not receive a step-up in tax basis. Stepped-up tax basis is discussed more fully later in this chapter.

All gifts in excess of the exempt amount are taxed at the rate schedule determined by federal tax law, at the maximum rate of 40 percent in 2019. See Appendix D. There are numerous other complexities involved with gifts—for example, whether the recipient has received ownership of the gift, whether it is partially delivered and partially retained—that is only available for the recipient part of the year. These complexities should be discussed with your estate planning attorney.

---

### IN PLAIN ENGLISH

If the gifts you give throughout your life are not already tax-free because of the yearly gift tax exemption and the total value of your estate when you die is greater than $11.4 million, your estate will pay very high taxes on that excess.

---

## INTER VIVOS GIFTS

As previously mentioned, in 2019 each individual can give away up to $15,000 per recipient per year without any federal tax consequences. If the individual making the gift is married and the spouse joins in the gift, the exempt amount increases to $30,000 per recipient per year. This means if you have ten family members and friends and you would like to give each of them $15,000, then you would be able to reduce your estate by $150,000 in the year the gift was made, and no federal gift tax would be required. Remember, gift tax laws require the *donor* to pay the gift tax. The recipient is not subject to any tax for a gift. This annual exemption does not apply to the federal lifetime exemption, or unified credit, discussed above.

There are some issues with respect to outright gifts that you should consider. These include the fact that you will no longer have that money or property available, and you will not be able to control its use after making the gift. Before making your annual gifts, you need to determine if there are any issues with the recipient that might put the gift in jeopardy, such as bankruptcy, creditor problems, a potential divorce, substance abuse, gambling addiction, or financial immaturity. If any of these are concerns, then the gift can be made by use of a trust, discussed more fully in Chapter 4 of this book.

One other very important consideration is whether you are able to afford the gift you would like to make, since once a gift is completed, the recipient, and not you, will own the gift.

By having an annual gifting program within the annual tax-free limit, you avoid gift tax, the recipients do not pay income tax, the annual gift does not reduce your lifetime exemption, and at death, you save about 40 percent in estate tax.

### IN PLAIN ENGLISH

Using the annual gift exclusion to reduce your estate is an excellent tool to reduce taxes. Just make sure you can afford to give the gift away!

## HEALTH AND EDUCATION EXEMPTION

Separate from and in addition to the annual gift exclusion amount, there is an unlimited federal gift tax exclusion for gifts related to health and education. To qualify for the health and education exemption, you must make direct payments for qualified medical and educational expenses. The relationship to the recipient does not matter, so this gift can be given to relatives, friends, or even strangers so long as the payments are made directly to the medical or educational provider.

Qualifying educational expenses include tuition, but not books, room and board, or other similar expenses. Qualifying medical expenses including costs for diagnosis, cure, mitigation, treatment or prevention of disease, and other essential medical treatments.

The qualified medical and educational gifting exclusion is in addition to and does not replace the annual exclusion for gifts.

### IN PLAIN ENGLISH

The unlimited education exclusion can also be used to *prepay* someone's tuition.

## GIFTS TO MINORS

Before 2018, gifts to minors did not qualify for the annual gift exclusion. The Uniform Transfer to Minors Act (UTMA) and the Uniform Gift to Minors

Act (UGMA) change that. Now, you can gift to minors and name a custodian to manage the gift until the minor reaches the age of majority. Under the UTMA and UGMA, the assets are considered a part of the *custodian's* taxable estate until the minor takes possession of them, even though the assets are owned by the minor. It is important that the custodian is aware of this, as it may put him or her in a higher tax bracket. Another important implication to note is that the assets will be considered if the minor applies for financial aid or need-based scholarships.

### IN PLAIN ENGLISH

The age of majority varies from state to state and can range anywhere from 18 to 25 years of age. Further, as of this writing, not every state has adopted the Uniform Transfer to Minors Act, and even the states which have adopted both Acts may have adopted different versions. You should work with an experienced attorney when dealing with this subject since your state may be one of the few which has not yet adopted these laws or the version adopted in your state may have important differences.

### Custodial Accounts for Minors

Under most state laws, the custodian of an account for a minor generally has the discretionary power to distribute funds, accumulate income, and accelerate the distribution of principal for the minor's benefit. As noted above, if you are a custodian for a minor's account, the assets will be considered part of your estate. This rule is applicable to custodial accounts where you are the donor and die while acting as the trustee or custodian before the minor attains majority and becomes the direct owner of the account assets. Giving stocks, bonds, and other property to children through a custodial account may result in the transferred property being included in your gross estate, unless someone other than you is named as the custodian of the gift.

## GIFTS TO A SPOUSE

Gifts to a spouse may be made outright, as joint ownership, or in trust. Apart from your personal motives in making gifts to your spouse, there are advantages and disadvantages for each of these methods of gift giving.

## Marital Deduction

Gifts between spouses are very common and enjoy an unlimited marital deduction for gift tax purposes. In most cases, there is no tax advantage in a transfer of property to a spouse during lifetime as compared with the transfer to that spouse at death. In either case, there will be no tax liability for the spouse making the gift. Instead, the transferred property will be taxable as part of the surviving spouse's estate.

## "Stepped-Up" Basis

A "step-up" basis is when the value of an asset is readjusted based on how much its value has gone up. While you own an asset—such as a piece of land—the value of that land may grow. When you sell that land, you will have a capital gain if the value increased or a capital loss if the value decreased. Capital gains are taxed at a high rate, so whenever possible, it is financially beneficial to reduce the amount of capital gain that will be taxed. When property that has gained or lost value is transferred to another person through a will, the property value is adjusted to the current market value so that the person receiving the property will minimize their capital gains, thus reducing their tax burden, if they were to sell the property.

If your spouse dies before you do and if the transferred property has a fair market value greater than the cost basis (the amount you paid for the property), the basis will be "stepped up" to market value sooner than if you had kept it. For example, if you personally own a rental house that you bought many years ago for $150,000 and that house is transferred to your spouse upon your death and it is then worth $300,000, the basis that your spouse would be able to claim in that house would be $300,000. That is, the basis would be "stepped up" based on the fair market value at the time of your death. The reason that this is important is that when that house is sold by your spouse for $305,000, only $5,000 of the profit would be taxable; whereas, if the original purchase price had been used, then the taxable amount would be $155,000. If, however, you make a gift of property to your spouse, your spouse then dies within one year of the gift, and you inherit the property back from your spouse, the basis of the gifted property will not be "stepped up."

There are some risks and disadvantages in this arrangement. The spouse who has received the gift might squander it. Divorce is sometimes a possibility. Some risks can be reduced by making a Qualified Terminable Interest Property (QTIP) gift in trust (see below), with your children receiving the remainder of the gift after the death of your spouse, or by purchasing life insurance on the life of your spouse naming your children as both beneficiaries and owners of the policy.

## Qualified Terminable Interest Property (QTIP) Gifts to a Spouse

With certain exceptions, if you give your spouse a gift of any kind other than an outright gift, the value of the gift will not qualify for the gift tax marital deduction. The one exception to this rule allows you to control who will receive the property when your spouse's interest terminates and permits a marital deduction for the property—that is a gift of Qualified Terminable Interest Property (QTIP). QTIP is property that you transfer to a trust created by you (either during your lifetime or at the time of your death) in which your spouse has a "qualifying income interest" for life. A qualifying income interest for life gives your spouse the right to all income from the property for his or her life, payable at least annually, and prohibits distributions of the property held in the trust to anyone other than your spouse during his or her lifetime. A QTIP gift to a spouse has the same advantages as any other spousal gift, in that it may augment your spouse's estate so as to take advantage of any available unified credit and marital deduction under the estate tax system while taking the property out of your estate. The amount of property in the trust at the time of your spouse's death equal to the credit amount could be passed on to remainder beneficiaries other than yourself, such as your children.

## Gifts to a Noncitizen Spouse

For gifts made to a noncitizen spouse, a $155,000 annual exclusion for transfers by gift is allowed but only for transfers that would qualify for the marital deduction if the recipient spouse were a US citizen. Thus, a gift in trust would not qualify for the annual exclusion unless it were within one of the exceptions to the terminable interest rule. The $155,000 annual exclusion for gifts to a noncitizen spouse is available regardless of whether the donor is a citizen, resident alien, or nonresident alien. On the other hand, a gift to a citizen spouse qualifies for gift tax marital deduction regardless of the citizenship of the spouse making the gift.

There is no exemption against the gift tax imposed on transfers by nonresident noncitizens. However, the applicable exemption credit is available for transfer by resident noncitizens.

## CHARITABLE GIFTS

Charitable gifts of cash, regardless of the amount, and charitable gifts of property, regardless of the value, qualify for the unlimited gift tax charitable deduction. A gift of a partial interest in property gives rise to more complex issues, is beyond the scope of this book, and should be discussed with a competent tax attorney.

## GIFTS MADE ON YOUR BEHALF

If you were to become incapacitated, your ability to continue giving gifts would be severely restricted unless you had a properly prepared durable power of attorney in effect. This document must specifically authorize another person, called an attorney-in-fact, to make gifts on your behalf. Without the specific language, the Internal Revenue Service would not recognize any such gifts. With regard to state gift taxes, the ability of an attorney-in-fact to make gifts without specific authorization depends upon state law.

## GIFTS BY A NONRESIDENT NONCITIZEN

If you are neither a citizen nor resident of the United States, the federal gift tax only applies to a transfer, by you, of property that is situated in the United States. If, therefore, the only property that you have is outside of the United States, then the gift tax will not apply to you. For situations in which you have both property in the United States and property abroad, the gift tax would only apply to your United States property.

## REFUSING A GIFT

A person may refuse to accept a gift by a signed, written disclaimer. The disclaimer will cause the interest in the gift to transfer to another person. That transfer will not be considered as a gift if the formalities for qualified disclaimer are followed. A qualified disclaimer must meet all of the following requirements:

- The disclaimer must be in writing—it must describe the interest disclaimed and must be signed by the disclaimant or his or her legal representative.

- The disclaimer must be received by the maker of the gift or executor (in the case of disclaimers of bequests) within nine months of the creation of the property interest (usually at the death of the estate owner) or nine months of the date the recipient of the gift turns twenty-one.
- The disclaimant must not have accepted the interest or any of its benefits.

## BARGAIN SALES

Property may be sold for less than its actual value. If the sale is bona fide, at arm's length, and there is no gift intention, there will be no gift. However, if property is sold at a price far below fair market value, such a sale will be treated as part sale and part gift under the Internal Revenue Code. To the extent that the consideration received is less than the fair market value of the property sold, there is a gift. A bargain sale that results in gift tax liability may also arise when the purchase price is equal to the fair market value of the property sold, but the notes given in exchange are for low or no interest.

### IN PLAIN ENGLISH

Arm's length is customarily defined in this context as both independent and on equal footing. That is, there is no relationship between the parties and the parties each have similar resources.

## CONSIDERATIONS IN MAKING GIFTS

You and your significant other should develop a sensible strategy for lifetime giving. You may have a variety of personal and financial reasons for making gifts. You may want to experience the pleasure of sharing accumulated wealth with family members, friends, or a favorite charity. You may wish to ensure that certain persons receive particular gifts now rather than risking uncertainty in distribution after your death. You may want to see firsthand the way your recipient handles the gift.

In order to select the most efficient and cost-effective way, you need to answer certain questions, such as the following:

- What should be given to one recipient rather than another?
- What is the most appropriate vehicle or instrument for making the gift?
- What time schedule for the gift is desirable?
- What are the financial and tax consequences of these choices?
- Are there less expensive alternatives available?

There is a worksheet at the end of this section for you to identify the individuals you would like to provide gifts, their contact information, the gift you would like to provide each of them, the timing of those gifts, and your understanding of the fair market value of the gift. In some cases, you may want to obtain appraisals for those items in order to determine fair market value.

## NET GIFT TECHNIQUE

If you wish to make a gift that may be taxable and you would like avoid that tax, there is a procedure, referred to as the *net gift technique*. The net gift technique involves a gift made on condition that the recipient of the gift pay the gift tax. However, this technique cannot be used until your yearly federal gift tax exemption for that person has been exhausted. In addition, if the gift tax paid by the recipient exceeds your cost basis in the property, you may have to pay income tax on the amount the recipient paid in gift tax.

## DEATHBED GIFTS

Generally, gifts made within three years of death are not included in your gross estate for potential estate tax purposes. The only gifts that are included in your estate would be the gift of a life insurance policy and gifts where you retain certain rights or control of the gift.

## STATE GIFT TAXES

Presently, there are a number of states that impose state gift taxes. In these jurisdictions, the gift tax regulations may be similar to the state's estate tax. See Appendix E.

---

A gift-giving plan can bring satisfaction by allowing you to see the pleasure the recipient receives and is an excellent tool to reduce estate taxes. However, giving large gifts can have hidden tax consequences that should be discussed with your estate planning attorney or accountant.

# CHAPTER 14

# Co-Ownership

Co-ownership of property should never be considered a substitute for a will or trust. If the joint owners were to die simultaneously and no will or trust exists, the assets could pass to those not intended, which would be the nearest blood relatives of each joint owner (on a one half each basis).

Although joint ownership of property allows you to avoid probate, it has distinct downsides. A joint owner could be subject to a creditor's claims to the asset. For potential transfer tax purposes, these deal mainly in the loss of a *stepped-up value* or *stepped-up basis* of the property at the time of the death of the co-owner. The stepped-up value is the value of the property increased to fair market value at the time of the owner's death, which becomes the tax basis to the heirs. The basis for tax purposes can be the fair market value of the property at the time of death or on the *alternate valuation date* (six months after the date of death). The increase in the basis value of the estate assets and can reduce or eliminate capital gains tax upon the asset's eventual sale. The failure to obtain a stepped-up value can result in adverse tax consequences to the heirs of an estate.

## JOINT TENANCY

Joint tenancy is the simplest way to avoid probate. In this type of ownership, each person's interest can be disposed of without the consent of the other owner. This means a joint tenant can sell or gift their ownership in the property without asking the other joint tenant(s) for permission. Importantly for estate planning, joint tenancy can include a *right of survivorship*, allowing the deceased owner's share to transfer automatically to the surviving joint owners(s) without going through probate.

In just over half of the states, a form of ownership called *tenancy by the entirety* is available for married couples only. This method offers the right of survivorship (like a joint tenancy), except that in a tenancy by the entirety, each joint tenant is deemed to own the entire interest. This prevents the sale or transfer of property without the consent of the other joint owner. An additional benefit to a tenancy by the entirety is that complete ownership of the whole by two individuals creates a distinct unit of ownership that prevents creditors of just one spouse from seizing the jointly owned property. Unfortunately, this form of ownership is not available to unmarried couples—even those in lifelong committed relationships.

The disadvantages of joint tenancy or tenancy by the entirety are, first, that joint ownership may have unforeseen tax implications on the estate of the second to die, including impacting the unified credit exemption and not having a stepped-up value in the property when the first joint tenant dies. Second, in certain instances, the creation of a joint interest may be subject to gift taxes. These risks can be analyzed and mitigated by your estate planning attorney and tax advisor.

## TENANCY IN COMMON

*Tenancy in common* is another form of joint tenancy that allows each owner to dispose of his or her ownership interest in the property independently. When one owner dies, that owner's share will usually pass on to their heirs rather than to the joint owner. Each individual's ownership interest in the property can be transferred to a trust to avoid probate and provide a survivorship feature.

## JOINT TENANCY AND COMMUNITY PROPERTY LAWS

Nine states—Arizona, California, Idaho, Louisiana, Nevada, New Mexico, Texas, Washington, and Wisconsin—have a form of co-ownership of property for spouses known as community property.

The community property system varies from state to state, but there are certain common concepts. All property acquired by spouses during the marriage, while they reside in a community property state, is community property. It belongs to each of the spouses, share and share alike. Community property also includes the income from the property and the salaries, wages, and other compensation for services earned during the marriage. Community property also includes debts acquired during the marriage.

Each spouse may still own separate property and the married couple can hold property between them in joint tenancy. A married couple can convert community property to separate property or vice versa. A change in the form of ownership must be decided by the couple. Any such changes should be formalized by an agreement in order to have a clear, written record of the parties' desire should a future dispute arise as to ownership rights.

Property owned by a spouse prior to marriage, property obtained after a legal separation, and any property received as a gift or inheritance during the marriage from a third party remains separate property. Additionally, spouses can agree prior to the marriage through a prenuptial agreement that they will not be bound by the community property laws of their state of residence.

In general, community property assets remain community property even after the parties have moved to a non–community property state, unless the parties expressly agree otherwise. Thus, if you are living in a community property state, you and your spouse may have acquired a community property bank account. If you move into a non–community property state and take the proceeds of the account with you, the money still retains its community property character. If the money is invested in real estate in your new home state, the real estate may still be viewed as a community property asset.

The reverse is not true: If you are a couple who moves from a separate property state to a community property state, the personal property acquired in the separate property state, whether tangible or intangible (stocks and bonds and the like), retains its character as separate, joint, or whatever other form of ownership it originally had. Real estate will retain the form of ownership assigned to it. Real estate in a community property state acquired by either spouse while married is considered community property without regard to the domicile or residence of the spouses. If the property generates income, the law of the state where the real estate is located determines whether the income is community property.

## TRANSFER ON DEATH DEEDS

Another kind of deed which can be used to transfer property on death and avoid having the property become part of the decedent's estate is a "Transfer on Death" deed. In this situation the owner or owners of the property identify the individual or individuals who will own the property after death. Those individuals will not have any interest in the property until the owner or owners die. At that time, the property will automatically pass to the identified individual or individuals. By structuring the arrangement this way, the property will not have to go through probate. Not every state has adopted laws permitting this type of arrangement. If you are interested in having this type of ownership for your property, you should consult an experienced estate planning attorney in order to determine whether your state permits this type of arrangement, and if it does not, whether any existing laws specifically prohibit this.

### Warning to Third Parties

If a spouse in a community property state purchases property in joint tenancy with someone other than his or her spouse, it is important to determine whether the purchased property is community property. If it is, the surviving spouse would have a claim for one half interest in the property. The surviving spouse could successfully contend that the deceased spouse had authority only to transfer his or her half of the community property into joint tenancy with someone else.

## NEW VALUE OF PROPERTY WHEN A JOINT TENANT DIES

The general rule is that the values for tax purposes of property acquired from a decedent is the fair market value of the property on the date of his or her death (or on the *alternate valuation date* if the executor so elects). Where property is held jointly by spouses and in common law states, the surviving spouse can receive a stepped-up basis (an increase in the value of the property from the price when purchased to the current fair market value) of the deceased spouse's half of the value only. This stepped-up value is added to the original basis of the surviving spouse to become the new basis in the property.

Example: Jamie and Shannon bought a small office building as joint tenants in 1980 for $100,000. $100,000 is the couple's tax basis in the building. In 2020, the building was valued at $600,000. If Jamie and Shannon were to sell the building, they would have a $500,000 capital gain on the building (Capital Gain = Sale Price [$600,000] – Tax Basis [$100,000]).

Sadly, Jamie passed away in 2020. Jamie's 50 percent ownership interest received a stepped-up value from $50,000 (half of the purchase price in 1980) to $300,000 (half of the fair market value in 2020). Shannon now owns 100 percent of the property, so we add Shannon's own tax basis in half the property ($50,000) to Jamie's stepped-up basis in half of the property ($300,000). Shannon's basis is $350,000. Now, if Shannon were to sell the office building for $600,000, the capital gain would only be $250,000—a significant tax savings.

## SIMULTANEOUS DEATH

If joint tenants die simultaneously, their interest in the property will pass according to their individual wills or trusts. If they do not have a will or trust, it will pass under the rules of intestacy (all of which will be discussed in future chapters). Usually, the residuary clause in the will passes the property on to the residuary beneficiaries of the estate. This cannot be done with a trust since it only works to dispose of property previously transferred into the trust. It may be appropriate to create a pour-over backup will to transfer the jointly owned property to a trust.

## JOINT TENANCY AND TAXABLE GIFTS

When a person purchases property in joint tenancy or holds property as a sole owner and later creates a joint tenancy in the property, the transfer of ownership will be a taxable gift unless each of the joint tenants contributes the same amount to purchase the property. There are some limited exceptions to this rule. If a joint bank account is created, with one person contributing all of the funds, no taxable gift is created at that time. The same is true for US savings bonds held in joint tenancy. However, when the joint tenant who did not contribute at least half of the original deposit or cost takes possession of more than their original contribution (by withdrawing money from the bank account, or selling interest in the bond), there may be a taxable gift.

No gift taxes are assessed against any gift made between spouses, however. Either spouse may transfer any separately owned property in joint tenancy to the other spouse without concern of the gift tax.

While co-ownership of property should never be considered a substitute for a will or trust, it can be a useful tool, especially for roommates, partners, and spouses that live together. Additional laws apply to spouses that will affect joint ownership and how property transfers after death. Be sure to discuss all of the property you own, whether jointly or individually, with your estate planning attorney.

# CHAPTER 15

# Bank Accounts and Insurance Policies

In this chapter, we will discuss some of the other situations in which probate can be avoided. These include joint ownership or pay on death designations for bank accounts and insurance policies. These tools can be used in connection with wills and trusts for a more complete estate plan.

## BANK ACCOUNTS

You can use joint tenancy bank accounts to avoid probate and provide funds to heirs. Most forms of bank accounts can be owned in joint tenancy, including checking, savings, and certificates of deposit. To open such an account, everyone involved signs as joint tenants with the right of survivorship. When one joint tenant dies, the survivor(s) can have access to the account, with no need to go through probate.

Under the Uniform Probate Code, a joint account belongs proportionately to each contributor, thereby permitting each to revoke the joint ownership at any time. Under the laws of many states, including the state of New York, each joint owner has the right to an equal percentage of the joint account.

Under a joint tenancy arrangement, ownership is automatically transferred to the surviving owner(s). Other forms of shared ownership, such as tenancy in common and community property, do not create a right of survivorship. In those cases, how each shared owner's interest will be disposed of is determined by a will or living trust.

Multiple individuals can own the same property as joint tenants provided that each has an equal interest. If they own different interests in the property, the form of ownership is tenancy in common, which does not allow the right of survivorship.

Most states allow the individuals who create the account to define the rights of the joint holders of the account per an agreement signed when the account is opened. Joint bank accounts generally fall into one of three of the following categories:

- **Joint tenancy with immediate vesting**: on the creation of the account, each joint owner acquires interest in one half of the funds deposited, and neither can withdraw more than half without accounting to the other.
- **Revocable account:** each joint owner can withdraw the full amount on deposit without accounting to the other. Avoid using this type of account if there is any serious possibility that the would-be named joint tenant would misappropriate the funds.
- **Convenience account:** one person deposits all the funds and has the sole right to the funds while both are alive; the other can make deposits and withdrawals only as an "agent" for the owner.

All three types provide for survivorship. In the case of the convenience account, however, while it is clear that the individual supplying the funds receives the funds when he or she is the survivor, if the other person survives, whether he or she receives the funds depends on the deposit agreement and the local law.

You can create a bank account to prevent a joint owner from withdrawing any funds before your death. In the state of New York, these accounts are commonly called a *Totten trust* account, and this form of nonprobate passing is limited only to bank accounts. During your lifetime, the beneficiary of such an account normally has no rights in the account and is entitled to such funds only after your death. If the beneficiary of such an account should predecease you, an account of this kind would pass under the residuary clause of your will or trust.

## PAY-ON-DEATH ACCOUNTS

A *pay-on-death* designation names a beneficiary to receive the account balance at the time of the account holder's death. Financial institutions will recognize the pay-on-death designation and transfer those assets without the need to go through probate.

## BANK AND CREDIT UNION ACCOUNTS

Sometimes a bank may not use the word beneficiary or Totten trust—it may call the account a "pay on death" (POD) or "transfer on death" (TOD) designation—but it amounts to the same thing. It does not matter what the bank or institution calls it, so long as the money ends up with the beneficiary without probate.

Once your bank and credit union accounts have a pay-on-death designation, you do nothing different from what you did before. Your checks do not have to have the name of the beneficiary printed on them. Upon death, the bank will likely request a death certificate before effecting any transfer.

### IN PLAIN ENGLISH

Create a list of institutions and accounts for your attorney or beneficiaries to send notification of death and a death certificate to upon your passing.

## SAFETY DEPOSIT BOXES

A joint tenancy in a safety deposit box can be a sensible place to keep important personal documents. Either joint tenant can obtain access to the documents when they are required.

In many states with state estate taxes, safety deposit boxes are sealed by the bank as soon as it is notified of the death of an owner. The contents cannot be released until the box is inventoried by a government official or a waiver is obtained, which is usually a relatively simple procedure. If more than one person owns the box as joint owners, and if the safety deposit box is sealed, even the other owner will not have access to it until it has been unsealed.

> **NOTE:** Because a safety deposit box may be sealed when the bank is made aware of the owner's death, you should not have any documents in the safety deposit box that need to be available on death. For example, wills, trusts, deeds, titles, and other documents that your estate planning attorney will need when you pass away should *not* be in the box.

## LIFE INSURANCE

Generally, a life insurance policy will pass to its named beneficiaries without having to go through probate. There are a few limited circumstances that require a life insurance policy to be probated. The first circumstance is when the beneficiary of the life insurance policy dies before the policy can be paid out. The risk of this happening can be reduced by naming co-beneficiaries or successor beneficiaries of the policy. The second circumstance in which a life insurance policy may need to go through probate is when the beneficiary is a minor. By law, a minor cannot take ownership of the benefits of a life insurance policy. The probate process will appoint a guardian who will hold on to the benefits and manage them until the minor turns eighteen. Establishing a trust for the minor and making that trust the beneficiary of the life insurance policy can eliminate the need for probate. This can also allow you to choose who will hold and manage the minor's insurance benefits. The third circumstance in which a life insurance policy must be probated is when the beneficiary of the life insurance policy kills the person whose life is insured. This situation can be avoided by naming co-beneficiaries or successor beneficiaries of the policy. See Chapter 8 for a more in-depth discussion of life insurance policies.

---

Joint ownership or pay-on-death designations for bank accounts and insurance policies are generally a useful way to distribute assets without going through the probate process. Check with your estate planning attorney to make sure you are complying with all rules and regulations to ensure there are no unintended consequences to your designations.

# CHAPTER 16

# Business Structures

If you want to transfer assets to your friends and family, but are concerned about the delay caused by probate and the burden of gift and estate taxes, a business structure can help you control and protect your assets during life and transfer ownership of those assets automatically upon your death.

## CHOOSING A BUSINESS STRUCTURE

The most common business structures used in estate planning are the Family Limited Partnership ("FLP") or a Limited Liability Company ("LLC"). The FLP is similar to a general partnership ("GP") where the general partners (often one or more parents) control and manage the FLP, while the limited partners (children and grandchildren) cannot be active in the management of the company. In an FLP, like a GP, the limited partners enjoy protection from personal liability in the case of debt, lawsuits, and other claims. Like all business structures, the FLP is created and controlled by state law. Each state will have slightly different requirements and restrictions on creating an FLP. The most common restriction is that membership in the FLP is limited to family members—whether by birth, adoption, or marriage.

In a LLC, the owners are not partners but members. Each member enjoys the same liability shield that the limited partners of an FLP enjoy. This enhanced liability shield for the managing members (often the parents) is one of the reasons that LLCs have become more popular for estate planning purposes than FLPs. An LLC established for estate planning purposes is formed under the state law for all-purposes LLCs, and therefore has no family restrictions. The same management structure that is attractive in the FLP—one or more parents managing assets while the children, grandchildren, and other beneficiaries have no management or voting rights—can be established using the governing document of the LLC, called an operating agreement. Like the bylaws of a corporation, an operating agreement governs the day-to-day operations and prescribes what will occur on certain events such as the death of one of the members. This is what allows the LLC assets to be transferred outside of probate law.

### Two Classes of Ownership

Regardless of the business structure that you choose to form, at least two classes of ownership need to be established to take full advantage of the estate planning benefits of using a family corporation, LLC, or FLP.

Each class of ownership should be assigned different rights and characteristics. For example, one class of ownership can be voting stock while the remainder of the ownership is in non-voting shares. For purposes of estate planning, one class of ownership could have no voting or distribution rights until the member with these rights dies. The death of the controlling owner would trigger the second class to "come alive" with all of the rights and responsibilities of full ownership.

By establishing multiple classes of ownership, a single LLC can accommodate generations of your family, incorporate close friends or family businesses, and is only bound by the creativity of your estate planning team.

## BUY-SELL AGREEMENTS

In a partnership or other business entity, a buy-sell agreement is a legally binding contract that governs how a partner's share of a business may be reassigned if that partner dies or otherwise leaves the business. Most often, the buy-sell agreement stipulates that the available share be sold to the remaining partners or to the partnership. A buy-sell agreement can also be used as part of an estate plan to put limitations on the future sale or transfer of real estate and other property. A buy-sell agreement is also known as a buy and sell agreement, a buyout agreement, a business will, or a business prenup.

For estate planning purposes, a buy-sell agreement allows a business owner's heirs to sell inherited shares in a business fast and for a guaranteed price per share. This may be important for heirs who have no interest in running the business and would prefer to cash out as soon as possible. It can also be structured to provide the decedent's estate with a vehicle whereby the estate receives cash and the other owners are not burdened by having an estate as a co-owner. This is also something important for the business owner to consider. If the partner would rather his or her interest in the business be continuously held by family members, he or she can find another way to bequeath the interest in the business.

Generally, a buy-sell agreement is not a document that designates who will inherit the shares. The person who owns the shares still has to make that designation in a will or trust or otherwise provide a way for the shares to be legally transferred after the business owner's death. Because the buy-sell agreement may come with restrictions on how a beneficiary inheriting shares may use them or sell them, it is important to inform beneficiaries of the existence of the agreement and its restrictions.

A buy-sell agreement may be used for virtually every type of business entity, including C corporations, S corporations, partnerships, and limited liability companies. Typically, the agreement applies to the shares of stock and any business real estate held by respective owners. Although variations exist, the agreement essentially provides for the sale of a business interest to other owners or partners, the business entity itself, or a hybrid. Alternatively, the agreement may cover a sale to one or more longtime employees.

The agreement, which is typically signed by all affected parties, imposes restrictions on the future sale of the business or property. For instance, if you intend to leave a business interest to your children, you may provide for each child to sell or transfer his or her interest to another party or parties named in the agreement, such as grandchildren or other relatives. Similarly, the agreement may include provisions relating to the distributions of assets to trusts and potential divorces of heirs. (Be aware that special rules may apply in community property states.)

There are two common forms of buy-sell agreements:

- In a **cross-purchase agreement,** the remaining owners purchase the share of the business that is for sale.
- In a **redemption agreement,** the business entity buys the share of the business.

Some partners opt for a mix of the two, with some portions available for purchase by individual partners and the remainder bought by the partnership.

In order to ensure that funds are available, partners in a business commonly purchase life insurance policies on the other partners. In the event of a death, the proceeds from the policy will be used toward the purchase of the deceased's business interest. If structured properly, there can be significant tax benefits: the premium may be tax deductible and the proceeds may also be tax free. This is frequently accomplished through the use of an insurance trust, which is discussed in more detail in Chapter 8.

When a sole proprietor dies, a key employee may be designated as the buyer or successor.

Buy-sell agreements are designed to help partners manage potentially difficult situations in ways that protect the business and their own personal and family interests. For example, the agreement can restrict owners from selling their interests to outside investors without approval from the remaining owners. Similar protection can be provided in the event of a partner's death.

A typical agreement might specify that a deceased partner's interest be sold back to the business or remaining owners. This prevents the estate from selling the interest to an outsider.

In addition to controlling ownership of the business, buy-sell agreements spell out the means used in assessing the value of a partner's share. This can have uses outside the question of buying and selling shares. For example, if there is a dispute among owners about the value of the company or of a partner's interest, the valuation methods included in the buy-sell agreement would be used.

As you might imagine, having a valid buy-sell agreement in writing removes much of the uncertainty that can occur when a business owner passes away. The agreement provides a "ready, willing and able" buyer who's arranged to purchase shares under the formula or at a fixed price. There's no argument about what the business is worth among co-owners, partners, or family members.

The buy-sell agreement addresses a host of problems about co-ownership of assets. For instance, if you have one partner who dies first, the partnership shares might pass to a family member who has a different vision for the future than you do.

An agreement also provides for a smooth transfer of the business in advance of specified events, such as the death of an owner. This can help minimize disruptions while the business recovers from the loss.

A buy-sell agreement can be a stand-alone document or may be incorporated into the operating agreement of an LLC, the bylaws of a corporation, or the partnership agreement of a partnership or FLP.

## TRANSFERRING OWNERSHIP DURING LIFE

Once you have established a family entity—be it an FLP or LLC—assets should be transferred to the company. To transfer an asset, you must first establish its market value. For some assets, this can be easy—an appraisal can establish the value of most physical assets, and cash will be valued at its face value. For other assets, valuation can be difficult. For example, the value of a family business or the rights in intellectual property like a copyright, trademark, or patent can be hard to establish. Your estate planning attorney can help you find the fair market value for these assets. Once the assets have been valued and transferred, you will need to translate the value of the entity's property into units of value—often called stocks, shares, percentage of ownership, etc. These units of value can then be transferred to members of the LLC or FLP.

One advantage of transferring assets using ownership interest in an entity, rather than transferring the asset directly, is that the value of an ownership interest can be greatly reduced—often up to 40 percent of its market value—when it is transferred to a non-managing member of an LLC or a limited partner in an FLP. This discount is based on the fact that without management rights, the unit of ownership becomes less marketable. This functions to reduce the tax burden on the recipients of the ownership interest, reduce the amount that would count against any gift tax exemptions, and reduce the overall value of your personal estate.

---

A family-owned LLC or FLP is a powerful tool for managing your assets and passing them along to your heirs. You can maintain control over your estate by assigning yourself as the manager of the LLC or general partner of the FLP, while providing significant tax benefits to both yourself and your children.

# WORKSHEET 2

In addition to the fillable pages included in this section, you should add supplemental pages whenever necessary and fasten them to this part of the book.

## GIFTS

| Individuals to Receive Gifts During My Lifetime | |
| --- | --- |
| Name | |
| Relationship to me | |
| Address | |
| Telephone number | |
| Email address | |
| Birth date (if a minor) | |
| Medical or health-care purpose? | |
| Gift & value (if known) | |
| Recurring gift? | |
| Name | |
| Relationship to me | |
| Address | |
| Telephone number | |
| Email address | |
| Birth date (if a minor) | |
| Medical or health-care purpose? | |
| Gift & value (if known) | |
| Recurring gift? | |
| Name | |
| Relationship to me | |
| Address | |
| Telephone number | |
| Email address | |
| Birth date (if a minor) | |
| Medical or health-care purpose? | |
| Gift & value (if known) | |
| Recurring gift? | |

| Individuals to Receive Gifts During My Lifetime, *continued* | |
|---|---|
| **Name** | |
| Relationship to me | |
| Address | |
| Telephone number | |
| Email address | |
| Birth date (if a minor) | |
| Medical or health-care purpose? | |
| Gift & value (if known) | |
| Recurring gift? | |
| **Name** | |
| Relationship to me | |
| Address | |
| Telephone number | |
| Email address | |
| Birth date (if a minor) | |
| Medical or health-care purpose? | |
| Gift & value (if known) | |
| Recurring gift? | |
| **Name** | |
| Relationship to me | |
| Address | |
| Telephone number | |
| Email address | |
| Birth date (if a minor) | |
| Medical or health-care purpose? | |
| Gift & value (if known) | |
| Recurring gift? | |

Additional information regarding gifts is located: _____

| Organizations or Charities to Receive Gifts During My Lifetime | |
|---|---|
| **Name of the Charity or Organization** | |
| Contact person | |
| Address | |
| Telephone number | |
| Email address | |
| Tax deductible gift? | |
| Charitable purpose | |
| Gift & value (if known) | |
| Recurring gift? | |
| **Name of the Charity or Organization** | |
| Contact person | |
| Address | |
| Telephone number | |
| Email address | |
| Tax deductible gift? | |
| Charitable purpose | |
| Gift & value (if known) | |
| Recurring gift? | |
| **Name of the Charity or Organization** | |
| Contact person | |
| Address | |
| Telephone number | |
| Email address | |
| Tax deductible gift? | |
| Charitable purpose | |
| Gift & value (if known) | |
| Recurring gift? | |

| Organizations or Charities to Receive Gifts During My Lifetime, *continued* | |
|---|---|
| **Name of the Charity or Organization** | |
| Contact person | |
| Address | |
| Telephone number | |
| Email address | |
| Tax deductible gift? | |
| Charitable purpose | |
| Gift & value (if known) | |
| Recurring gift? | |
| **Name of the Charity or Organization** | |
| Contact person | |
| Address | |
| Telephone number | |
| Email address | |
| Tax deductible gift? | |
| Charitable purpose | |
| Gift & value (if known) | |
| Recurring gift? | |
| **Name of the Charity or Organization** | |
| Contact person | |
| Address | |
| Telephone number | |
| Email address | |
| Tax deductible gift? | |
| Charitable purpose | |
| Gift & value (if known) | |
| Recurring gift? | |

Additional information regarding gifts is located: _____

# JOINTLY OWNED PROPERTY

| Real Property (Land and Buildings) | |
|---|---|
| **Type of Property** (house, condo, apartment, etc) | |
| Co-owner | |
| Address | |
| If a deed (or lease) is recorded, where? | |
| **Type of Property** (house, condo, apartment, etc) | |
| Co-owner | |
| Address | |
| If a deed (or lease) is recorded, where? | |

| Vehicles | |
|---|---|
| **Year, Make, Model** | |
| VIN | |
| License | |
| Co-owner | |
| Title is located where? | |
| **Year, Make, Model** | |
| VIN | |
| License | |
| Co-owner | |
| Title is located where? | |

| Other Tangible Property | | | |
|---|---|---|---|
| **Item** | **Location** | **Value (if known)** | **Co-Owner** |
| | | | |
| | | | |
| | | | |
| | | | |
| | | | |
| | | | |
| | | | |
| | | | |

| Intangible Assets (include licenses, copyrights, patents, trademarks, and other rights) | | | |
|---|---|---|---|
| Item | Location | Value (if known) | Co-Owner |
| | | | |
| | | | |
| | | | |
| | | | |
| | | | |
| | | | |
| | | | |
| | | | |

## BANK ACCOUNTS & SAFETY DEPOSIT BOXES

| Bank Accounts | |
|---|---|
| **Name of Institution** | |
| Names on the account | |
| Pay-on-death account? | |
| Account number | |
| Branch address | |
| Telephone number | |
| Beneficiaries of the account (transfer on death) | |
| Online account information | |
| **Name of Institution** | |
| Names on the account | |
| Pay-on-death account? | |
| Account number | |
| Branch address | |
| Telephone number | |
| Beneficiaries of the account (transfer on death) | |
| Online account information | |

| Bank Accounts, *continued* | |
|---|---|
| Name of Institution | |
| Names on the account | |
| Pay-on-death account? | |
| Account number | |
| Branch address | |
| Telephone number | |
| Beneficiaries of the account (transfer on death) | |
| Online account information | |

| Safety Deposit Box | |
|---|---|
| Name of Institution | |
| Names on the account | |
| Key location | |
| Box number | |
| Branch address | |
| Telephone number | |
| Name of Institution | |
| Names on the account | |
| Key location | |
| Box number | |
| Branch address | |
| Telephone number | |
| Name of Institution | |
| Names on the account | |
| Key location | |
| Box number | |
| Branch address | |
| Telephone number | |
| Name of Institution | |
| Names on the account | |
| Key location | |
| Box number | |
| Branch address | |
| Telephone number | |

# BUSINESS INTERESTS

| Business Interests | |
|---|---|
| **Name of Entity** | |
| State of formation | |
| EIN | |
| Structure of the entity (LLC, Corporation, etc.) | |
| Class of ownership | |
| Characteristic of your class of ownership | |
| Entity's assets | |
| Value of the assets when acquired | |
| Your contribution to the entity | |
| Current fair market value (or most recent valuation) | |
| Co-owners & contact information | |
| **Name of Entity** | |
| State of formation | |
| EIN | |
| Structure of the entity (LLC, Corporation, etc.) | |
| Class of ownership | |
| Characteristic of your class of ownership | |
| Entity's assets | |
| Value of the assets when acquired | |
| Your contribution to the entity | |
| Current fair market value (or most recent valuation) | |
| Co-owners & contact information | |

Additional information regarding business interests can be found: _____

# PART III
# The Probate Process

# CHAPTER 17

# Testate

In the next two chapters, we will discuss the different processes an estate goes through when a person dies with a will and without a will. First, we address the probate process that each estate should go through when a person dies with a valid will. As you contrast this experience with the process your loved ones must go through if you die without a will, we hope it will encourage you to seek the advice of an estate planning attorney sooner, rather than later.

## WHAT IS DYING TESTATE?

Dying *testate* means that you died having left a valid will. Dying *intestate* means you died without a will or the will that you had was invalid for some reason or another. We will discuss the intestate process in Chapter 18.

## OPENING THE ESTATE

First, your survivors should locate and read your will. This document, along with the instructions you have written down in this book, should have instructions regarding your funeral, cremation, or burial, and name the personal representatives, executors, trustees, and guardians or conservators that will carry out your requests. Your survivors or the personal representative should keep the will in a safe place until it can be given to the lawyer who will assist you in settling the estate. For this reason, you should let the person whom you have identified as the personal representative know where your original will is located.

Before meeting with the attorney, it will be helpful for the survivors for you to list the names, addresses, phone numbers, dates of birth, Social Security numbers, and email addresses of everyone mentioned in the will. This will include all of the named beneficiaries and unnamed beneficiaries. For example, if the will leaves a gift to each of the grandchildren and some of those grandchildren were born after the will was written, these grandchildren's names will not be in the will but need to be written down. All of the people named in the will that may have passed away should also be recorded.

It will also be helpful for the survivors to list all of the assets that you had at the time of your death. If you have completed all of the worksheets in this book, you will have identified all of the important papers, accounts, policies, titles, and deeds, and told your survivors where to find them. This will be a great start, and all they will need to do is identify any assets that you have acquired after making that list or forgot to record. The fact that an asset cannot be located may mean that it was disposed of before you died or that it is simply lost. For this reason, it is a good idea to periodically review the lists in this book and update them.

In addition to the assets, your survivors should prepare a final list of all liabilities. Again, if you have completed all of the worksheets in this book, you will have identified the mortgages, taxes, fees, loans, credit cards, and bills including the account information they will need to locate and address each liability. Your survivors will need to simply access those accounts and verify the final amounts owing. Here, too, periodic updates will be beneficial.

Finally, your survivor should secure proof of death. Some courts, banks, lenders, and other institutions will require an original death certificate, where others will accept a copy. If your survivors did not receive a death certificate or it was lost, your attorney can help secure another one from the appropriate state agency. There are several different types of death certificates available throughout the United States, and your personal representative will need to know which types of death certificates will be required for the various purposes. For example, in order to obtain life insurance benefits, the life insurance company will likely require a certified "long" version that includes the cause of death. Funeral homes customarily assist in obtaining the original death certificates and they generally know how many copies of which form your personal representative will likely need.

If possible, all beneficiaries named in the will should meet with the attorney to discuss the will and plan to probate the estate. If that is impossible or impractical, it will be essential that the personal representative meet with the attorney. If an in-person meeting is still impossible, the personal representative should at least meet with the attorney by phone. The estate's attorney will help your personal representative draft the court documents required to open the probate estate. In most cases, the attorney will have other documents for the beneficiaries and others named in the will to review and sign as well. These documents will vary depending on what state you are in and what choices you made in your estate plan. Generally, these forms include a petition for probate administration; the oath and acceptance of the personal representative or executor; the appointment of a resident agent, joinders, waivers, and consents; a petition to waive bond; an order admitting the will to probate; an order appointing the personal representative or executor; an order waiving the bond; and letters of administration or letters testamentary. If a bond is required, the attorney will assist in acquiring the bond. Most individuals will instruct the attorney who drafts the will to waive the requirement of having the estate purchase an expensive bond, since the personal representative or executor selected will be someone you trust to handle your estate. A properly drafted will is likely to state explicitly that no bond shall be required.

## APPOINTING THE PERSONAL REPRESENTATIVE

After the petition or application for probate has been filed—along with the death certificate and the original copy of the will—the probate court will appoint the person named as executor or personal representative in the will. The terms *executor* and *personal representative* are interchangeable, and which term is used will be determined by state law. If that person is unable or unwilling to serve, the court will appoint the successor executor identified in the will.

Probate courts generally grant authority to estate administrators by issuing letters testamentary. Once these letters are issued, the executor or personal representative is authorized to make financial transactions on behalf of the estate, such as accessing the bank accounts of the person who died.

## NOTIFYING CREDITORS

Once an executor or personal representative obtains the letters testamentary, the executor must notify all heirs or beneficiaries identified in the will of that appointment. Probate courts generally require that notification to heirs or beneficiaries be sent via certified mail, as proof of mailing the notification is required. Furthermore, the estate's creditors must be notified of the pending probate proceedings because creditors have a right to submit claims to the probate court so that the executor may pay the claims using estate assets. If the creditors are known, they should be contacted directly by certified letter. In addition, it is generally required that a notification of the probate be published for several weeks in a newspaper of general circulation in the county where the probate is filed.

## PRESERVING THE ASSETS OF THE ESTATE

It is the executor's job to keep estate assets safe until they are distributed to the people who inherit them. It's the executor's responsibility to manage the estate's finances and debts. The executor will be required to open an estate bank account for all financial activity involving the estate to pass through. This bank account should be used to pay debts like a mortgage or to make car payments, and to deposit any money the estate is owed, such as wages, pension, life insurance, Social Security, and so on.

If the executor must sell property to either liquidate assets or pay debts, the estate account will be necessary to hold the funds and keep track of all deposits and disbursements.

The executor will also have to manage day-to-day affairs of the estate, like canceling credit cards, Internet and cable services, phone and utility bills, and any subscriptions you had. The executor should also notify health-care professionals like doctors, therapists, etc., as well as recreational facilities, gyms, or clubs to close the accounts. Many of these individuals or organizations will require a death certificate, and most will require proof that the executor has the appropriate authority. This proof is the letters testamentary previously referred to. It is best practice to inform the post office to either have mail forwarded or the service canceled.

The executor has a fiduciary duty to ensure all assets and property are protected while your last wishes are administered. A good practice is for your executor to take better care of estate assets than the executor would take care of their own property. Certain valuables or property, like collectibles or art, should be insured for the estate and the beneficiaries. This is important because if anything happens to these assets while they are under the executor's cares, the executor could be held personally liable for damages, and if the bond was waived, the executor will have to personally pay for those damaged assets.

## Household and Personal Items

Especially if a lot of relatives and friends will be in and out of the home, put valuable items away where they can't be taken. That includes cash, jewelry, art, collectables, or anything else you think might catch someone's eye. Unfortunately, it's not uncommon for people to help themselves to items that they believe were promised to them or that they think you would want them to have.

It's easiest for the executor to give anyone who asks for something the same answer: no, or at least "not yet." They may explain that as executor, they have a legal responsibility not to let even the smallest item out of the house until they have inventoried everything and been given the probate court's blessing to make distributions. It may calm them down to hear that the executor is not giving anything to anyone else, either, until the proper procedures have been followed.

## Land and Buildings

Make sure land and buildings, legally referred to as real property, are safe, secure, and maintained. The executor must keep making mortgage payments and pay local property tax bills on time to avoid penalties or default. The executor must also pay any property insurance premiums as they come due. If the insurance lapses, and there is fire or other damage, theft, or a personal injury claim (someone trips on the front stair, for example), the executor could end up personally liable for the loss.

It's the executor's job to ensure the property receives basic regular maintenance. The yard must be mowed, the snow shoveled, the gutters cleaned out. In cold weather, the executor needs to know that the furnace is working, so pipes don't freeze and burst. And of course, the executor must repair any damage that occurs, such as a broken window or step, or a roof that starts to leak.

It's a good idea to put some lights on a timer to make the property look occupied, and ask a neighbor to pick up any free newspapers or advertising flyers that get deposited on the porch or in the yard. If the executor does not live close enough to keep an eye on the property, the executor should find a trustworthy neighbor to go in and walk around the property every week or so just to make sure everything is okay.

## Cars and Other Vehicles

If there's a car, truck, or boat in the estate, the executor will need to make some effort to see that it keeps its value until it can be sold or turned it over to whoever inherits it. The executor must find or collect all the keys and find a place to store the vehicle, preferably off the street where break-ins are unlikely.

The other crucial things to take care of are insurance and maintenance. The executor must keep making insurance payments. If the vehicle is sold or transferred to a new owner before the policy period is over, the executor must get a refund from the company. The executor must also keep up with regular maintenance, such as periodic oil changes and tire inflation checks. Even if a car isn't driven, it still needs to be looked at regularly.

The executor may not have to keep a car around until the probate process is over. Depending on how the car was owned and who inherits it, you may be able to take advantage of several shortcuts for transferring cars to their new owners. The executor may also want to sell the car during the probate process; whether or not this will be possible depends on what the will says and on the wishes of the beneficiaries.

## Investments

An executor must safeguard the investments of the estate, but is not required to undertake a comprehensive evaluation of your investment strategy and shift assets around in an attempt to get the greatest return. In other words, the executor's goal is to not lose money. Generally, that means the executor can leave investments pretty much as they were. The executor might wish to retain the services of a qualified investment advisor. If significant investments are involved, the executor and estate planning attorney should establish a plan for conserving those assets for the estate.

Of course, there are times when a leave-things-as-they-are strategy could actually be reckless. For example, if the executor found that you had recently moved money out of conventional investment vehicles into something that looks too speculative or suspect, then the executor should discuss the situation with the estate planning attorney and request advice from that attorney. In this type of situation, it would like be best for the executor to enlist the aid of an experienced and qualified investment advisor to assist with the investment.

Needless to say, the executor's fiduciary responsibility obligates that person to act with absolute integrity when dealing with estate assets. The executor should never use the assets in a way that benefits the executor personally. For example, the executor should never invest estate money in the executor's own business or sell assets to friends or relatives at less than their market value. This kind of behavior will surely get the executor in legal trouble.

## EXECUTING THE WILL

After all debts have been paid, the remainder of the estate and whatever specific property or gifts named in the will can be transferred to the beneficiaries, including any donations to charities specified in the will. Some people gift property like vehicles or money (either in the form of a specific dollar amount or a percentage of the residue of their estate). Lastly, the executor may be entitled to an executor fee (commonly 5 percent of the residue of the estate) depending on your state's laws.

## FINAL INCOME TAXES

One of the executor's most important duties is to file your final taxes. The executor should enlist the aid of an accountant or tax preparer when doing this as there are some additional estate-related documents that must be filed in order to complete the process.

Keep in mind that the executor will also have to file tax returns for any years preceding your death if you didn't file tax returns for those years.

## ANNUAL ACCOUNTINGS

Smaller estates may be probated within one year and the executor will, with the aid of the estate planning attorney, prepare and file a final accounting. Once the final accounting is reviewed and approved by the court, an order will be issued allowing the estate assets to be distributed and the estate closed. The executor will receive any payment due and the executor will be discharged. The estate will then be closed.

If the estate cannot be probated within one year, then the executor, with the assistance of the estate's attorney, will need to file an annual accounting providing the probate court with a report about the estate's activities for that year. The probate judge will review that report and determine whether there is anything in it that must be explained. If the court believes an explanation is necessary, the executor and the estate's attorney will be required to provide an explanation either in person or through a written report, depending upon the probate judge's requirements.

Larger estates will likely remain open for many years and annual accountings will need to be filed with the probate court by the executor, with the assistance of the estate's attorney, every year until the estate is ready to be closed. At that time, the executor and the estate's attorney will prepare a final accounting, and the process described above for final accountings will occur.

## INTERIM PAYMENTS

A probate commonly takes at least nine to twelve months to complete, but this does not mean that beneficiaries will necessarily need to wait until the probate has finished to receive any money from the estate. It may be possible for some payments to be made to beneficiaries while the estate administration is still ongoing—these are called interim payments.

The probate process involves a significant amount of legal, tax, and administrative work, and some estates will take longer than others to complete. At the end of the estate administration, beneficiaries will be paid their final distribution from the estate.

Interim means "in the intervening time," and interim payments are when beneficiaries are paid a portion of their share while the estate administration is still ongoing.

An interim payment may not always be possible. It will be up to the executor to assess the risks and determine how much money, if any, can be paid out to beneficiaries as interim payments. Additionally, in some states the executor must obtain the probate court's approval to make any interim payments to beneficiaries. While the estate will pay the ongoing legal costs incurred throughout the probate process, the estate's attorney will typically not be paid fees until the final accounting is approved by the probate court. If the estate remains open for an extended period of time, the attorney may request permission from the probate court to obtain interim or periodic payments.

## LIQUIDATING OR DISTRIBUTING ASSETS

Once the court has issued the order allowing the estate to be closed, the executor will pay all outstanding bills, distribute all assets to the beneficiaries, close all accounts, and wind up the estate. The final report discussed below will then be prepared.

## CLOSING THE ESTATE

After the probate court issues an order allowing the estate to be closed, the executor must organize and file all financial data, including the records of activity in the estate account (income and disbursements), close the estate bank account, and send statements of estate activity to all beneficiaries.

When that's completed, the executor will file a closing statement or affidavit with the court. The type of document that must be filed varies from state to state, but it will essentially declare that the last wishes of the deceased have been carried out and advise the probate court that the estate has been closed.

Once the estate is closed, the duties of the executor are complete and the executor is discharged. As stated earlier, this process can take anywhere from a few months to many years depending on how complicated or large the estate is.

---

Now that you are familiar with the testate probate process, read the following chapter to see how state law will step in and determine how your assets are distributed in the absence of a valid will. Even if you have a valid will, or plan to have one very soon, understanding the intestate process is necessary so you will know what the default rules are, and what may happen if a portion of your will is invalidated.

# CHAPTER 18

# Intestate

If you die without having a valid will, then you will have died intestate, and the intestate laws of the state where you died will establish the rules for distributing your assets. See Appendix E for the intestate laws of all fifty states.

In this chapter, we will explain what it means to "die intestate" and the probate process that each estate should go through when a person dies without a valid will.

## WHAT IS INTESTATE?

Dying *intestate* means that you died without a will or the will you had was invalid for some reason or another.

## OPENING A FILE WITH THE COURT

To begin with, if you die without a will, the person who needs to obtain legal access to the property you leave behind will need to arrange to have your estate probated. That person may be able to accomplish this without the assistance of an attorney—though we recommend that a estate planning attorney be used for this purpose.

The person or the attorney will need to open the estate by filing the appropriate documents with the probate court. In virtually every state, the court will then require the estate administrator to purchase a bond. This requires the payment of a significant fee to a bonding company for a probate bond. Customarily, the fee is a percentage of the value of the estate, a percentage that varies from state to state and from bonding company to bonding company.

## APPOINTING AN ADMINISTRATOR

After the petition or application for probate has been filed—along with the death certificate—the probate court will appoint the person who is deemed to have priority over others to administer the estate. For example, surviving spouses typically have priority over other relatives. See Appendix E: State Laws on Intestate Succession. Many probate courts require the person who seeks appointment to send notification of their request to heirs who have priority. If those heirs object to the appointment, the probate court may choose an heir with priority to administer the estate instead.

Probate courts generally grant authority to estate administrators by issuing letters of administration (as opposed to letters testamentary, as discussed in the previous chapter). Once these letters are issued, the administrator is authorized to make financial transactions such as accessing bank accounts and safe deposit boxes.

## COMPLYING WITH STATE LAW

The administrator is required to comply with the intestate laws of the state in which you died. In order to be sure that all laws are being complied with, the administrator should work with an estate planning attorney, since the laws vary from state to state and few individuals have the knowledge and experience necessary to comply with those laws.

## NOTIFYING CREDITORS

As discussed in the preceding chapter, the administrator must notify all of the creditors of the estate that you died, and that the administrator will be assuming responsibility for all of your debts. If the creditors have been identified, as for example in the listing found in this book, then the administrator will typically be required to send each of those creditors a certified letter requesting that the creditor submit a written claim within a prescribed period of time. In addition, the administrator will typically be required to publish a notice in a newspaper of general circulation in the county where the probate was filed advising all creditors that a probate has been opened and requesting that anyone who believes they are owed money by the estate should file a claim within the prescribed period of time. This publication should run for the time required by state law.

## PRESERVING ASSETS

In addition to notifying all creditors, the administrator must preserve the estate's assets in the same manner as the executor is required to as described in the preceding chapter.

## PAYING CLAIMS, ATTORNEYS, AND ADMINISTRATOR

The intestate estate will be required to pay the claims that have been received and the administrator believes are valid. Determining which claims are valid may be complex and, therefore, we strongly recommend that the administrator enlist the aid of an estate planning attorney when making this determination.

Once all valid creditor claims have been paid, the remaining assets must be distributed in accordance with the laws of intestacy, which are listed in Appendix E. In the event that the assets are not sufficient to pay all creditors, then the administrator must review the state laws of intestacy in order to determine the priority of the creditors. Since each state's laws may be different, it is important for an administrator to work with an estate planning attorney in this situation.

Generally, the law requires the estate to pay all of the claims with priority first. These typically include child and spousal support, expenses of administering the estate, funeral expenses, hospital and medical expenses of the decedent's last illness, wages due for labor performed immediately preceding death, debts incurred under federal law (taxes), taxes or debts owed to the state, judgments, and other claims. If there aren't sufficient assets to pay all of the priority claims, then the amount paid will be prorated. Once the priority claims have been paid, then the other creditors will receive full payment of their claims. If the assets are insufficient to pay all claims, a prorated portion will be paid. Once the remaining creditors are paid, any remaining assets may be distributed to the heirs in accordance with state law.

## SMALL ESTATES

Most states have laws that allow for a simpler process if the intestate (or testate) estate is small. The definition of a small estate varies from state to state and, therefore, the person who will serve as the administrator should check the state law in order to determine the definition in the state where you died. See Appendix E for those laws.

The small estate process is very similar to the intestate process described above, though it is customarily faster and less expensive to comply with. If the individual who will serve as administrator feels comfortable in handling a small estate without assistance, the probate court clerk may be able to assist, though we recommend that an estate planning attorney be consulted even for a small estate.

## BENEFITS OF HAVING A WILL

Since the intestate process requires the estate administrator to purchase a bond, which is customarily quite expensive, and since the assets of an intestate estate will be distributed in accordance with the laws of the state where you die rather than in accordance with your wishes, you should decide whether you believe that taking the time to prepare a will is appropriate. If you are willing to have your estate pay a significant amount for a bond and have your assets distributed in accordance with the laws described in Appendix E, then you should not worry about having a will. If, on the other hand, you prefer to conserve the assets you worked hard to obtain and have those assets available for your loved ones after you die, and if you would prefer to identify the people who will receive those assets after you die, then it is important for you to work with an estate planning attorney and have a will in place. By having a will that you have thought through and worked out, you will maximize the value of your estate and determine how it is being distributed. The choice is yours.

---

In the event you decide that you do not want to spend the time preparing a will and working with an estate planning attorney in order to ensure that the will is properly executed and valid, then your assets will need to be handled through the intestate process when you die. As pointed out in this chapter, the process requires the purchase of a bond, and the intestate laws will govern the individuals who will be entitled to receive your assets. If this is an acceptable arrangement for you, then you will not have to waste any time preparing a will. Few individuals believe that this is acceptable to them and, for this reason, most individuals do prepare an appropriate estate plan. The fact that you are reading this book means that you too believe that estate planning is important.

# PART IV

# Guidance for Survivors

The following chapters in Part IV are intended to be used as a resource for your loved ones who survive you. As such, these chapters speak directly to those survivors and give you the opportunity to provide them with additional information necessary to administer your estate.

# CHAPTER 19

# In the Event of Death

This chapter is intended to provide guidance by you to your survivors immediately upon your death. The chapter contains what to do in the case of an accidental or unexpected death, your personal information, instructions of whom to call, and a list of your current medications. When the immediate needs of your death have been managed, your survivors can turn to the following chapter for information about notifying your friends and family, your wishes concerning organ donation, and funeral arrangements.

The information that follows is confidential and sensitive. Please take care to ensure only trusted individuals use the information that you have written throughout this book. Up until this chapter, we have been advising you. From this point forward, the material is intended for your survivors, and for that reason, it is structured so that you will be communicating with your survivors.

## WHAT TO DO IN CASE OF AN ACCIDENTAL OR UNEXPECTED DEATH

1. Call 911 or instruct someone to call 911 if you are administering first aid. Identify yourself. Tell the 911 dispatcher where you are, what happened, or what you discovered. Follow the instructions of the dispatcher.
2. Give first aid if it is appropriate. Continue first aid until either the authorities arrive or it is clear that I have died. If you have first aid training, rely on that training to determine when it is appropriate to stop giving first aid. If you do not have first aid training, ask the 911 operator to talk you through how and when to administer first aid.

3. If death occurred on a job site, contact my supervisor.

4. Do not disturb any property on or around my body unless it is necessary to give lifesaving first aid. If possible, make an inventory of the belongings I have with me including valuable items like jewelry or a wallet. You may need to take my car keys to retrieve my parked vehicle.

5. Wait for the authorities to arrive. When they arrive, cooperate fully, identify yourself, and tell them what happened or what you discovered.

6. Follow up with my family and friends. If you were the last person to see me alive, your memory may be important for them to achieve closure. Since memories quickly fade, it is important for you to write down, dictate, or otherwise preserve as much as you remember of the situation as promptly as possible.

7. If death occurred at home and calling 911 is not appropriate, for example, if I died in my sleep, call the mortuary (listed in a later section called At the Time of My Death). The mortuary will arrange for the care of my body and help you with the other arrangements. If you do not know which mortuary I have selected, then you may wish to call my religious organization in order to determine which mortuary it would recommend.

8. If I have a religious preference that prohibits parts of my body being removed after death for an autopsy, that should be told to the person that picks up my body.

9. If you are the person who will manage my affairs, review the instructions in the rest of this book and contact a professional advisor, such as an attorney, about your duties.

**NOTE:** These are guidelines to follow in the case of accidental or unexpected death. They are not meant to be a substitute for first-aid training or certification. We recommend that you take a first-aid or cardiopulmonary resuscitation class to learn more.

## MY PERSONAL INFORMATION

When I pass away, you will need a lot of information about me. Below are the basics. The remainder of the worksheets in the book will guide you to other information you will need in the coming days and months.

Name: _____

Aliases/Maiden Name: _____

Address: _____

Telephone: _____

Date of Birth: _____

Place of Birth: _____

Social Security Number: _____

Spouse/Significant Other: _____

Children: _____ Date of Birth: _____

_____ Date of Birth: _____

_____ Date of Birth: _____

_____ Date of Birth: _____

_____ Date of Birth: _____

_____ Date of Birth: _____

_____ Date of Birth: _____

Religious Preferences: _____

## UPON MY DEATH

This person may be able to help you and be with you. The individual(s) listed below may be a religious leader, family member, friend, or other person that has experience dealing with the emotional issues surrounding death.

Call: _____

At: _____

Alternate Number: _____

OR

Call: _____

At: _____

Alternate Number: _____

## AT THE TIME OF MY DEATH

There are some technical issues that you will need to oversee. I have listed professionals that will be able to help. This is likely to be a very emotional time for you. These professionals should assist you with the technical issues and are experts at dealing with death.

**If I am in the hospital:**
Tell the hospital staff to:

Call this mortuary: _____

Mortuary Phone Number: _____

and ask them to pick up my body.

**If I am under at-home hospice care:**
Call the hospice:

Hospice: _____

Hospice Phone Number: _____

and tell them that I have passed away.

**If I am at home and not under hospice care:**
Call 911. Tell the dispatcher that I died at home.
When an officer arrives, tell the officer:

- Cause of death (if known)
- Medications I am taking (see below)

When the body is released, call the mortuary listed above.


## MY CURRENT MEDICATIONS

| Name of Drug | Dosage | Prescribing Physician's Contact Information |
|---|---|---|
| *Example:* | | |
| Lisinopril | 20 mg/1x day | Dr. John Doe, (555) 555-1234 |
| _____ | _____ | _____ |
| _____ | _____ | _____ |
| _____ | _____ | _____ |
| _____ | _____ | _____ |
| _____ | _____ | _____ |
| _____ | _____ | _____ |

Last Updated: _____

*Update this list whenever your medications change.*

# CHAPTER 20

# General Information about Handling the Death of a Loved One

In this chapter, we discuss the information needed in the hours, days and weeks following your death. It includes a list of the items we believe are important. This information is likely to also be confidential and therefore it should be handled in the same manner as the information discussed in the preceding chapter.

## FAMILY AND FRIENDS TO NOTIFY

Please notify the following people in order. Let them know of my passing and ask them to notify others that might not be on this list. Please ask them not to post about my death on social media until you have completed notifying the entire list.

| Name | Number |
|------|--------|
|      |        |
|      |        |
|      |        |
|      |        |
|      |        |
|      |        |
|      |        |

For additional people to notify, please see the list on page: _____

## NOTIFY MY PRIMARY CARE DOCTOR

There is no need to call my doctor immediately in nonemergency situations. Please wait until regular business hours unless it is an emergency.

Name: _____

Clinic Name: _____

Address: _____

Telephone Number: _____

Email address: _____

Fax Number: _____

For additional doctors and specialists that should be notified, please see the list on page: _____

## ORGAN DONATIONS

☐ I want to donate all of my usable organs.

☐ I **do not** want to donate my organs.

☐ I want to donate my eyes and tissue.

☐ I **do not** want to donate my eyes and tissue.

_____        _____

Signature                                                    Date

If my organs are to be donated, please contact my doctor or the hospital immediately as organs can begin to deteriorate within hours of my death. Please also notify those responsible for my body of my intent. Keep in mind that many states include a designation of organ donorship on a driver's license or state issued identification. Please check my license if I have one.

## Organ and Tissue Donor Card

NAME: _____

(Print or type name of donor)

In the hope that I may help others, I hereby make the anatomical gift, if medically acceptable, to take effect upon my death. The words and marks below indicate my desires. I give:

☐ any needed organs or tissues.
☐ only the following organs or tissues (Specify the organ(s) or tissue(s)):

_____

_____

_____

for the purposes of transplantation, therapy, medical research, or medical education.
☐ my body for anatomical study if needed.

Limitations or special wishes: _____

_____

_____

Signed by the donor and the following two witnesses in the presence of each other:

_____      _____
(Signature of Donor)                    (Date of Birth of Donor)

_____      _____
(Date Signed)                    (City and State)

_____      _____
(Witness)                    (Witness)
(Preferably Next of Kin)

This is a legal document under the Uniform Anatomical Gift Act or similar laws.

## FUNERAL ARRANGEMENTS

If you have not already done so, call the mortuary and arrange to have them pick up my body. If death occurred at night, you may reach an answering service.

Call this mortuary: _____

Mortuary Phone Number: _____

If the mortuary or funeral parlor is not known, then contact the religious organization that I affiliate with in order to determine what it recommends.

The disposition of my remains is stated in my estate planning documents. If those documents are not complete, please notify my executive or personal representative that I wish to be: _____ (cremated, buried, other).

Please order _____ (at least four) death certificates from the mortuary. The number ordered should be a reasonable amount depending on the number of accounts that I have and whether the account holders will require an original or certified copy death certificate. For more information about this, see the discussion in Chapter 17.

### Memorial Service

Call the contact person below to notify them of my death. That person will coordinate with you to prepare the memorial service, as well as burial, entombment, etc.

Memorial service to be held at: _____

Contact Person: _____

Phone Number: _____

Please coordinate a reception following the memorial/grave/entombment service. It is important that family and friends be able to attend the services and reception unless I leave specific instructions here:

_____

_____

_____

_____

I was a member of the armed services and the military should be notified of my death and appropriate arrangements should be made to honor my service. The military will pay a portion of the cost of the services, provide an appropriate ceremony, and, if desired, allow the use of a military cemetery.

Once the dates and times are arranged, call family and friends listed on page _____ to notify them of the scheduled service. Do not publish notice of my service in the paper because there is a risk of home invasion and burglary if people are aware that no one will be home.

If I have prearranged or prepaid for cremation, burial, or funeral home services, my receipts are papers are located: _____

The following section has specific instructions about my funeral.

## Memorial Directive

In lieu of flowers at my funeral or memorial service, I would like memorials or remembrances in my name be for the benefit or use of: _____

_____

_____

Contact Person: _____

Email Address: _____

Telephone Number: _____

Address: _____

City, State, Zip: _____

Contributions should be sent to the above organization with a note indicating that the contribution is in my name and for the benefit of the above-named organization.

Copies of this information should be given to:

    ☐ Those attending my funeral or memorial service
    ☐ Friends and family
    ☐ Attached to my will and given to each heir or beneficiary
    ☐ Published along with my obituary
    ☐ Other: _____

Contributions may be tax deductible. Donors should contact the organization and their tax advisor to discuss available tax deductions.

_____    _____

Signature                              Date

## Funeral Instructions

Please have the organist play appropriate music and include the following hymns or songs:

_____

_____

Please have flowers for the location. In lieu of other memorial flowers, I request a memorial contribution to the following charity or organization(s):

_____

_____

I request the following readings at my service. If I have selected no specific readings, I request that my family and memorial service personnel choose appropriate readings:

_____

_____

Please have the following people speak at my service:

_____

_____

Please allow anyone who would like to speak to come forward.
Please have the following people act as pallbearers:

_____

_____

Additional instructions:

_____

_____

More instructions can be found:

_____

My signature below certifies that the above hymns, readings, and request for flowers or contributions are my wishes for my service.

_____        _____

Signature                                                Date

## Burial Arrangements
### My Preference for Burial Options
First Choice: _____

Second Choice: _____

Third Choice: _____

Check with the funeral home to make sure this option is available. In some locations, certain types of burials may not be permitted. For example, in areas where ground water is a problem, underground burial is not permitted.

It is important that the burial option chosen conforms to my religious preferences.

### Casket Options
First Choice: _____

Second Choice: _____

Third Choice: _____

It is important that the casket option chosen conforms to my religious preferences.

### Grave Marker Options
Text to appear on the marker: _____

The options available for grave markers and the text which may appear are numerous. You should discuss this with the funeral home representative in order to determine what that person recommends in the location where the grave is located. In addition, you can search online for grave marker options. Other choices: _____

_____

_____

Some religions permit the installation of a grave marker immediately while other delay the installation for a prescribed period. It is important to determine what my religion requires with respect to the time the marker is to be installed and whether there are any religious preferences with respect to the type of marker to be used.

### Grave Tending Services
The cemetery in which my grave is located may have ongoing maintenance taken care of automatically as part of the cost of my burial plot. In that case, there is nothing more for you to do unless I have requested that some particular

events be recognized with flowers. For example, on the anniversary of my death or Veterans Day or Memorial Day. If, on the other hand, the cemetery requires periodic payments for maintenance, then those payments need to be made. Generally, the cost of ongoing payment will continue to increase and if I have established a trust for those payments, then the trust should be used to make the periodic payments. Many cemeteries provide for an arrangement whereby a single, specified payment will be required for perpetual grave maintenance. If the cemetery I have selected for my grave has that kind of arrangement, then it would be appropriate to determine whether it is more cost-effective to make the single payment or to pay the periodic fees. More likely than not, the single payment will be better since that will end the requirement for ongoing mainte-nance, whereas ongoing fees will continue and likely increase.

If the cemetery does not have a single-payment arrangement, then estab-lishing a perpetual trust for periodic maintenance payments will be neces-sary in order for my grave to continue receiving maintenance. The trust I have created addresses this situation.

Grave tending service will be provided by: _____

I hereby instruct my personal representative to:

    ☐ Establish a trust to pay for grave tending services to be funded with
       $ _____
    ☐ Pay the above-named grave tending service a one-time pay-
       ment of $ _____
    ☐ Other: _____

## Burial Out of State

In some situations, the individual who dies will wish to be buried in another state. This can be a complex and expensive process. It can also be difficult if appropriate plans have not been made in advance of death. For this reason, it is important to have a plan in place while I am still alive.

To begin with, if I died in one state and wish to have my remains interred in another state, it is important to determine where my funeral will take place. That is, in the state where I died, in the state where I am to be buried, or both. Second, the state in which I die must permit my remains to be transported to the state where I am to be buried and you must obtain appropriate permits from both of those states. Third, you will need to arrange for my body to be transported to the state where I am to be laid to rest. This can be by plane or ground transport. Appropriate arrangements must be made. The cost of the move can be significant and a fund may be created for that purpose before I die. That fund should be secured and the person responsible for the arrangement should know where the fund is and have the documents necessary to access that fund. In some situations, the funeral home selected to receive my remains may assist with this arrangement.

## MY OBITUARY

It is common for an obituary to appear in newspapers, religious publications, and online. The obituary can be written after my death or it can be written by me and updated after my death. The benefit in having it written by me is that I will have the time and ability to be sure that everything I want the obituary to contain is in my obituary.

My obituary should contain at least the following information:

☐ Name: _____
☐ Age when I died: _____
☐ Family relationships: _____
☐ Military or other service organizations: _____
☐ Religious preferences: _____
☐ Accomplishments: _____
☐ Awards: _____
☐ Education: _____
☐ Important life events: _____
☐ Photo: _____
☐ Praise for those who assisted me during my life and at the time
   of my death: _____
☐ Requests for donations in lieu of flowers: _____
☐ Quotes (by me): _____
☐ Quotes (that I lived by): _____

Publications where my obituary should appear:

☐ Newspapers: _____
☐ Online: _____

&#9633; Organizational newsletters: _____

&#9633; Professional publications: _____

&#9633; Religious publications: _____

## MY PHOTOS

&#9633; Please select an appropriate and recent photograph of me for my service and remembrances.

&#9633; Attached below is a photograph of myself that I would like used at my memorial service and any remembrances, if appropriate.

&#9633; A digital copy of the photograph of myself that I would like used at my memorial services and any remembrances, if appropriate, is located:

&#9633; I do not want any photographs of me used. Please select appropriate designs and decorations for my memorial service and any remembrances.

&#9633; (Attach Photo Here)

## MY PROFESSIONAL ADVISORS

| | |
|---|---|
| **Attorney:** | |
| Address: | |
| Phone: | |
| **Accountant:** | |
| Address: | |
| Phone: | |
| **Financial Planner:** | |
| Address: | |
| Phone: | |
| **Insurance Agent:** | |
| Address: | |
| Phone: | |
| **Banker:** | |
| Address: | |
| Phone: | |

| Property Manager: |
|---|
| Address: |
| Phone: |
| **Other:** |
| Address: |
| Phone: |

## OTHER PEOPLE TO NOTIFY

Below I have listed employers, IRA account holders, credit card companies, banks, DMV, Social Security office, licensing boards, health insurance companies, the U.S. Post Office, utilities including gas, electric, water, sewer, sanitation, etc., security patrol or local police, and social service organizations that you will need to contact in order to wrap up my affairs.

| Name (Role) | Number |
|---|---|
| Example:<br>Smith Financial (IRA account holder) | (555) 555-1234 |
| | |
| | |
| | |
| | |
| | |
| | |

My Social Security number is: _____

# CHAPTER 21

# Miscellaneous Instructions

My clothing should be disposed of as follows:

_____
_____
_____
_____

Other personal property should be distributed as provided in my will or letter of instruction in my estate planning documents.

Additional instructions:

_____
_____
_____
_____

## FAMILY INFORMATION

| Relationship | Name | Still Living? | Contact Information |
|---|---|---|---|
| My Mother | | | |
| My Father | | | |
| My Sibling | | | |

| Relationship | Name | Still Living? | Contact Information |
|---|---|---|---|
| My Sibling | | | |
| My Spouse or Significant Other | | | |
| My Spouse or Significant Other's Mother | | | |
| My Spouse or Significant Other's Father | | | |
| My Spouse or Significant Other's Sibling 1 | | | |
| My Spouse or Significant Other's Sibling 2 | | | |
| My Child | | | |
| | Child's spouse: | Child's other parent: | Child's children and grandchildren: |
| My Child | | | |
| | Child's spouse: | Child's other parent: | Child's children and grandchildren: |

Additional family members are listed on page _____

## PETS AND ANIMALS

I have the following pets/animals:

| Type of Pet | Name |
|---|---|
|  |  |
|  |  |
|  |  |

If willing, I would like _____ to take care of my pets. If that person is not willing, I would like my pets:

☐ To be sold or given to a loving family chosen by _____.
☐ To be cared for at a local animal shelter for the remainder of their lives and instruct my personal representative to made a donation of $_____ to the animal shelter. I recognize that if I want to make this gift binding, I need to do so in my will.
☐ Other: _____

_____

## Pet Care

Below are the care instructions for each pet including special needs, medication, diet, exercise, medical history, and veterinarian information

| Pet Name | Special Instructions & Veterinary Information |
|---|---|
|  |  |
|  |  |
|  |  |
|  |  |
|  |  |
|  |  |
|  |  |
|  |  |
|  |  |
|  |  |
|  |  |
|  |  |
|  |  |

# CHAPTER 22

# Important Documents and Where to Find Them

## WHERE TO FIND VITAL DOCUMENTS

Below is information on where to find vital documents. Policy and other relevant information is located later in this chapter.

| Estate Related | Location of Originals |
| --- | --- |
| Letter of Last Instruction | |
| Will | |
| Trust | |
| Power of Attorney | |
| Advance Directive | |

| Insurance Policies | Location of Originals |
| --- | --- |
| Auto | |
| Disability | |
| Health | |
| Life | |
| Homeowners/Renters | |
| Other | |

| Deeds and Legal Documents | Location of Originals |
|---|---|
| Automobile Titles | |
| Birth Certificates | |
| Marriage Certificates | |
| Passports | |
| Real Estate Deeds | |
| Other | |

| Payable on Death Policies | Location of Originals |
|---|---|
| 401(k) | |
| IRA | |
| 403(b) | |
| Other | |

| Investments | Location of Originals |
|---|---|
| Certificates of Deposit | |
| Brokerage Records | |
| Savings Passbooks | |
| Stock Certificates | |
| Other | |

| Tax Records | Location of Originals |
|---|---|
| Last Year's Tax Return | |
| Last 7 Years' Tax Return Records | |
| Other | |

| Loans and Credit Cards | Location of Originals |
|---|---|
| Credit Cards | |
| | |
| | |
| Loan Notes | |
| | |
| | |

## ESTATE PLANNING DOCUMENTS

I have executed the following estate planning documents:

☐ **Wills:**
Date executed: _____
Copies are located: _____
The original is located: _____
The attorney who assisted drafting the document: _____

☐ **Codicils (Amendments to the will):**
Date executed: _____
Copies are located: _____
The original is located: _____
The attorney who assisted drafting the document: _____

☐ **Trusts:**

| Trusts | |
|---|---|
| **Trust 1** | |
| Trustee(s) | |
| Date executed | |
| The original trust document is located | |
| Copies are located | |
| The attorney who assisted drafting the document | |
| **Trust 2** | |
| Trustee(s) | |
| Date executed | |
| The original trust document is located | |
| Copies are located | |
| The attorney who assisted drafting the document | |
| **Trust 3** | |
| Trustee(s) | |
| Date executed | |
| The original trust document is located | |
| Copies are located | |
| The attorney who assisted drafting the document | |

Information about additional trusts is located: _____

☐ **Advance Medical Directive:**

Date executed: _____

Copies are located: _____

The original is located: _____

The attorney who assisted drafting the document: _____

☐ **Power of Attorney:**

Date executed: _____

Copies are located: _____

The original is located: _____

The attorney who assisted drafting the document: _____

☐ **Personal Property Memorandum:**

Date executed: _____

Copies are located: _____

The original is located: _____

The attorney who assisted drafting the document: _____

☐ **Other:** _____

Date executed: _____

Copies are located: _____

The original is located: _____

The attorney who assisted drafting the document: _____


Information about additional documents is located: _____


# BENEFICIARY DESIGNATIONS

Beneficiary information for 401(k)s, IRAs 403(b)s, insurance policies, and other payable on death (POD) policy information can be found: _____

## LOCATION OF SAFETY DEPOSIT BOX

I have safety deposit box(es) located at:

| Bank | Box # |
|------|-------|
|      |       |
|      |       |
|      |       |
|      |       |
|      |       |

The keys for the above boxes are located: _____

## PERSONAL AND CONFIDENTIAL INFORMATION INSTRUCTIONS

Following this page is a worksheet that contains instructions for handling very personal or embarrassing information. The information can be copied onto separate sheets of paper or the pages should be removed from this book and put into an envelope labeled "Personal and Confidential Information." Seal the envelope and write the following on the envelope:

Only _____, as my chosen representative, should be allowed to open this sealed envelope, and if that person is not my executor or personal representative, then my executor or personal representative should forward the sealed envelope to the named person immediately upon my death.

It is my specific intent that the person named above be as discreet as possible with such personal items and/or information so as not to cause undue harm or unnecessary embarrassment to myself or others.

The envelope is located: _____

## Personal and Confidential

Specific items or information:

_____

_____

_____

_____

_____

Specific handling/disposition instructions:

_____

_____

_____

_____

_____

WARNING: Do not use this form to pass property of value as the property may not pass as intended and may need to be disclosed to the personal representative, executor, trustee, administrator, or court for legal reporting purposes.

## INSURANCE POLICIES

| Auto | |
|---|---|
| Company: | |
| Policy Number: | |
| **Disability** | |
| Company: | |
| Policy Number: | |
| **Health** | |
| Company: | |
| Policy Number: | |
| **Life** | |
| Company: | |
| Policy Number: | |

| Homeowners/ Renters | |
|---|---|
| Company: | |
| Policy Number: | |
| **Other** | |
| Company: | |
| Policy Number: | |

## DEEDS AND DOCUMENTS

| | |
|---|---|
| Automobile Titles | |
| Birth Certificates | |
| Marriage Certificates | |
| Passports | |
| Real Estate Deeds | |
| Other | |

## INVESTMENTS

| | |
|---|---|
| Certificates of Deposit | |
| Brokerage Records | |
| Savings Passbooks | |
| Stock Certificates | |
| Other | |

## TAX RECORDS

**My tax records are located:**

Last year's tax return: _____

Last 7 years of tax return records: _____

Other: _____

**For other questions, contact my tax preparer or accountant:**

Name: _____

Contact Information: _____

## LOANS AND CREDIT CARDS

| | |
|---|---|
| **Credit Cards** | |
| | |
| | |
| | |
| **Loan Notes** | |
| | |
| | |
| | |

# CHAPTER 23

# Digital Assets, Accounts, and Passwords

The following information is incredibly sensitive. It should be kept safe and confidential at all times.

## Hardware Access

Information to access computers, external hard drives, flash drives, tablets, smartphones, digital music players, e-readers, digital cameras, DVRs, any other digital device that has a password should be recorded here.

| Device | Username | Password/PIN | Recovery Email/Phone Number |
|--------|----------|--------------|------------------------------|
|        |          |              |                              |
|        |          |              |                              |
|        |          |              |                              |
|        |          |              |                              |
|        |          |              |                              |
|        |          |              |                              |
|        |          |              |                              |

## Email Accounts

| Account | Username | Password | Recovery Email/Phone Number |
|---------|----------|----------|-----------------------------|
|         |          |          |                             |
|         |          |          |                             |
|         |          |          |                             |
|         |          |          |                             |
|         |          |          |                             |
|         |          |          |                             |
|         |          |          |                             |

## Social Media Accounts

| Account | Username | Password | Recovery Email/Phone Number |
|---------|----------|----------|-----------------------------|
|         |          |          |                             |
|         |          |          |                             |
|         |          |          |                             |
|         |          |          |                             |
|         |          |          |                             |
|         |          |          |                             |
|         |          |          |                             |

## Data Storage Accounts

| Account | Username | Password | Recovery Email/Phone Number |
|---------|----------|----------|-----------------------------|
|         |          |          |                             |
|         |          |          |                             |
|         |          |          |                             |
|         |          |          |                             |
|         |          |          |                             |
|         |          |          |                             |
|         |          |          |                             |

## Shopping Accounts

| Account | Username | Password | Recovery Email/Phone Number |
|---------|----------|----------|------------------------------|
|         |          |          |                              |
|         |          |          |                              |
|         |          |          |                              |
|         |          |          |                              |
|         |          |          |                              |
|         |          |          |                              |
|         |          |          |                              |

## Photo- and Video-Sharing Accounts

| Account | Username | Password | Recovery Email/Phone Number |
|---------|----------|----------|------------------------------|
|         |          |          |                              |
|         |          |          |                              |
|         |          |          |                              |
|         |          |          |                              |
|         |          |          |                              |
|         |          |          |                              |

## Gaming Accounts

| Account | Username | Password | Recovery Email/Phone Number |
|---------|----------|----------|------------------------------|
|         |          |          |                              |
|         |          |          |                              |
|         |          |          |                              |
|         |          |          |                              |
|         |          |          |                              |
|         |          |          |                              |

## Websites, Blogs, and Domain Names

| Account | Username | Password | Recovery Email/Phone Number |
|---|---|---|---|
|  |  |  |  |
|  |  |  |  |
|  |  |  |  |
|  |  |  |  |
|  |  |  |  |
|  |  |  |  |
|  |  |  |  |

## Financial Accounts

| Account | Username | Password | Recovery Email/Phone Number |
|---|---|---|---|
|  |  |  |  |
|  |  |  |  |
|  |  |  |  |
|  |  |  |  |
|  |  |  |  |
|  |  |  |  |
|  |  |  |  |

## Subscription Accounts

| Account | Username | Password | Recovery Email/Phone Number |
|---|---|---|---|
|  |  |  |  |
|  |  |  |  |
|  |  |  |  |
|  |  |  |  |
|  |  |  |  |
|  |  |  |  |
|  |  |  |  |

## Security Questions

| Question | Answer |
|---|---|
|  |  |
|  |  |
|  |  |
|  |  |
|  |  |
|  |  |

# CHAPTER 24

# Immediate Care of Property and Obligations

In this chapter we will detail many of the important steps that must be taken when a loved one has passed away. Because each life and circumstance is unique, this chapter cannot cover every eventuality. It is our hope that the material we included will provide a foundation of information and give you some additional resources to guide you through the legal steps you must take. While these tasks may be tedious, difficult, or even emotionally overwhelming, keep in mind that this is the last great service you are providing for someone who cannot do this for himself or herself. It says much about your character that you are willing to perform these selfless acts in such a thoughtful manner.

Many religious, fraternal, and senior organizations, such as the AARP, have advice and help lines with individuals who are available around the clock to advise and assist when a loved one dies.

## LEGAL JARGON ALERT

In this chapter, we will be referring to your deceased loved one by the legal term that means one who has passed away—*decedent* (\duh-see-dent\). It is not our intention to be cold, confusing, or overly technical. In our experience, using the legal term rather than colloquial terms like *loved one* can help the survivors perform the many legal and practical tasks required of them in a businesslike and efficient way.

It is vital that you process through the grief that you experience and take the time you need to reflect and grieve—even during the early days following your loved one's death that require so much levelheaded effort.

However, many of the people we have worked with have found that the time to process and feel that grief is not while you are on the phone with the florist or the bank. Even though the word *decedent* is not In Plain English® and we would normally choose a less formal term, it is our hope that this helps you as well.

## REPORT THE DEATH

Each death must be reported to state and local officials. If the decedent passed away at the hospital or other medical center, the staff is trained to handle the immediate concerns of death. This includes notifying the officials and disposition of the body. While the exact procedures will vary from institution to institution, each facility will have paperwork you need to fill out to certify the death for state records.

If the death occurs at home, immediately call 911 and report the death. The 911 operator will assist you in taking the appropriate steps. For more information on this, see Chapter 19.

The individuals who were present at the time of death or immediately thereafter will need to complete paperwork with the assistance of mortuary personnel in order to properly record the death.

No matter where the death occurs, it is a good idea to discuss whether an autopsy is appropriate with the hospital, physician, or other staff members at the mortuary. Sometimes understanding the reason for death is a vital element of closure for the surviving friends and family. Be aware, however, that the decedent's religious or personal preferences may preclude an autopsy.

In addition to reporting the death to state and county officials, the Social Security office, and, if appropriate, the US Department of Veterans Affairs, should be notified as soon as possible. A death benefit payment may be available. If the decedent was already receiving benefits, you may need to reimburse the government for the benefits that were received after death.

If the decedent has a will, it will appoint a personal representative. If the decedent had a trust, the trust documents will appoint a successor trustee. If the decedent died without a will, the court will appoint an administrator for the estate. In all of these cases it will take some time for a personal representative, successor trustee, executor, or administrator to be officially appointed. This means that there are some things that need to be done immediately and then reported to the person in charge of administering the estate once that person is appointed. The fact that you are reading this book indicates that that person is probably you.

## SECURE AND INVENTORY PROPERTY

Even before the body has been disposed of and the death has been reported, it may be necessary to secure the decedent's property. It is important that neither you nor anyone else that is present at the time of death disturb any of the decedent's property unless it is necessary for safekeeping. It is common for valuable personal property such as rings, watches, wallets, and purses to disappear following a death. It is important that you secure these items and keep an inventory of their location. Some religions or personal preferences prohibit the removal of certain items from the body or the decedent's residence. If you are concerned about protecting valuable property, contact an attorney immediately and ask for guidance.

Most people have several keys to their property whether they live in an apartment or own their own home. Copies of these keys may be in the possession of several different people including other family members, nurses, housekeepers, and neighbors. If the decedent lived alone, it may be necessary to have the locks in the house changed and arrange for security measures such as an alarm system or cameras, asking someone to periodically check on the property, or installing automatically timed indoor lights.

If death occurred in a medical facility, you can request a list of personal property that belonged to the decedent or was in their possession at the time of death. Use this list to identify what property may still be at the facility and secure that property. If the property was already returned, this list should include information about who received the property.

Take inventory of the property at the decedent's home. The personal representative, executor, or administrator of the estate will need this list at some point in the future. A thorough and complete inventory is crucial to the administration of the estate and can make the probate process proceed more efficiently.

## CONTACT FAMILY AND FRIENDS

A list of individuals that you can call for emotional support and the friends and family that should be notified of the decedent's passing is located in

Chapter 19. We strongly recommend setting up a network with friends and family so that no one has to do all of the calling and no one gets overlooked. When you contact friends and family, be sensitive to the needs of those that may be grieving and assist them emotionally when possible.

Obtain a list of local service agencies, clergy, or trained counselors that are experienced in grief counseling. If you speak to someone who may need the help of these services, or if you need the services yourself, give the numbers out freely.

If there are family members or friends who are unable to cope with the loss and you are fearful for their safety or health, it may be necessary to contact a family physician or therapist. If you are concerned that someone may take his or her own life, call 911 immediately or take the individual to the emergency room.

Be cautious about intervention. Each individual has a different way of coping with death. Even denying the need for assistance can be a symptom of grief. Check in with your own emotions often and seek support, even if that support is just a quick check-in with a friend.

## LOCATE ESTATE PLANNING DOCUMENTS

The location of estate planning documents is listed in Chapter 22. The estate planning attorney may know where the documents are and have a copy of them, but most attorneys do not keep original copies of the estate planning documents. Other family members or friends may also know where the decedent's written instructions are located. When death is expected, locating these documents is usually easier because the decedent likely told someone where they are. If death was unexpected, it may be more difficult to locate these documents.

Estate planning documents are customarily stored in safety deposit boxes, home safes, strongboxes, or other secured locations where important documents such as birth certificates, passports, and Social Security cards are kept.

In some cases, more than one document may surface. This happened recently in the estate of Aretha Franklin as discussed earlier in Chapter 3. While her family was going through her effects in her home, they located a number of handwritten wills. The family struggled to determine which will was the most recent and whether the documents invalidated prior wills, amended prior wills, or were invalid themselves. If you find multiple wills, each one will need to be examined by an attorney or perhaps even analyzed by the court to determine which will governs. If you cannot find a valid estate plan, the person is said to have died intestate and the state law will determine who receives the property. To learn more about the intestate process, see Chapter 18 of this book.

Once you find the estate planning documents, it will be important to safeguard them. They may be delivered to an attorney for safekeeping. Unauthorized destruction of estate planning documents is illegal in all fifty states.

## IDENTIFY THE FIDUCIARIES

*Fiduciaries* are the individuals who will have some responsibilities, obligations, or duties to the estate of the decedent. The executor or personal representative of the estate is a *fiduciary*. A trustee of a trust is a *fiduciary*. The guardian of minor children, pets, or disabled family members is a *fiduciary*.

Fiduciaries are bound by certain standards that are called fiduciary duties. These duties are spelled out in state law. Fiduciaries must be honest, prudent, loyal, impartial, and patient. Some people are not allowed to be a fiduciary. In most states a minor, a legally incompetent person, or a felon may be prevented from serving as a fiduciary.

The powers of a fiduciary are governed by state law. During the administrative process, fiduciary positions including the executor, personal representative, administrator, trustee, or guardian, are very important. The person chosen for each of these positions should have good judgment and a history of reasonable actions. There are some fiduciary positions that may require special skill. For example, if a trustee is appointed to file a patent application for an invention, the trustee should be familiar with the invention and the patent process. If a guardian is appointed to care for a family member with special needs, that guardian should be familiar with the individual's needs and be able to provide that care.

Now that the decedent has died, you must identify who each of these individuals are and ensure that they are willing and able to perform their fiduciary duties. The will or trust document should name each of the fiduciaries, and the best estate planning documents will also name replacement individuals who will serve if the person originally named has died or is otherwise unable or unwilling to perform the duties. If no one has been named in the will or trust, or all of the individuals named are unable to perform, you should contact an attorney to help you identify the proper fiduciary.

If the decedent had a valid will, it should name a personal representative or executor to manage and close the decedent's affairs. You should contact the personal representative or executor immediately if you have not already done so.

Once the fiduciaries have been identified, those people should take over the administration of the estate, trust, or guardianship. This person will have fiduciary duties to fulfill. One of these duties is to keep certain people, including the heirs and beneficiaries of the estate, updated with status reports. In some cases, the executor or personal representative may be required to obtain a bond to guarantee that that person will act appropriately and comply with the fiduciary duties. The estate plan may waive this requirement and some state laws may not require one. See Chapter 17 for more information about bonds.

One of the most important duties of the executor or personal representative is to follow the decedent's wishes for disposition of the body. See Chapters 19 and 20 of this book for details about mortuary and memorial instructions. If the decedent left no instructions, you will need to comply with state law. In most jurisdictions, this means that the family must decide, and if they cannot agree, a legal conflict can arise—which is expensive and typically causes emotional pain for the parties involved. If there is some question as to the disposition of the body, contact an attorney for assistance immediately. Because this is a task that can only happen once, it should be done right the first time.

The executor or personal representative should contact an attorney to discuss the administration and closing of the estate. If this is not done correctly, that person might face personal liability for claims by creditors, heirs, or beneficiaries. Someone who is inexperienced with the requirements, documents, court filings, and deadlines that accompany administrating an estate is vulnerable to making well-intentioned mistakes. Protect yourself by asking for help if you are charged with the responsibility of a fiduciary role.

Once the immediate concerns regarding disposition of the body and funeral arrangements have been made, dependents and pets are cared for, and the decedent's property is secure, there are very few tasks that must be completed in a hurry during the administration of the estate. That is not to say that you should allow time to pass unnecessarily, but it is to say that you should get plenty of rest, and make sure all of the heirs and beneficiaries have enough time to relax and reflect on the life of the decedent. You should do everything to take care of yourself since it is important for you to be comfortable and alert during this process. There is a greater chance of tempers flaring and disputes arising if everyone is tired, stressed, or still reeling from loss.

## FIDUCIARY RESPONSIBILITIES

A fiduciary will have responsibilities specific to the task assigned; however, all fiduciaries share certain duties imposed by law to perform honestly, diligently, and with reasonable care. Below is an explanation of these general duties.

### Prudent Investment

One duty that a personal representative, executor, or trustee has is to invest the decedent's interests wisely. For example, an executor who sells the decedent's stock and invests that money in a lottery ticket is not acting in the best interest of the estate and is probably acting illegally. The fiduciary should consider the best interests of current and future beneficiaries of the estate and follow reasonable investment principles such as diversification and engage in appropriate risk analysis. Fiduciaries can enlist the help of a professional but are not required to be professional themselves. Many states have laws that guide investment strategies, so it will be important for you to contact an attorney to determine what your fiduciary duties are in respect to investments.

### Duty of Responsible Delegation

The executor, personal representative, or administrator of the estate may not be able to perform all of the duties required to maintain the estate property. It is perfectly appropriate for the executor to delegate some of these responsibilities to another person. It is a fiduciary duty to delegate responsibilities to someone who is qualified and capable of performing the duty. In addition, the duty to perform the delegated responsibility does not end simply because it is delegated to another person. The fiduciary must check up on the progress regularly and keep appropriate records. Even if the task has been delegated, the fiduciary is ultimately responsible for how things are handled and must ensure the person assigned to complete the task acts responsibly.

## Duty of Faithfulness and Impartiality

All of the fiduciaries must faithfully and impartially fulfill their duties. This means the executor must faithfully administer the estate, a trustee must faithfully manage or distribute trust assets, and a guardian must faithfully care for their charges. This means that a fiduciary cannot favor certain heirs or beneficiaries and may not put their own interests above that of the estate. Fiduciaries often run afoul of this duty when they sell things to themselves at below market cost or enlist the services of their own company on behalf of the estate. Failing to faithfully and impartially fulfill a duty is also called self-dealing, because you are putting yourself before your duty to perform your tasks faithfully.

## Duty of Accounting and Furnishing Information

The executor, administrator, or personal representative of the estate is responsible to provide complete information to the beneficiaries and the court. Some fiduciaries fail to properly account for the assets in the estate or keep track of when the assets are sold or disposed of. This could be a serious problem for the estate, and for the fiduciary personally. State law will likely have a limit as to how often beneficiaries can reasonably request an accounting, but an accounting should generally be done and available at all times.

The estate administrator should keep a separate accounting of all estate assets, although there is no standard accounting system or practice for fiduciary accounting. In addition, each estate will have its own unique requirements based on the nature of the assets. In general, the estate administrator or executor should have an initial entry or opening balance sheet recording the receipt of all assets. The accounting should include earnings, gains, receipts, costs, expenses, and expenditures. The accounting should have a record of all distributions made from income and principal of any accounts. All receipts from income and principal, records of payments and invoices must be kept as well. An attorney or accountant can be of great assistance to determine whether a distribution was from principal or income and give advice as to what software programs might be available to track all of this information.

## Example of Duties

Once a fiduciary has been identified, the court will officially appoint the fiduciary and give either *letters of administration* in the case of a decedent who died intestate or *letters testamentary* if the decedent died with a will. See

Chapters 17 and 18 for more information. These documents give the fiduciary authority to act on behalf of the estate. The court will send these documents to the fiduciary who is named, and that person should keep several copies of the document on hand at all times. The executor or administrator will need to provide these documents whenever they are signing papers or conducting transactions on behalf of the estate. There are ways to structure an estate plan to avoid probate. In that case, fiduciary letters may not be needed. It is important to contact an attorney to determine whether this applies to you.

Once you have the fiduciary letters, you should immediately open a bank account so that all transactions on behalf of the estate are handled through that account.

Some of the responsibilities that an executor, administrator, or personal representative may include notifying individuals who are named in the will, or will inherit through an intestate process, of all probate proceedings; notify banks, stockbrokers, insurance agencies, accountants, and lawyers of the death; take possession of, inventory, and preserve the assets of the estate; collect insurance benefits, veteran benefits, and refunds on prepaid services such as magazine subscriptions; obtain a valuation or appraisal of valuable assets; make sure all assets remain properly insured; continue to pay property insurance premiums, utility bills, and property taxes; and obtain a tax identification number for the estate and pay all estate and income taxes for the decedent. An estate planning attorney will assist you in performing your proper role.

## FUNERAL ARRANGEMENTS AND MEMORIAL SERVICES

The decedent's wishes for funeral arrangements and memorial services are listed in Chapter 20. If you have not already done so, you should call the mortuary and make arrangements to receive the body. If you do not know which mortuary or funeral parlor to contact, you should contact the religious, fraternal, or senior organization that the decedent affiliated with in order to determine what it recommends.

The mortuary will be able to assist with funeral arrangements and ordering death certificates. Order at least four death certificates. The number ordered should be a reasonable amount depending on the number of accounts that the decedent had and whether the account holders will require an original or certified copy of the death certificate. Additional certificates can be ordered later, but there is likely to be a delay in acquiring them, and there will be an additional charge. It is more efficient to obtain the appropriate number of death certificates initially. As discussed in Chapter 17, there are several different types of death certificates and the estate planning attorney can assist you in determining how many are recommended and the types recommended.

The name and contact information for the location of the memorial service is also located in Chapter 20. If no location is listed or otherwise known, the decedent's religious, fraternal, or senior organization or mortuary may have recommendations. It is important that family and friends be able to attend the services and reception.

If the decedent was a member of the armed services, the military should be notified of the death and appropriate arrangements should be made to honor the decedent's service. The military will pay a portion of the cost of the services, provide an appropriate ceremony, and allow the use of a military cemetery if that is the decedent's wish.

The decedent may have completed a separate memorial directive that details decedent's wishes regarding funeral arrangements and memorial services. The decedent's wishes should be followed as closely as practicable.

## Grave Marker

Some religions permit the installation of a grave marker immediately, while others delay the installation for a prescribed period. It is important to determine what the decedent's religion or personal preferences require with respect to the time the marker is to be installed and whether there are any religious preferences with respect to the type of marker to be used.

## Grave Maintenance

The cemetery in which the decedent's grave is located may have ongoing maintenance taken care of automatically as part of the cost of the burial plot. In that case, there is nothing more for you to do unless the decedent or other family members have requested that some particular events be recognized. For example, flowers may be placed on the grave on the anniversary of the decedent's death or flags placed on Veterans Day or Memorial Day. If, on the other hand, the cemetery requires periodic payments for maintenance, then those payments need to be made. Generally, the cost of ongoing payments will continue to increase, and if the decedent has established a trust for those payments, then the trust should be used to make the periodic payments.

Many cemeteries provide for an arrangement whereby a single, specified payment will be required for perpetual grave maintenance. If the cemetery has that kind of arrangement, then it would be appropriate to determine whether it is more cost-effective to make the single payment or to pay the periodic fees. More likely than not, the single payment will be better since that will end the requirement for ongoing maintenance whereas ongoing fees will continue and likely increase.

If the cemetery does not have a single-payment arrangement, then establishing a perpetual trust for periodic maintenance payments will be necessary in order for the decedent's grave to continue receiving maintenance. Some families would rather personally maintain the graves of their loved ones, and if that is the family preference, then appropriate arrangements should be made for the periodic maintenance. No matter which of these is applicable, some arrangement for maintenance of the decedent's grave should be established and followed so that the grave remains as the decedent would wish.

---

There are many steps you must take once your loved one has passed away. Delegate those tasks that can be delegated to responsible individuals, enlist the aid of the estate's attorney and other professionals whenever appropriate, and remember that these tasks were not meant to be done in a day. You must take time to deal with the loss and care for yourself in the midst of taking care of the estate. If you become overwhelmed, confused, or exhausted, reach out to friends and family or to religious, fraternal, and senior organizations, such as the AARP, that are prepared to advise and assist when a loved one dies.

# CHAPTER 25

# Identifying and Caring for Estate Property

The fiduciary described and identified in the previous chapter will have a multitude of duties. This chapter will describe some of the duties. As prescribed throughout this book, we recommend that you work with an experienced estate planning attorney in order to ensure that all of the fiduciary tasks are properly fulfilled and that all of the laws that apply to the estate you will be representing are complied with.

## REAL PROPERTY

Real property is defined as land as well as buildings (including homes, apartments, condominiums, and commercial buildings such as offices, factories, stores, restaurants, and every other kind of building).

If the decedent owned any real property as described above, then it is important to determine the method by which the real property was owned. There should be a document describing the character of the ownership of the property. The document will either be a deed, if the decedent owned the land and buildings on the land; a lease, for land or buildings which are leased for a particular period of time; a mortgage or deed of trust, if there are loans against the property; and in some cases, the decedent may have occupied a building without any documentation. You should obtain the addresses of all buildings the decedent lived in for residential real property and all buildings the decedent owned or occupied for commercial activity. A list of this real property is located in the worksheet at the end of Chapter 11.

Once you have identified the appropriate list of real properties owned by the decedent, you should determine whether that real property automatically transferred to another individual when the decedent died—for example, if a residence is owned by a husband and wife as tenants by the entirety, then on the death of either spouse, the survivor will automatically own that property. Other forms of deeds such as joint tenants may have similar rules. You should check with the estate planning attorney in order to determine whether the transfer is automatic or requires some additional documentation.

Commercial property must also be dealt with. If the decedent owned commercial property, and it remains part of the decedent's estate, the fiduciary will need to make the appropriate transfer of that property either in accordance with the will, trust, or in accordance with the laws of intestacy if no estate plan was in place. Here too, the estate planning attorney should assist.

If the decedent did not own commercial property but merely rented it, and there is a written lease, the estate will need to contact the landlord or the landlord's representative and work out an acceptable arrangement for the leased property. If there was no written lease, and the commercial property is occupied through an oral arrangement, then the state law of the state where the property is located will determine the rules regarding proper arrangements when the person occupying that property dies. Working with an experienced estate planning attorney in this situation is essential so that you do not violate those laws.

As the material presented above makes clear, real property is very important and it is likely that the decedent owned or occupied some form of real property. The estate planning attorney should be consulted in order to properly deal with the decedent's real property.

## PETS

Many individuals have one or more pets, and those pets must be cared for after the decedent dies. Dogs, cats, fish, hamsters, lizards, and other forms of pets require food, water, cleaning, and other care in order to survive. It is likely that the decedent identified pets and provided information regarding their ongoing care after death in Chapter 21 of this book. If so, the request(s) provided in that section should be followed. If not, then you should consult with the estate's attorney and find out what that attorney recommends for the care and maintenance of the decedent's pet(s).

Finally, keep in mind that not all animals are pets. Livestock, work animals, and animals bred for sale are not pets but still need to be cared for on a daily basis. While these animals have the same need to be fed, sheltered, and tended to, they will be distributed more like property than a pet. You may also have additional decisions to make regarding their sale or slaughter in order to avoid waste and prudently manage the estate.

## BANK ACCOUNTS

Virtually everybody has one or more bank accounts. This includes accounts in banks, credit unions, and other commercial institutions such as investment companies. It is essential for you to identify all of the decedent's bank accounts. If the decedent either omitted an account or failed to make appropriate requests for an account, then you will need to comply with the terms of the decedent's will, trust, or, if the decedent died without an estate plan, the intestacy laws. It is also prudent for you or the estate's lawyer to conduct an unclaimed property search for every state in which the decedent ever resided in order to determine whether the decedent has any unclaimed property, such as unclaimed bank accounts.

All of the money in the decedent's bank accounts should be transferred into the estate's bank account so that it can all be accounted for. In addition, all securities such as stocks and bonds should be transferred into an estate account as well. None of the assets of the estate should be transferred out of the estate account until a transfer is authorized by a probate court.

Once all of the assets of the estate have been collected, then the estate's attorney will assist in paying all bills, and satisfying all approved claims against the estate. After those payments are made, then any funds remaining will be available for distribution in accordance with the estate plan if one exists or the intestate laws of the state where the decedent died. For a list of those laws, see Appendix E. If the estate is unable to pay all creditors and approved claims, then a percentage of the claims and debts will be paid. Since this is an extremely important responsibility, you should work closely with the estate's attorney before making any payments.

## STOCKS AND BONDS

Many individuals have money invested in stocks, bonds, or both. These are commonly referred to as *securities*. Securities are typically held by investment banks for financial services companies such as Morgan Stanley, Goldman Sachs, and Charles Schwab. When a decedent dies having a security investment, it is important for you, as a fiduciary, to immediately notify the company that manages that investment. The company should then obtain the value of the decedent's investment on the date of death, since this information will be necessary for ultimately completing the estate. It should then be determined whether there are any co-owners. If there are co-owners, ownership of the securities may have transferred automatically on the decedent's death. If not, the securities will belong to the estate. If funds are needed to satisfy state creditors or approved claims against the estate, then some or all of the securities will need to be sold. If this is the case, you should work with the estate's attorney or investment advisor in order to obtain the maximum benefit from the sale. If the estate has sufficient funds to satisfy all debts and approved obligations, then you, the attorney, and the investment advisor should determine whether it would be best to merely transfer the securities to the intended beneficiaries or sell some or all of those securities and transfer the proceeds in order to obtain the maximum financial benefit for the estate. Since this is a very technical area requiring a great deal of knowledge and skill, you should work closely with the estate's lawyer and review the decedent's preferences, which are located in Chapter 22 of this book.

## AUTOMOBILES AND OTHER VEHICLES

Virtually every individual owns a vehicle such as a car, truck, boat, airplane, motorcycle, RV, or any other vehicle that customarily has a legal title that is issued by the state's department of motor vehicles. The list of vehicles owned by the decedent is contained in Chapter 22 of this book. You should identify the vehicles and arrange to have the vehicle transferred to the appropriate person. In order to accomplish this, you will need to have the legal title transferred from the decedent to the identified beneficiary, if any. You will need the letters testamentary/administration and possibly a copy of the death certificate in order to complete the transfer. Timing is important since it might be a problem to have the decedent's vehicle remain idle while the estate is being administered, and some vehicles, like airplanes, require a great deal of maintenance. The vehicle should be properly stored in the meantime. It is also very important to determine whether the vehicle was owned by the decedent alone or with someone else, and whether it is secured by a loan. It is also important to maintain insurance on the vehicle until the vehicle is properly transferred to the new owner. As you can see, there are a number of important issues you must consider and deal with regarding vehicles, and state law must be complied with. We strongly recommend that you work closely with the estate's attorney with respect to the decedent's vehicles.

## INCOME AND PAYMENTS TO THE ESTATE

Unless the decedent was retired before death, it is likely that income for work performed before death will be owed to the decedent, and that income will be an asset of the estate. In addition, if the decedent had life insurance that remained in the decedent's control at the date of death, then the proceeds of that insurance will be an asset of the estate as well. The estate will also be entitled to the decedent's Social Security death benefits and other death benefits payable through employment programs. If the decedent had investments, then dividends will be payable to the estate and, if the decedent was entitled to receive the proceeds of loans, they too will be payable to the estate. In fact, every financial benefit the decedent was entitled to before death, as well as every death benefit not properly transferred to another, will remain an asset of the estate. A list of those assets should be found in Chapter 22 of this book. The value of all of those assets, plus all of the other assets of the estate, will need to be determined in order to prepare the required documents for both the Internal Revenue Service and the probate court. You will need to work with the estate's attorney and accountant in order to be sure that all of the legal and tax requirements are properly complied with. As a fiduciary, you are obligated to strictly follow the law's requirements.

## OBLIGATIONS OF THE ESTATE

Virtually every individual will die owing some money, even if the debt is for utilities, insurance, and credit card balances that have not yet been paid. As the fiduciary representing the estate, you will need to determine all of the debts the decedent had on the date of death. Since this is ever-changing, it is impossible for the material in this book to identify all of them. You should certainly check the material in Chapter 22 in order to identify some of the debts such as mortgage payments, vehicle loan payments, insurance premiums, personal loans, and other debts that the decedent identified. In addition, you should check regular household expenses such as utilities (gas, electric, water, sewer, garbage, etc.), cell phone and Internet bills, and, if the decedent owned a business, all possible business obligations as well. You should check the decedent's personal and business mail to locate additional bills. The estate's attorney will be able to assist you in identifying a list of expenses that are typical in estates such as the one you are representing. Cancel or forward the mail while you're at it.

Since many individuals use automatic payments, you should audit the decedent's accounts to determine whether there are additional obligations you will need to deal with. Cancel automatic withdrawals. Since the estate will publish a notice requesting that all claims against the decedent be submitted within a prescribed period of time in accordance with state law, additional debts may arise. By diligently examining all of the items described above and by following the publication requirement of the decedent's state, you will have fulfilled your fiduciary duty to the estate, and any creditor that is not located and does not submit a timely claim will not be able to be paid for the debt once the estate closes.

Here too, it is essential for you, as a fiduciary, to collect all assets diligently and pay all estate bills, as well as approved claims. It is very important for you to work closely with the estate's attorney in order to be sure that you are complying with the law.

## MISCELLANEOUS

Since every estate is unique and it is impossible for us to list everything that might be included in an estate, you need to evaluate the particular situation you will be dealing with. Some individuals store items in storage lockers, warehouses, or other off-site storage locations, which might contain very valuable items such as antiques, art, precious metals, and other collectables. Some storage lockers merely contain old clothing and discarded furniture. You should check Chapter 22 to see if the decedent identified any such off-site storage facility and if so, you should inventory the items in that facility. If you believe they have value, then they should be added to the estate and dealt with appropriately. If not, then they should be donated to an appropriate charity and the cost of maintaining the facility should end.

In the event you find that the decedent possessed illegal drugs, unlicensed firearms in states where firearm licenses are required, or other items that you believe might be unlawful, then you must report them to the authorities in order to avoid legal problems. The items themselves should be turned over to the authorities.

As noted above, many individuals have safes, lockboxes, and safety deposit boxes. These should be identified in Chapter 22 of this book and you should access them in order to obtain their contents for the estate. In addition, some people stash valuables in strange places—for example, putting money under a mattress or burying treasure in the backyard. Hopefully these items will be identified and their location pointed out in Chapter 22. If not, then you should try your best to make a thorough search, and question relatives and friends in order to determine whether there are any other assets that should be included in the estate. Do the best you can to find those assets.

If the assets of the estate have been identified for a particular person or group, then the decedent's wishes should be followed. If the assets are valuable, then you should determine the best way to handle those assets—for example, liquidation or transfer to the estate's beneficiaries. If, on the other hand, the assets are not valuable and their maintenance is higher than their value, then you should discuss the problem with the estate's attorney and decide whether it would be best to dispose of those assets as soon as possible in order to reduce the estate's overhead until it is completed.

As pointed out throughout this book, it is important for you to work closely with an experienced lawyer when acting as a fiduciary for an estate, in order to comply with all complex tax and legal requirements.

# CHAPTER 26

# The Decedent's Businesses

In this chapter, we describe what you, as a fiduciary, need to deal with for decedents who are employed by others and for those who have their own businesses. As a fiduciary, you are obligated to obtain everything that the decedent was entitled to in order to provide the maximum benefit to the heirs and beneficiaries of the estate.

## EMPLOYERS

If the decedent was employed by a company, then the company will be responsible for making all final payments and taking care of anything else that the decedent's estate is entitled to receive from the company. You should merely contact the decedent's employer and request that the employer provide you with a list of the items the decedent is entitled to receive now that death has occurred.

## WHAT SHOULD BE DONE WITH THE BUSINESS

If the decedent owned a business, either individually or with others, then you will need to deal with that business interest. If the decedent was a co-owner of the business, then the business will probably have a buy-sell agreement in place so that the decedent's interest will be available for the other owner(s) to acquire. If not acquired by the other owner(s), then the entity may acquire that interest and, if the entity does not acquire it, it may be sold to third persons. It is very common for buy-sell agreements to be funded by insurance. In this event, the insurance proceeds will be used to purchase the decedent's interest and the estate will receive the proceeds. Check Chapter 22 in order to determine whether the decedent acquired a business interest and whether that interest was covered by a buy-sell agreement. You should then contact the other owner(s) to determine whether the agreement was funded by key person life insurance. If so, you will need to provide the necessary documentation to obtain the benefits from that insurance. It is appropriate for you to work with both the estate lawyer and the attorney representing the business so that they can assist you with this process. More on insurance and buy-sell agreements is discussed in Chapter 8.

If the decedent owned the business individually, then there may still have been a buy-sell arrangement between the decedent and the business entity that could also have been funded by insurance. Chapter 22 should describe this situation if it exists. In this arrangement, since the business was owned solely by the decedent, it will be important for you, the estate's attorney, and the business's attorney to determine whether the business may be able to continue under someone else, whether the business must be sold as part of the estate, or whether the business will cease to exist. Hopefully the decedent made appropriate arrangements for this type of business so that it can achieve maximum benefit for the estate. The attorneys should be able to assist you with this type of arrangement.

## CONTROLLING THE ASSETS

Whether the business is owned by the decedent and others or by the decedent alone, it must be valued as of the date of the decedent's death and its assets must be properly preserved. A valuation will be necessary for estate tax purposes since the decedent's interest must be counted as part of the value of the estate on the date of death. The value will also be necessary if the interest will be sold through a buy-sell agreement or to a new owner since the estate would receive fair value for the decedent's interest.

You are also required to keep accurate records of the value of an estate in order to work with the estate's attorney in filing annual estate accountings and the final estate accounting.

## TIME IS OF THE ESSENCE

Since a business, whether owned by the decedent alone or with others, must continue operating if it is to survive, time is an important factor. Any delay in dealing with an operating business can be fatal to its ongoing success. For this reason, it is essential for you to attend to the business immediately and be sure that either the other owners, replacement owner, or person desiring to continue the business, immediately implements whatever succession plan has been prepared. Chapter 22 will contain the succession plan or identify its location of one if it is necessary for a business.

---

Make sure to communicate often with business partners, professionals, employees, and coworkers that were involved in the decedent's business. If you are unfamiliar with the day-to-day operations or the best way to wind up a business, reach out to the estate's attorney for advice on where to look for help.

# CHAPTER 27

# Insolvent Estates

While most individuals hope they will die with enough assets to pay all bills and have assets available for their heirs and beneficiaries, there are some situations in which the decedent's estate will be worthless or insolvent. In this unfortunate situation, the estate will either be totally insolvent, in which nothing more will need to be done by you, and the estate's attorney should be contacted so that the lawyer can deal with unhappy creditors.

Regrettably, this type of situation is occurring more often since individuals are living longer and outliving their resources.

If the estate is not totally insolvent, and it has some resources but they are not sufficient to satisfy all outstanding claims, then the law does establish a list of priorities as to how the estate's assets must be applied.

To begin with, you should work with an estate attorney in opening this type of estate. Either through the probate process described in Chapter 17, if there is an estate plan, or if there is no estate plan, through the intestacy process described in Chapter 18. Once the estate is open, obtain all of the assets of the estate in the same manner as you would if the estate were solvent. This process has been described more fully in Chapter 25 of this book. Once those assets have been acquired, you and the estate lawyer will need to prepare a distribution plan.

There are seven categories of priority payments which must be followed. The estate's assets must be applied to pay creditors in each of the categories until that category is fully satisfied. If additional assets remain, then payment will be applied to the next category. If the assets are not sufficient to fully satisfy a category, then each of the creditors in that category will receive a percentage of their debt or approved claim. The categories identified by the law are as follows:

1. Cost and expenses of administration—this includes attorney's fees and expenses such as hiring a dumpster to clean out mom's house. This is the first category and all of the items in this category must be paid in full. If not, each of the claimants will be entitled to receive a percentage of the debt or approved obligation.

2. Reasonable funeral expenses

3. Debts with preference under federal law (e.g., federal taxes)

4. Reasonable medical/hospital/nursing expenses pertaining to final illness. If another person guaranteed the medical bill, for example, a spouse, then the hospital or physician will likely seek recovery of the guaranteed amount from that person in addition to seeking payment from the estate.

5. Reasonable medical/hospital expenses for the year preceding death. Here too, if another individual guaranteed the bill, that individual will likely be obligated to pay any portion of the bill not covered by the estate.

6. Debts with preference under state law (e.g., state taxes). See Appendix D for a list of the state estate and inheritance tax schedule.

7. Any other claims of unsecured debt (e.g., credit cards). If a credit card has been issued to a business and an individual or if more than one individual was on the credit card, then the party, other than the decedent, will be required to satisfy credit card claims that are not paid for by the estate. It should be noted that many credit card companies are willing to negotiate the debt owed by simply asking.

Most states have a homestead exemption for a specified amount. The amount of the homestead exemption may be transferred to beneficiaries even if the estate is insolvent. This is a very technical and complex area and you should consult with an attorney if you believe a homestead exemption is involved.

There is a potential trap for unwary fiduciaries: Creditors have a full four-month window to submit their claims, and the creditors should be aware of this by virtue of the publication discussed in Chapters 17 and 25. If you start writing checks to persistent creditors such as a pushy credit card company, and three months later you uncover a higher priority item (like federal tax debt), you will be liable to cover the higher priority debt after all the estate's assets have been exhausted. For this reason, you should work with an estate attorney and you should advise all creditors that they will be paid after the time for submitting claims is over. In this way, you will have all valid debts and approved obligations in hand so that you and the estate's attorney can establish a payment program.

As this chapter makes clear, there are a number of potential pitfalls when dealing with insolvent estates, and you may have some risks if the estate is not handled properly. It is therefore important for you to work with the estate's attorney throughout this process.

# CHAPTER 28

# Finding a Lawyer and an Accountant

Most individuals expect to seek the advice of a lawyer only occasionally, for counseling on important matters such as employment contracts or real estate considerations. If this is your concept of the attorney's role, you need to reevaluate it. Most individuals would operate more efficiently and effectively in the long run if they had a relationship with an attorney more like that of a family doctor and patient. An ongoing relationship that allows the attorney to get to know you well enough to engage in preventive legal counseling and to assist in planning makes it possible to solve many problems before they occur.

If you are financially challenged, you are doubtless anxious to keep costs down. You probably do not relish the idea of paying an attorney to get to know you if you are not involved in an immediate crisis. However, it is a good bet that a visit with a competent lawyer right now will raise issues vital to your future. Ready access to legal advice is something you should not deny to yourself at any time, for any reason. As pointed out in numerous places throughout this book, the cost of hiring an estate planning lawyer will be far less than the cost your estate will incur if an appropriate estate plan has not been created. Review the recent problem of the Aretha Franklin estate discussed in Chapters 1 and 3.

An attorney experienced in estate planning can give you important information regarding the risks unique to your estate. Furthermore, a lawyer can advise you about your rights and obligations in your relationships with creditors, partners, and others whom you should consider when creating your estate plan. Since each state has its own laws related to probate, trusts, estate planning formalities, and intestacy, state laws must be consulted on many areas covered in this book. A competent local estate planning attorney is, therefore, your best source of information on many issues that will arise in creating your estate plan or serving as a fiduciary for a decedent's estate. Many law firms have attorneys who are licensed in several jurisdictions, and others have relationships with attorneys in other locales.

---

### IN PLAIN ENGLISH

Most legal problems cost more to solve or defend after they arise than it would have cost to prevent their occurrence in the first place. Litigation is notoriously inefficient and expensive. You do not want to sue or to be sued, if you can help it.

---

## FINDING A LAWYER

If you do not know any attorneys, ask other people if they know any good ones. You want either a lawyer who specializes in estate planning law or a general practitioner who has many satisfied estate planning clients. Finding the lawyer who is right for you may require that you shop around a bit. Most local and state bar associations have referral services. A good tip is to find out who is in the estate planning law section of the state or local bar association or who has served on special bar committees dealing with law reform. It may also be useful to find out if any articles covering the estate planning law have been published in either scholarly journals or continuing-legal-education publications and if the author is available to assist you.

It is a good idea to hire a specialist or law firm with a number of specialists rather than a general practitioner. While it is true that you may pay more per hour for the expert, you will not have to pay for the attorney's learning time. Experience is valuable. In this regard, you may wish to keep in mind that it is uncommon for a lawyer to specialize in estate planning law and also handle criminal matters.

## EVALUATING A LAWYER

One method by which you can attempt to evaluate an attorney in regard to estate planning law is by consulting the *Martindale-Hubbell Law Directory* in your local county law library or online at www.martindale.com. While this may be useful, the mere fact that an attorney's name does not appear in the directory should not be given too much weight, since there is a significant charge for being included and some lawyers may have chosen not to pay for the listing. You can also consult Avvo (www.avvo.com), Google (www.google .com), and Yelp (www.yelp.com). Many law firms have established websites. The larger firms usually include extensive information about the firm, its practice areas, and its attorneys.

After you have obtained several recommendations for attorneys, it is appropriate for you to talk with them for a short period of time to determine whether you would be comfortable working with them. Do not be afraid to ask about their background, experience, and whether they feel they can help you.

## USING A LAWYER

Once you have completed the interview process, select the person who appears to best satisfy your needs. One of the first items you should discuss with your lawyer is the fee structure. You are entitled to an estimate. However, unless you enter into an agreement to the contrary with the attorney, the estimate is just that. Lawyers generally charge by the hour, though you may be quoted a flat rate for a simple estate or drafting a specific document such as a simple will or advance directive.

Once you have selected an estate planning lawyer, you should begin filling out the information in this book and provide it to that lawyer so that the attorney can begin planning your estate. In addition, contact your lawyer whenever you believe a legal question has arisen. The attorney should aid you in identifying which questions require legal action or advice and which require personal decisions. Generally, lawyers will deal only with legal issues, though they may help you to evaluate other related issues.

Some attorneys encourage clients to feel comfortable calling at the office during the day or at home in the evening. Other lawyers, however, may resent having their personal time invaded. Many, in fact, do not list their home telephone numbers. You should learn the attorney's preference early on.

The attorney-client relationship is such that you should feel comfortable when confiding in your attorney. You lawyer will not disclose any confidential communications; in fact, a violation of this rule, depending on the circumstances, can be considered an ethical breach that could subject the attorney to professional sanctions.

If you take the time to develop a good working relationship with your attorney, it may well prove to be one of your more valuable assets.

## FINDING AN ACCOUNTANT

In addition to an attorney, most fiduciaries will need the services of a competent accountant to aid with the estate's accounting, including the necessary filings with the IRS and the probate court. Finding an accountant with whom you are compatible is similar to finding an attorney. You should ask around and learn which accountants are servicing other estates similar to the one you are involved with. State professional accounting associations may also provide a referral service or point you to a directory of accountants in your area. You should interview prospective accountants to determine whether you feel that you can work with them and whether you feel their skills will be compatible with your needs.

Like your attorney, your accountant can provide valuable assistance in planning for the future of your estate or the estate of the decedent. It is important to work with professionals you trust and with whom you are able to relate on a professional level.

For an online newsletter that covers many of the issues discussed in this book and updates that information on a regular basis, go to www.dubofflaw .com and join the mailing list.

# Common Estate Acronyms

## BASIC ACRONYMS

| | |
|---|---|
| AHCD | Advance Health Care Directive |
| CP | Community Property |
| DPA/DPOA | Durable Power of Attorney |
| EP/ESP | Estate Planning |
| GPOA | General Power of Appointment |
| I&A | Inventory and Appraisal |
| JTWROS | Joint Tenancy with Right of Survivorship |
| LPOA | Limited Power of Appointment |
| POA | Power of Attorney |
| PR | Personal Representative |
| PRO | Public Records Office |
| SPOA | Springing Power of Attorney |
| TA | Taxing Authority |
| TBE | Tenancy by the Entirety |
| TIC | Tenancy in Common |
| TPP | Tangible Personal Property |

## TRUST RELATED

| | |
|---|---|
| CLAT | Charitable Lead Annuity Trust |
| CLT | Charitable Lead Trust |
| CLUT | Charitable Lead Unitrust |

| | |
|---|---|
| CRAT | Charitable Remainder Annuity Trust |
| CRT | Charitable Remainder Trust |
| CRUT | Charitable Remainder Unitrust |
| ESBT | Electing Small Business Trust |
| GRAT | Grantor Retained Annuity Trust |
| GRIT | Grantor Retained Income Trust |
| GRUT | Grantor Retained Unitrust |
| IDGT | Intentionally Defective Grantor Trust |
| ILIT | Irrevocable Life Insurance Trust |
| PRT | Personal Residence Trust |
| QDOT | Qualified Domestic Trust |
| QPRT | Qualified Personal Residence Trust |
| QSST | Qualified Subchapter S Trust |
| QTIP | Qualified Terminable Interest Property |
| RLT | Revocable Living Trust |
| SAT | Spousal Access Trust |
| SLAT | Spousal Lifetime Access Trust |
| SNT | Special Needs Trust |
| UDT | Under Declaration of Trust (U/D/T) |
| UTA | Under Trust Agreement |

## STATUTES

| | |
|---|---|
| CUTMA | California Uniform Transfers to Minors Act |
| DOMA | Defense of Marriage Act |
| ERISA | Employee Retirement Income Security Act |
| HIPAA | Health Insurance Portability and Accountability Act |
| IAEA | Independent Administration of Estate Act |
| TRA | Tax Relief Act |
| TRUIRJCA | Tax Relief Unemployment Insurance Reauthorization, and Job Creation Act |
| UGMA | Uniform Gift to Minors Act |
| UTMA | Uniform Transfer to Minors Act |

## FINANCE RELATED

| | |
|---|---|
| ESA | Education Savings Account |
| IRA | Individual Retirement Account |
| ITF | In Trust For |
| POD | Pay on Death |
| RBD | Required Beginning Date |
| RMD | Required Minimum Distribution |
| SCIN | Self-Canceling Installment Note |
| TOD | Transfer on Death |
| TSA | Tax-Sheltered Annuity |

## TAX RELATED

| | |
|---|---|
| DSUEA | Deceased Spousal Unused Exclusion Amount |
| EIN | Employer Identification Number |
| ETIP | Estate Tax Inclusion Period |
| PTIN | Preparer Tax Identification Number |
| TIN | Taxpayer Identification Number |

## BUSINESS RELATED

| | |
|---|---|
| FLP | Family Limited Partnership |
| GP | General Partnership |
| LLC | Limited Liability Company |
| LLP | Limited Liability Partnership |
| LP | Limited Partnership |

## OTHER

| | |
|---|---|
| IP | Intellectual Property |
| SSDI | Social Security Disability Insurance |
| SSN | Social Security Number |
| VA | US Department of Veterans Affairs |

# Information Sources

## SENIOR ASSOCIATIONS

60 Plus Association: 60plus.org

American Association of Retired Persons (AARP): https://www.aarp.org/

American Seniors Association (ASA): https://www.americanseniors.org/

Association of Mature American Citizens (AMAC): https://amac.us/

Christian Seniors Association (CSA): https://csabenefits.site-ym.com/

National Association of Conservative Seniors (NAOCS): http://naocs.us/

The Seniors Coalition (TSC): http://www.senior.org/

## GOVERNMENT RESOURCES

Medicaid: www.medicaid.gov

Social Security Administration: www.ssa.gov

## ADVANCE DIRECTIVES

Link to state forms can be found at the National Hospice and Palliative Care Organization: http://www.caringinfo.org/i4a/pages/index.cfm?pageid=3289

## TAX INFORMATION

Internal Revenue Service:
  www.irs.gov

## ATTORNEY REFERRALS

Martindale: www.martindale.com

Avvo: www.avvo.com

State Bar Associations

# State Estate and Inheritance Tax Schedules

Alabama: No estate tax or inheritance tax

Alaska: No estate tax or inheritance tax

Arizona: No estate tax or inheritance tax

Arkansas: No estate tax or inheritance tax

California: No estate tax or inheritance tax

Colorado: No estate tax or inheritance tax

Connecticut: The top estate tax rate is 12 percent and is capped at $15 million (exemption threshold: $3.6 million; the exemption amount will rise to $5.1 million in 2020, $7.1 million in 2021, $9.1 million in 2022, and is scheduled to match the federal amount in 2023)

Delaware: No estate tax or inheritance tax

Florida: No estate tax or inheritance tax

Georgia: No estate tax or inheritance tax

Hawaii: The top estate tax rate is 16 percent (exemption threshold: $5.49 million)

Idaho: No estate tax or inheritance tax

Illinois: The top estate tax rate is 16 percent (exemption threshold: $4 million)

Indiana: No estate tax or inheritance tax

Iowa: The top inheritance tax rate is 15 percent (no exemption threshold)

Kansas: No estate tax or inheritance tax

Kentucky: The top inheritance tax rate is 16 percent (exemption threshold for Class C beneficiaries: $500; exemption threshold for Class B beneficiaries: $1,000; Class A beneficiaries, which is the majority, pay no inheritance tax)

Louisiana: No estate tax or inheritance tax

Maine: The top estate tax rate is 12 percent (exemption threshold: $5.6 million)

Maryland: The top estate tax rate is 16 percent (exemption threshold: $5 million); the top inheritance tax rate is 10 percent (no exemption threshold)

Massachusetts: The top estate tax rate is 16 percent (exemption threshold: $1 million)

Michigan: No estate tax or inheritance tax

Minnesota: The top estate tax rate is 16 percent (exemption threshold: $2.7 million; this increases to $3 million in 2020)

Mississippi: No estate tax or inheritance tax

Missouri: No estate tax or inheritance tax

Montana: No estate tax or inheritance tax

Nebraska: The top inheritance tax rate is 18 percent (exemption threshold: $10,000)

Nevada: No estate tax or inheritance tax

New Hampshire: No estate tax or inheritance tax

New Jersey: The top inheritance tax rate is 16 percent (no exemption threshold)

New Mexico: No estate tax or inheritance tax

New York: The top estate tax rate is 16 percent (exemption threshold: $5.749 million)

North Carolina: No estate tax or inheritance tax

North Dakota: No estate tax or inheritance tax

Ohio: No estate tax or inheritance tax

Oklahoma: No estate tax or inheritance tax

Oregon: The top estate tax rate is 16 percent (exemption threshold: $1 million)

Pennsylvania: The top inheritance tax rate is 15 percent (no exemption threshold)

Rhode Island: The top estate tax rate is 16 percent (exemption threshold: $1,561,719)

South Carolina: No estate tax or inheritance tax

South Dakota: No estate tax or inheritance tax

Tennessee: No estate tax or inheritance tax

Texas: No estate tax or inheritance tax

Utah: No estate tax or inheritance tax

Vermont: The top estate tax rate is 16 percent (exemption threshold: $2.75 million)

Virginia: No estate tax or inheritance tax

Washington: The top estate tax rate is 20 percent (exemption threshold: $2.193 million)

Washington, DC (District of Columbia): The top estate tax rate is 16 percent (exemption threshold: $5.6 million)

West Virginia: No estate tax or inheritance tax

Wisconsin: No estate tax or inheritance tax

Wyoming: No estate tax or inheritance tax

# State Probate and Intestate Laws

**Alabama**

Title 43, Chapter 2: Administration of Estates—http://www.legislature.state
.al.us/CodeofAlabama/1975/128505.htm

Title 43, Chapter 8: Probate Code—http://www.legislature.state.al.us/
CodeofAlabama/1975/130738.htm

**Alaska**

Title 13: Decedents' Estates, Guardianships, Transfers, and Trusts—http://
www.legis.state.ak.us/basis/folioproxy.asp?url=http://wwwjnu01.legis
.state.ak.us/cgi-bin/folioisa.dll/stattx09/query=*/doc/{t5180}?

Title 13, Chapter 16: Probate of Wills and Administration—http://www
.legis.state.ak.us/basis/folioproxy.asp?url=http://wwwjnu01.legis.state
.ak.us/cgi-bin/folioisa.dll/stattx09/query=*/doc/{t5309}?

**Arizona**

Title 14: Trusts, Estates and Protective Proceedings—http://www.azleg.gov/
ArizonaRevisedStatutes.asp?Title=14

Title 14, Chapter 3: Probate of Wills and Administration—http://www.azleg
.gov/ArizonaRevisedStatutes.asp?Title=14

**Arkansas**

Title 28: Wills, Estates, and Fiduciary Relationships—http://www.lexisnexis
.com/hottopics/arcode/Default.asp

### California

California Probate Code—http://www.leginfo.ca.gov/cgi-bin/
calawquery?codesection=prob&amp;amp;codebody=&amp;
amp;hits=20

### Colorado

Title 15: Probate, Trusts, and Fiduciaries—https://leg.colorado.gov/sites/
default/files/images/olls/crs2016-title-15.pdf

### Connecticut

Title 45a: Probate Courts and Procedure—https://www.cga.ct.gov/current/
pub/title_45a.htm

### Delaware

Title 12: Decedents' Estates and Fiduciary Relations—https://delcode
.delaware.gov/title12/

### Florida

Title XLII: Estates and Trusts—http://www.flsenate.gov/Laws/Statutes/2011/
Title42/#Title42

### Georgia

Title 53: Wills, Trusts, and Administration of Estates—http://ga.elaws.us/
law/53

### Hawaii

Title 30A: Uniform Probate Code—http://www.capitol.hawaii.gov/
hrscurrent/vol12_ch0501-0588/hrs0560/hrs_0560-.htm

### Idaho

Title 15: Uniform Probate Code—https://legislature.idaho.gov/statutesrules/
idstat/title15/t15ch1pt1/

### Illinois

Chapter 755: Estates—http://www.ilga.gov/legislation/ilcs/ilcs3
.asp?ActID=2104&ChapterID=60
Chapter 760: Trusts and Fiduciaries—http://www.ilga.gov/legislation/ilcs/
ilcs2.asp?ChapterID=61

### Indiana

Title 29: Probate—http://iga.in.gov/legislative/laws/2019/ic/titles/029
Title 30: Trusts and Fiduciaries—http://iga.in.gov/legislative/laws/2019/ic/
titles/030

## Iowa

Title XV, Chapter 633: Probate Code—https://law.justia.com/codes/
iowa/2015/title-xv/subtitle-4/chapter-633/

## Kansas

Chapter 59: Probate Code—http://www.kslegislature.org/li/b2011_12/
statute/059_000_0000_chapter/

## Kentucky

Title XXIV, Chapter 394: Wills—https://apps.legislature.ky.gov/law/statutes/
chapter.aspx?id=39195

Title XXIV, Chapter 395: Personal Representatives—https://apps.legislature
.ky.gov/law/statutes/chapter.aspx?id=39197

## Louisiana

Civil Code 1570 et seq.—http://legis.la.gov/Legis/Laws_Toc.aspx?folder
=67&level=Parent

## Maine

Title 18: Decedents' Estates and Fiduciary Relations—http://www
.mainelegislature.org/legis/statutes/18/title18ch0sec0.html

Title 18-A: Probate Code—http://www.mainelegislature.org/legis/
statutes/18-A/title18-Ach0sec0.html

## Maryland

The Office of the Register of Wills (Estates and Trusts, Titles 1–16)—http://
registers.maryland.gov/main/

## Massachusetts

MGL, Part II, Title II: Descent and Distribution, Wills, Estates of Deceased
Persons and Absentees, Guardianship, Conservatorship and Trusts—
http://www.malegislature.gov/Laws/GeneralLaws/PartII/TitleII

## Michigan

Chapters 701-713: Probate Code—http://www.legislature.mi.gov/
(S(aqwkluqyogktck55nmgw2paw))/mileg.aspx?page=getObject&objectN
ame=mcl-Act-288-of-1939

## Minnesota

Chapter 524: Uniform Probate Code—https://www.revisor.leg.state.mn.us/
statutes/?id=524

**Mississippi**

Title 91: Trusts and Estates—http://www.lexisnexis.com/hottopics/mscode/

**Missouri**

Title XXXI, Chapters 456–475: Trusts and Estates of Decedents and Persons Under Disability—http://www.moga.mo.gov/STATUTES/STATUTES.HTM#T31

**Montana**

Title 72: Estates, Trusts, and Fiduciary Relationships—http://leg.mt.gov/bills/mca_toc/72.htm

**Nebraska**

Chapter 30: Decedents' Estates; Protection of Persons and Property—https://nebraskalegislature.gov/laws/browse-chapters.php?chapter=30

**Nevada**

Title 12: Wills and Estates of Deceased Persons—http://www.leg.state.nv.us/NRS/Index.cfm

**New Hampshire**

Title LVI: Probate Courts and Decedents' Estates—http://www.gencourt.state.nh.us/rsa/html/NHTOC/NHTOC-LVI.htm

**New Jersey**

Title 3A: Administration of Estates—Decedents and Others—https://law.justia.com/codes/new-jersey/2013/title-3a/

Title 3B: Administration of Estates—Decedents and Others—https://law.justia.com/codes/new-jersey/2013/title-3b/

**New Mexico**

Chapter 45: Uniform Probate Code—http://law.justia.com/codes/new-mexico/2011/chapter45/

**New York**

New York Court Probate Forms—https://www.nycourts.gov/forms/surrogates/probate.shtml

General overview of NY Probate—https://www.nycourts.gov/courthelp/WhenSomeoneDies/probate.shtml

**North Carolina**

Chapter 47: Probate and Registration—http://www.ncga.state.nc.us/gascripts/Statutes/StatutesTOC.pl?Chapter=0047

**North Dakota**

Title 30.1: Uniform Probate Code—http://www.legis.nd.gov/cencode/t30-1
  .html

**Ohio**

Title 21: Courts—Probate—Juvenile—http://codes.ohio.gov/orc/21

**Oklahoma**

Title 58: Probate Procedure—http://www.oscn.net/applications/oscn/index
  .asp?ftdb=STOKST58&amp;amp;level=1

Title 60: Property—http://www.oscn.net/applications/oscn/Index
  .asp?ftdb=STOKST60&level=1

Title 84: Wills and Succession—http://www.oscn.net/applications/oscn/
  index.asp?ftdb=STOKST84&amp;amp;level=1

**Oregon**

Title 12, Chapters 111–118—https://www.oregonlaws.org/ors/volume/3

**Pennsylvania**

Title 20: Decedents, Estates and Fiduciaries—http://www.legis.state.pa.us/
  cfdocs/legis/LI/consCheck.cfm?txtType=PDF&ttl=20

**Rhode Island**

Title 33: Probate Practice and Procedure—http://webserver.rilin.state.ri.us/
  Statutes/TITLE33/INDEX.HTM

**South Carolina**

Title 62: Probate Code—http://www.scstatehouse.gov/code/title62.php

**South Dakota**

Title 29A: Uniform Probate Code—http://legis.state.sd.us/statutes/
  DisplayStatute.aspx?Type=Statute&Statute=29A

**Tennessee**

Title 32, Chapter 2—http://www.lexisnexis.com/hottopics/tncode/

**Texas**

Texas Probate Estates Code—http://www.statutes.legis.state.tx.us/Docs/ES/
  htm/ES.102.htm#00

**Utah**

Title 75: Uniform Probate Code—https://le.utah.gov/xcode/Title75/75.html

**Vermont**

Title 14, Chapter 3: Probate and Procedure for Construction of Wills—
https://legislature.vermont.gov/statutes/chapter/14/003

**Virginia**

Title 64.2: Wills, Trusts, and Fiduciaries—https://vacode.org/2016/64.2/

**Washington**

Title 11: Probate and Trust Law—http://leg.wa.gov/CodeReviser/
RCWArchive/Documents/2016/Title%2011%20RCW.pdf

**Washington, DC**

Filing a Will in the District of Columbia (pdf)—https://www.dccourts.gov/
sites/default/files/matters-docs/DecedentsWils-Brochure.pdf
Large Decedents' Estates (ADM)—https://www.dccourts.gov/services/
probate-matters/large-decedents-estates-adm
Small Decedents' Estates (SEB)—https://www.dccourts.gov/services/probate
-matters/small-estates-seb

**West Virginia**

Chapter 44: Administration of Estates and Trusts—http://www
.wvlegislature.gov/WVCODE/Code.cfm?chap=44&art=1

**Wisconsin**

Chapters 851–882—http://docs.legis.wisconsin.gov/statutes/prefaces/toc

**Wyoming**

Title 2: Wills, Decedents' Estates and Probate Code—https://wyoleg.gov/
statutes/compress/title02.pdf

# State Digital Estate Planning Laws

Almost all fifty states have passed a law to give an estate's digital agent the right to access and manage digital assets of the decedent. If your state is not listed below, that means your state had not yet passed laws to address these issues when this book was published. At the time of publication, Kentucky, Louisiana, and Washington, DC, have yet to enact any digital estate planning laws. The laws are constantly changing, so we recommend that you consult your estate planning attorney to create a digital estate plan specific to the laws of your state.

### Alabama
Law: HB 138 Revised Uniform Fiduciary Access to Digital Assets Act
Full Bill: https://legiscan.com/AL/text/HB138/id/1501753

### Alaska
Law: HB 108 Revised Uniform Fiduciary Access to Digital Assets Act
Full Bill: http://www.legis.state.ak.us/PDF/30/Bills/HB0108A.PDF

### Arizona
Law: SB 1413 Revised Uniform Fiduciary Access to Digital Assets Act
Full Bill: https://www.azleg.gov/legtext/52leg/2r/bills/sb1413p.htm

### Arkansas
Law: HB2253 Revised Uniform Fiduciary Access to Digital Assets Act
Full Bill: https://law.justia.com/codes/arkansas/2017/title-28/subtitle-5/
  chapter-75/

## California
Law: AB-691 Revised Uniform Fiduciary Access to Digital Assets Act
Full Bill: https://leginfo.legislature.ca.gov/faces/billTextClient.xhtml?
  bill_id=201520160AB691

## Colorado
Law: SB 88 Revised Uniform Fiduciary Access to Digital Assets Act
Full Bill: http://leg.colorado.gov/sites/default/files/2016a_088_signed.pdf

## Connecticut
Law: SB 262 Public Act No. 05-136
Full Bill: https://www.cga.ct.gov/2005/act/Pa/2005PA-00136-R00SB
  -00262-PA.htm

## Delaware
Law: Title 12 Fiduciary Access to Digital Assets and Digital Accounts
https://delcode.delaware.gov/title12/c050/index.shtml

## Florida
Law: SB 494, Chapter 740 Florida Fiduciary Access to Digital Assets Act
Full Bill: https://www.flsenate.gov/Laws/Statutes/2016/Chapter740

## Georgia
Law: SB 301 Revised Uniform Fiduciary Access to Digital Assets Act
Full Bill: https://casetext.com/statute/code-of-georgia/title-53-wills-trusts
  -and-administration-of-estates/chapter-13-revised-uniform-fiduciary
  -access-to-digital-assets-act/article-2-disclosure-of-digital-assets

## Hawaii
Law: SB2298 Revised Uniform Fiduciary Access to Digital Assets Act
Full Bill: https://www.capitol.hawaii.gov/session2016/bills/SB2298_CD1
  _.htm

## Idaho
Law: SB 1303 Revised Uniform Fiduciary Access to Digital Assets Act
Full Bill: https://legislature.idaho.gov/wp-content/uploads/statutesrules/
   idstat/Title15/T15CH14.pdf

## Illinois
Law: HB 4648 Revised Uniform Fiduciary Access to Digital Assets Act
Full Bill: http://www.ilga.gov/legislation/publicacts/fulltext.asp?
   Name=099-0775

## Indiana
Law: SB 253 Revised Uniform Fiduciary Access to Digital Assets Act
Full Bill: https://law.justia.com/codes/indiana/2016/title-32/article-39/

## Iowa
Law: SF 333 Revised Uniform Fiduciary Access to Digital Assets Act
Full Bill: https://www.legis.iowa.gov/docs/publications/iactc/87.1/CH0079
   .pdf

## Kansas
Law: SB 63 Revised Uniform Fiduciary Access to Digital Assets Act
Full Bill: http://kslegislature.org/li_2018/b2017_18/measures/documents/
   sb63_enrolled.pdf

## Maine
Law: LD 846 Revised Uniform Fiduciary Access to Digital Assets Act
Full Bill: https://legislature.maine.gov/legis/bills/getPDF
   .asp?paper=HP0595&item=1&snum=128

## Maryland
Law: SB239/HB507 Maryland Fiduciary Access to Digital Assets Act
Full Bill: https://law.justia.com/codes/maryland/2016/estates-and-trusts/
   title-15/subtitle-6

## Massachusetts
Law: HD 3489 Revised Uniform Fiduciary Access to Digital Assets Act
Full Bill: https://malegislature.gov/Bills/190/H3083/House/Bill/Text

## Michigan
Law: HB 5034 The Fiduciary Access to Digital Assets Act
Full Bill: http://www.legislature.mi.gov/documents/2015-2016/publicact/
pdf/2016-PA-0059.pdf

## Minnesota
Law: HF 200 Minnesota Statutes Chapter 521A Revised Uniform Fiduciary
Access to Digital Assets Act
Full Bill: https://www.revisor.mn.gov/bills/text.php?number=SF0476&
session=ls89&version=latest&session_number=0&session_year=2015&
format=pdf

## Mississippi
Law: HB 489 Revised Uniform Fiduciary Access to Digital Assets Act
Full Bill: http://billstatus.ls.state.ms.us/documents/2017/pdf/HB/0800-0899/
HB0849SG.pdf

## Missouri
Law: HB 1250 Revised Uniform Fiduciary Access to Digital Assets Act
Full Bill: https://legiscan.com/MO/text/HB1250/2018

## Montana
Law: SB 118 Revised Uniform Fiduciary Access to Digital Assets Act
Full Bill: https://legiscan.com/MT/text/SB118/2017

## Nebraska
Law: LB 829 Revised Uniform Fiduciary Access to Digital Assets Act
Full Bill: https://nebraskalegislature.gov/laws/statutes.php?statute=30-502

## Nevada
Law: SB 131
Full Bill: https://www.leg.state.nv.us/Session/77th2013/Bills/SB/
SB131_EN.pdf

## New Hampshire
Law: SB 147 Revised Uniform Fiduciary Access to Digital Assets Act
Full Bill: https://legiscan.com/NH/text/SB147/id/1863599

**New Jersey**
Proposed Law: SB 2527 Uniform Fiduciary Access to Digital Assets Act
Full Bill: https://www.njleg.state.nj.us/2016/Bills/S3000/2527_I1.PDF

**New Mexico**
Law: SB 60 Revised Uniform Fiduciary Access to Digital Assets Act
Full Bill: https://www.nmlegis.gov/Sessions/17%20Regular/final/SB0060
.PDF

**New York**
Law: AB A9910A Revised Uniform Fiduciary Access to Digital Assets Act
Full Bill: https://www.nysenate.gov/legislation/bills/2015/A9910

**North Carolina**
Law: SB 805 Fiduciary Access to Digital Assets
Full Bill: https://www.ncleg.net/Sessions/2015/Bills/Senate/PDF/S805v3.pdf

**North Dakota**
Proposed Law: HB 1455
Full Bill: https://www.legis.nd.gov/assembly/63-2013/bill-actions/ba1455
.html

**Ohio**
Law: HB 432 Revised Uniform Fiduciary Access to Digital Assets Act
Full Bill: http://codes.ohio.gov/orc/2137

**Oklahoma**
Law: HB 2800
Full Bill: http://webserver1.lsb.state.ok.us/cf_pdf/2009-10%20ENR/hB/
HB2800%20ENR.PDF

**Oregon**
Proposed Law: SB 1554 Revised Uniform Fiduciary Access to Digital Assets
Act
Full Bill: https://www.oregonlegislature.gov/bills_laws/lawsstatutes/2016
orLaw0019.pdf

**Pennsylvania**
Proposed Law: SB 518 Revised Uniform Fiduciary Access to Digital Assets
Act, Amending Title 20 (Decedents, Estates and Fiduciaries)
Full Bill: https://www.legis.state.pa.us/cfdocs/legis/PN/Public/btCheck
.cfm?txtType=PDF&sessYr=2015&sessInd=0&billBody=S&billTyp
=B&billNbr=0518&pn=0483

**Rhode Island**
Law: Title 33: Probate practice and procedure, Chapter 33-27: Access to
Decedents' Electronic Mail Accounts Act, Section 33-27-3
Full Bill: http://webserver.rilin.state.ri.us/Statutes/TITLE33/33-27/33-27-3
.HTM

**South Carolina**
Law: SB 908 South Carolina Uniform Fiduciary Access to Digital Assets Act
Full Bill: https://www.scstatehouse.gov/sess121_2015-2016/bills/908.htm

**South Dakota**
Law: HB1080 Uniform Fiduciary Access to Digital Assets Act
Full Bill: http://sdlegislature.gov/Legislative_Session/Bills/Bill.aspx?File
=HB1080ENR.htm&Session=2017&Bill=1080

**Tennessee**
Law: SB 326 Uniform Fiduciary Access to Digital Assets Act
Full Bill: http://www.epcchattanooga.org/assets/Councils/Chattanooga-TN/
library/Farinato-SB0326-Tennessee-02.10.15.pdf

**Texas**
Law: SB 1193 Revised Uniform Fiduciary Access to Digital Assets Act
Full Bill: https://capitol.texas.gov/tlodocs/85R/billtext/pdf/SB01193F
.pdf#navpanes=0

**Utah**
Law: HB 13 Uniform Fiduciary Access to Digital Assets Act
Full Bill: https://le.utah.gov/~2017/bills/static/hb0013.html

**Vermont**

Law: HB 152 (Act 13) Uniform Fiduciary Access to Digital Assets Act

Full Bill: https://legislature.vermont.gov/bill/status/2018/H.152

**Virginia**

Proposed Law: SB 914

Full Bill: http://leg1.state.va.us/cgi-bin/legp504.exe?131+ful+SB914+pdf

**Washington**

Law: SB 5029 Revised Uniform Fiduciary Access to Digital Assets Act

Full Bill: http://lawfilesext.leg.wa.gov/biennium/2015-16/Pdf/Bill%20
Reports/Senate/5029-S.E%20SBR%20FBR%2016.pdf

**West Virginia**

Law: SB 102 Uniform Fiduciary Access to Digital Assets Act

Full Bill: http://www.wvlegislature.gov/Bill_Status/bills_text.cfm?billdoc
=SB102%20SUB1%20ENR.htm&yr=2018&sesstype=RS&i=102

**Wisconsin**

Law: AB 695 Revised Uniform Fiduciary Access to Digital Assets Act

Full Bill: http://docs.legis.wisconsin.gov/2015/related/proposals/ab695

**Wyoming**

Law: SF0034 Uniform Fiduciary Access to Digital Assets Act

Full Bill: https://www.wyoleg.gov/2016/Enroll/SF0034.pdf

# Glossary

## 123

**401(k)** is a type of plan provided by an employer for its employees that requires periodic payments during employment so that the employee can obtain post-retirement income benefits. Its name is derived from the initial section of the Internal Revenue Code that created it.

## A

**A trust** is the surviving spouse's portion of an A-B trust. Also called *marital trust* or *survivor's trust.*

**A-B trust** is a trust that includes a tax-planning provision that lets you provide for your surviving spouse and keep control over who will receive your assets after your spouse dies.

**Ab initio** is a Latin phrase that literally means "from the beginning." When a will is void ab initio, it is completely invalid and the court will disregard it as though it had never been written.

**Acceptance** is a term used in contract law to describe an element of a contract, which occurs after an offer has been made. See *contract, offer.*

**Accountant** is a trained profession who provides accounting services such as setting up and maintaining a company's books and tax preparation. See *certified public accountant.*

**Accounts payable** is an accounting term used to define monetary obligations owed by one to another. See also *accounts receivable.*

**Accounts receivable** is an accounting term used to define monetary obligations that one is entitled to from another. See also *accounts payable.*

**Action**, sometimes referred to as "cause of action," is the legal claim or right that one has against another. It is frequently written in the form of a legal document known as a *complaint*, which is filed in court and used to begin a lawsuit.

**Addendum** is a document attached at the end of another document and is customarily intended to supplement the terms of the document to which it is attached. See *contract*.

**Adjusted basis** is a term used to describe a tax concept. The "basis" of an item is its cost or fair market value that is "adjusted" for tax purposes by deducting depreciation and other offsets allowable under the Internal Revenue Code. This concept is frequently used when valuing property for tax or related purposes. See also *tax*.

**Administration** is the court-supervised distribution of an estate during probate. Also used to describe the same process for a trust after the grantor dies.

**Administrator** is the person or organization named by the court to represent a probated estate when there is no will or the will did not name an executor. A female administrator may be called an administratrix. Also called a *personal representative*.

**Affidavit** is a statement sworn to or affirmed by the party making the statement, who is known as an "affiant." Affidavits are written and the signature is notarized. Because of this, affidavits carry a great deal of weight and may be used in legal proceedings or other official purposes, such as in real estate transactions or in legal proceedings when a sworn oath is required.

**Agency** is the relationship between one person, known as the *principal*, and another, known as the *agent*. Customarily, the agent works for or on behalf of the principal and is subject to the principal's control or right of control. Typically, the agent owes a duty to the principal. See also *principal*.

**Agent**. See *agency, principal*.

**Agreement** is an arrangement, written or oral, whereby two or more parties reach an understanding. When conforming to the requirements of contract law, it is known as a *contract*. If one or more of the requirements for a legal contract are missing, the agreement may be subject to certain legal defenses and, thus, not enforceable. See also *contract*.

**Aleatory** is an adjective that describes any contract that is contingent on a certain event happening before the provisions are triggered. In the case of a will, it is said to be aleatory because it is contingent upon the death of the person who made the will. In other words, the assets cannot be distributed under the will unless and until the testator has died.

**Alternate beneficiary** is a person or organization named to receive your assets through a will or trust if the primary beneficiaries die before you do.

**Amendment** is the term used when an agreement is modified, as when a contract is changed. See also *contract*.

**Americans with Disabilities Act of 1990 (ADA)** is a federal statute enacted by Congress for the purpose of providing individuals with defined disabilities the opportunity to obtain fair treatment in employment, housing, transportation, and the like. The courts have been wrestling with the definition of "disability" for purposes of interpreting the statute and with the amount of "reasonable accommodation" required to be provided under the act.

**Ancillary administration** is an additional probate in another state. This is typically required if you own real estate in another state that is not titled in the name of your will or trust.

**Annual exclusion** is the amount you can give away each year without having to file a gift tax return or pay gift tax.

**Antidilution** is a term used in trademark law to describe one of the forms of protection available to trademark owners under the law. It prohibits another from weakening, tarnishing, disparaging, or otherwise undermining the strength and credibility of the protected trademark. See also *trademark*.

**Antitrust laws** are the laws used to prevent monopolies and unlawful arrangements that are intended to manipulate or control a particular market and unlawfully affect pricing, as well as other key market factors. The antitrust laws are enforced by both government regulation (federal and state) and by litigation.

**Apparent authority** is a legal term used to define the authority an agent appears to have when dealing with third persons. This is intended to protect the third person's reasonable expectations when dealing with the agent and is available for third-person protection even when contrary to the express instructions of the principal. See also *agency, principal*.

**Appreciate** and **appreciation** are financial and accounting terms used to define the increase in value of property, whether tangible or intangible, that occurs over time. Thus, a house frequently appreciates in value as real estate prices increase. Similarly, a copyright, which is intangible, may increase in value when the protected work has received positive critical acclaim or popularity. See also *depreciate, depreciation.*

**"Articles of incorporation"** is a legal document filed with the state in which a company desires to do business as a corporation and is the "charter" or creating instrument for the corporation. It defines the authority granted by the state for the company to be conducted in the corporate form and is analogous to a constitution. All business corporations are created under the law of the state in which they are incorporated and may do business in other states by filing the appropriate document(s) in those states as a "foreign" (corporation chartered in another state) corporation doing business in that state. The only entities incorporated under federal law are federally charted banks and certain federally mandated organizations, such as the Smithsonian Institution and the US Postal Service. See also *articles of organization, bylaws, corporation, partnership.*

**"Articles of organization"** is a legal document filed with the state in which a business desires to do business as a limited liability company (LLC), and is the "charter" or creating instrument for the LLC. It defines the authority granted by the state for the company to be conducted as an LLC and is analogous to a constitution. All LLCs are created under the law of the state in which they are created and may do business in other states by filing the appropriate document(s) in those states as a "foreign" (LLC chartered in another state) LLC doing business in that state. See also *articles of incorporation, bylaws, limited liability company, partnership.*

**Assets** are anything that you own, including your home and other land and buildings, bank accounts, insurance policies, investments, furniture, art, collectibles, jewelry, clothing, automobiles, and digital files.

**Assignment** is a document that transfers your interest in an asset from you to another person. It is often used when transferring assets to a trust.

**Assignment for the benefit of creditors** is a legal term used in bankruptcy and collections law to define an arrangement whereby assets of a debtor are assigned to another, either the creditor, trustee, or receiver, for the benefit of one or more creditors. This can take the form of a formal court-administered plan or an informal arrangement worked out between the parties. See also *bankruptcy, debt, receiver, trustee.*

**Attorney,** also known as a lawyer, is a professional who has been licensed to practice law in the state or other jurisdiction by which the license has been issued and whose conduct is regulated by state bar associations and the highest court of the state or jurisdiction. Attorneys must be licensed to practice in every court in which they appear. Customarily, attorneys are graduates of postgraduate law schools and have passed one or more bar examinations.

**Attorney-client privilege** is a legal doctrine established for the purpose of enabling a client to communicate freely with his or her attorney. All communications between the client and attorney (or attorney's staff) that are not in the presence of any other person are privileged and may not be disclosed by the attorney without the client's permission.

**Attorney-in-fact** is a person who is not actually a lawyer but, rather, is a person authorized to perform a specific act or combination of acts described in a document known as a "power of attorney" on behalf of the person granting the power. The person granting the power must sign this document and that person's signature must be notarized. The power may be general or specific, as defined in the document. In some jurisdictions and for some purposes, a power of attorney may be "recorded"—that is, filed with the appropriate governmental agency.

**Audit** is an accounting term used to describe a review, typically of financial statements or tax returns. The audit is intended to verify the accuracy of the document and is conducted by an *auditor*, who is typically a skilled professional.

**Authority** is the power granted by law or by a principal to a person to perform a prescribed act or combination of acts. The act or combination of acts, when performed, will be legally binding. See also *agency, attorney-in-fact, principal.*

# B

**B trust** The deceased spouse's portion of an A-B trust. Also called *credit shelter* or *bypass trust.*

**Bankruptcy** is the legal term defining the consequences of insolvency. In other words, when liabilities are greater than assets or when bills cannot be paid in the ordinary course of one's business, one is technically insolvent or bankrupt. Laws have been enacted that provide relief for those who are insolvent, as well as for their creditors. See also *receiver, trustee.*

**Basis** is what you paid for an asset. This value is used to determine your gain or loss when you sell, gift, or otherwise dispose of the asset.

**Beneficiaries** are the persons or organizations who receive the benefits of a trust or will after death.

**"Blue sky" law** is a common term used to define state securities laws enacted for protection of those who invest in businesses. The term comes from a statement in Congress during the aftermath of the 1929 depression which referred to the victims of the depression who bought securities whose values were artificially inflated as people who obtained nothing more than chunks of "blue sky."

**Board of directors** is the governing board of a business entity charged by statute with responsibility for administering the business and affairs of that entity. It is frequently used in the context of corporate boards of directors, though it can refer to the administrative board of other types of entities, such as nonprofit corporations, limited liability companies, or the like. See also *corporation, limited liability company, partnership*.

**"Branding"** is the term used to describe the identification and reputation of a product or service. This modern concept has been used by businesses to describe the process of identifying the qualities, unique characteristics, reputation, market awareness, and the like of specific products or services. One of the most famous "brands" in the world today is Coca-Cola.

**Buy-sell agreement** is a document customarily used by business organizations for the purpose of establishing a formal arrangement whereby the ownership interest in the business may be sold or transferred only in accordance with the terms of the agreement. These agreements typically impose restrictions on sale or transfer to "outsiders" and establish methods for valuing the interest when the owner desires to transfer the interest, dies, or becomes incapacitated. These agreements are frequently used in closely held businesses, as distinguished from those that are publicly traded.

**Bylaws** are formal documents adopted by corporations for administering the internal affairs of the company. They typically cover the rules and regulations for calling meetings, defining key positions, and the like. Bylaws may not be broader in scope than the company's articles of incorporation. Articles of incorporation are analogous to a constitution and define the boundaries of a company's power and authority. The bylaws are analogous to laws and statutes and are the rules and regulations for implementing the powers and authority. Bylaws are not filed with any governmental agency but are kept in the corporation's minute book. See *articles of incorporation, corporation.*

**Bypass trust** is another name for the deceased portion of an A-B trust. Also called a *B trust* or *credit shelter.*

# C

**C trust** is another name for a QTIP.

**Cash discount** is a reduction granted a customer for paying cash on delivery, rather than obtaining credit and delaying payment.

**Cashier's check** is purchased from a bank and is issued by the bank. See also *certified check, money order.*

**Certificate of incorporation** is the document issued by many states evidencing the formation of a corporation in that state. It is used to establish that a corporation is "in good standing" in that state. It may be required when a corporation desires to do business in another state.

**Certificate of trust** is a shortened version of a trust that verifies that the trust exists, identifies the trustee(s) and successor trustees (if any), and the powers given to the trustee. The certificate of trust does not contain any information about the trust assets or beneficiaries.

**Certified check** is a check that has been "certified" by the issuing bank, which means that the bank segregates adequate funds from the depositor's account to pay the check, and the certification means that the bank is guaranteeing payment of the check. See also *cashier's check, money order.*

**Certified public accountant (CPA)** is a professional who has passed the examinations required by the appropriate state agency to provide kinds of accounting services. These services include, for example, setting up and maintaining a company's books and tax preparation. One of the services unique to CPAs is providing audited financial statements. See *accountant, audit.*

**Chapter 7** is a type of federal bankruptcy for individuals and businesses whereby all "non-exempt" assets are made available to creditors, who are paid in a prescribed order according to an approved schedule, and the debtor is "discharged" from all further outstanding obligations to the listed creditors. See also *Chapter 11, Chapter 13.*

**Chapter 11** is a type of federal bankruptcy for businesses, which permits the debtor to propose a plan to pay creditors according to a specific schedule and "discharge" all outstanding debts. See also *Chapter 7, Chapter 13*.

**Chapter 13** is a type of federal bankruptcy for individuals, which permits the debtor to propose a plan to pay creditors according to a specific schedule and "discharge" all outstanding debts. See also *Chapter 7, Chapter 11*.

**Check** is a financial instrument whereby the payor (person writing the check) instructs the bank to pay the defined amount to the order of the designated payee (person or entity to whom the check is written).

**Children's trust** is a trust established for a beneficiary who is not of legal age. The trust will be managed by a trustee until the child reaches the age of majority or some other age identified in the document that establishes the trust.

**Civil law** is the body of law adopted in some jurisdictions, including Louisiana and California, based on the Napoleonic Code and following prescribed rules or statutes, rather than adhering to past practices or precedent, as in the "common law." See also *common law*.

**Civil liability** is the legal process for recovery of money or property or compelling the doing of things for the benefit of individuals and businesses, rather than imposing penalties or extracting obligations to the governmental jurisdiction. It is administered by private attorneys and individuals, rather than through a district or prosecuting attorney on behalf of the government.

**Closely held business** is a business owned by a small number of people or other business, rather than one that is publicly held or traded on the stock markets. It is frequently a business arrangement between one or more family groups or groups of friends, though the term could describe a larger group of owners, so long as the group is small enough to avoid the necessity of complying with the technical requirements set forth in the state and federal securities laws for publicly held businesses. See also *corporation, limited liability company, partnership*.

**Codicil** is a written amendment to a will.

**Co-grantors** are two or more people who establish a single joint trust together.

**Collective works** are works defined by the federal copyright statute as including periodicals, anthologies, or encyclopedia in which contributions consisting of separate and independent works themselves are assembled into a collective whole. See also Section 101 of the Copyright Revision Act of 1976, as amended.

**Collusion** is a legal term defining an unsavory arrangement between two or more entities for an improper purpose.

**Commingling** means combining assets from two or more sources. The commingling could be legitimate where, for example, a husband and wife have a joint checking account. It could also be improper, as in situations where a "mom and pop" corporation pays the personal obligations of the owners from corporate funds and/or corporate obligations from the owners' individual funds.

**Common law** is the legal system based on "English Common Law" and follows past practice or legal precedent, known as stare decisis. In this process, rules established in court cases become binding and are followed until modified, extended, or reversed. This should be distinguished from "civil law," which is based upon the Napoleonic Code and is limited to statutory pronouncements. See *civil law*.

**Common stock** is the form of stock issued by a corporation that has unrestricted voting rights, dividend rights, and ownership in the corporation. It is the kind of stock every corporation must have, and is distinguished from "preferred stock," which must, by definition, must have some form of "preference" in either dividends or distribution on dissolution, or both. See also *preferred stock*.

**Common trust** is one trust established by two or more people (commonly a married couple).

**Community property** includes all of the assets a married couple acquires by joint effort during the marriage if they live in a community property state. Each spouse owns half of the assets in the event of death or divorce.

**Complaint** is the legal document filed in a court that begins a lawsuit. This document, along with the summons, must be properly served on behalf of the complainant (plaintiff) on the other party (defendant) in order to continue the lawsuit.

**Confirming memorandum** is a written document sent by one party to another for the purpose of confirming the terms of an oral arrangement.

**Conflict of interest** is an ethical concept whereby a party has divided loyalties. For example, when a partner in a partnership is given a cash payment of $10 for a service rendered and belatedly realizes that, instead of one crisp $10 bill, there were two stuck together, the partner is forced to decide whether he should disclose to his partner the fact that the client overpaid. A lawyer who represents two parties who have opposing interests is in a conflict of interest and may, under the rules of many bar associations, be required to suspend representation of both parties. Alternatively, if the conflict is merely theoretical, then most bar associations permit the lawyer to continue representing both parties, provided the facts are disclosed to both parties in writing and there is an appropriate written waiver of the theoretical conflict by all.

**Conservator** is a person who is legally responsible for the care and well-being of another person. If a court appoints the conservator, the court will supervise the conservatorship. Also called a *guardian*.

**Conservatorship** occurs when a conservator is appointed to be responsible for the care of another individual. Also called a *guardianship*.

**Consideration** is a contract element that requires the giving or receiving of something of value by one party in exchange for something of comparable value from the other party. Consideration can be in the form of money, property, services, or an agreement to refrain from some action. Historically, consideration did not have to be comparable, as when "token" consideration was used for transactions, such as the classic use of "a single peppercorn." Today, the law tends to require the parties to give or receive things of comparable potential value in order for the "consideration" to be deemed valid.

**Consignment** is a legal arrangement whereby the property of one party is entrusted to another for purposes of sale. The person who entrusts the property, who must be the owner or lawful possessor, is known as the "consignor" and the person receiving the property is known as the "consignee." The consignment agreement may be oral or written and, if in writing, it may be recorded with the appropriate government office. Many states have enacted special legislation dealing with unique forms of consignment, such as fine art, crafts, and collectibles.

**Consumer Price Index (CPI)** is a financial tool used to define the increase or decrease in a defined list of consumer products and services in a particular geographic area during a specified period of time.

**Contest** is to dispute or challenge the terms of a will or trust.

**Contract** is a legal concept whereby one offers consideration to another in exchange for the other's providing comparable consideration. To be legally valid, all contracts require an offer, acceptance, and consideration. They may oral or written. There are other legal requirements for certain types of contracts; for example, contracts for the sale of real property (land) and contracts for personal property worth $500 or more must be in writing. See *acceptance, consideration, offer.*

**Cooling-off period** is a concept whereby a consumer is given a specified period of time to reflect on an otherwise valid contract and, if desired, rescind it before it is performed by either party. For example, many states permit a three-day period within which a consumer may cancel contracts obtained by door-to-door salespeople.

**Copyright** is the right whereby any original work of "authorship" which is put in a tangible form is protected by law. In the United States, the copyright laws have been enacted pursuant to the enabling provision set forth in Article I of the United States Constitution. The most recent copyright statute was enacted in 1976 and became effective January 1, 1978. This law continues to evolve and has been amended a number of times. It is known as "the Copyright Revision Act of 1976, as amended." There are numerous treaties throughout the world dealing with copyright on a multinational level.

**Corporate shield** and **corporate veil** are the terms used to define the limited liability available for those who conduct business through corporate or other business entities. It is said that shareholders in corporations and owners of limited liability companies are "shielded" by the limitation of liability available to them when they properly conduct business through these entitles. Creditors cannot "pierce the corporate veil" or "penetrate the corporate shield" without establishing a valid legal reason to do so, and the reasons available are very limited.

**Corporate trustee** is an institution, generally a bank or trust company, that specializes in managing trusts.

**Corporation** is a business entity created by one or more persons pursuant to the corporate code of the state in which the business is to be formed. See *common stock, preferred stock, articles of incorporation, certificate of incorporation.*

**Cotrustees** are two or more individuals or organizations who are named to act together to manage a trust's assets.

**Counteroffer** is an offer presented by an "offeree," or recipient of an offer, from another, which rejects the original offer and provides a new offer. It converts the original "offeror" into an "offeree." Once the "give and take" is completed and an agreement is reached, there is a contract. See *contract, offer.*

**Credit shelter trust** is the deceased spouse's portion of an A-B trust. Also called *B trust* or *bypass trust.*

**Creditor** is one who is owed an obligation, usually money, by another, known as a "debtor."

**Custodian** is the person named to manage assets left to a minor. In most states, the minor will receive the assets when the child reaches the legal age or majority.

# D

**Damages** is the compensation sought or awarded for legal injury sustained.

**Debentures** and **bonds** are legal debt instruments frequently used by corporations to evidence debt. When the debt is secured by one or more identified assets, such as a mile of railroad track, the instruments are "bonds." When the debt is secured by all of the debtor's assets, the instruments are known as "debentures." Bonds are also issued by governmental entities for specific designated purposes, such as building libraries, schools, and the like, or funding a particular project. See also *debt.*

**Debt** is an obligation owed by one ("debtor") to another ("creditor"). See also *creditor, debtor.*

**Debtor** is one who is owes an obligation to another, known as a "creditor." In business, the term is more commonly used to define one who owes money.

**Deceased** is the person who has died.

**Deed** is a document that transfers the title of real estate to another person.

**Defined benefit plan** is a retirement plan that pays a specific amount after the employee retires. This payment stream is used to determine the method and amount necessary to fund the plan. See also *defined contribution plan.*

**Defined contribution plan** is a retirement plan that establishes the amount to be paid into the plan, and the benefits then flow from the preretirement contribution. See also *defined benefit plan*.

**Depreciate** and **depreciation** are financial and accounting terms whereby the useful life of an item is "guesstimated" and the value of the item is reduced on a yearly basis according to a prescribed schedule. For tax purposes, the Internal Revenue Service has established prescribed periods of depreciation for various items. See also *appreciate, appreciation*.

**Derivative work** is a copyright concept whereby a work is taken from, or based on, a prior work. See Section 101 of the Copyright Revision Act of 1976, as amended.

**Design defect** is a defect in the design of a product that results in the product being defective and may result in liability for the designer of the product. This should be distinguished from a manufacturing defect, where liability would fall to the manufacturer of the product.

**Discharge** is the legal concept whereby a debtor in bankruptcy is permitted to extinguish all pre-bankruptcy debts when the legal requirements of the bankruptcy law are followed. See *bankruptcy, creditor, debtor*.

**Disclaim** is to refuse to accept a gift or inheritance so the gift goes to the next recipient in line.

**Disclaimer** is a legal device whereby a party may avoid responsibility for warranties that have either been expressly given or are implied by law. In order for a disclaimer to be valid, it must comply with the legal requirements set forth in the statute governing warranties and disclaimers. See Article 2 of the Uniform Commercial Code.

**Discretion** is the full or partial power to make a decision or judgment.

**Disinherit** is to prevent someone from inheriting from you.

**Dissolution.** An entity, such as a corporation, limited liability company, limited partnership, or the like, may end its existence by a formal process known as "dissolution." This can either be mandatory, by court order, or voluntary. It can also be involuntary, as when the annual report is required by state law and the accompanying annual fees are not tendered.

**Distribution** is payment in cash or asset(s) to the one who is entitled to receive it.

**Dividend preference** is a payment defined by a preferred stock instrument setting forth the amount (in either dollars or percentage) that must be paid to the holders of the preferred stock before any dividends are paid to the holders of common stock. See *common stock, preferred stock.*

**Durable Power of Attorney for Asset Management** is a legal document giving another person full or limited legal authority to sign your name on your behalf. It is valid during incapacity but ends at death.

**Durable Power of Attorney for Health Care** is a legal document giving another person the authority to make health-care decisions for you if you are unable to make them for yourself. It is valid during incapacity but ends at death. Also called *health-care proxy* or *medical power of attorney.*

# E

**e-commerce** is shorthand for "electronic commerce," which is the practice of engaging in commercial activities using the computer network known as the Internet and/or World Wide Web.

**Electronic signature** is the electronic communication adopted by a party for purposes of taking advantage of the E-Sign statute and consummating contracts through "e-commerce." See *e-commerce, Electronic Signature in Global and National Commerce Act (E-Sign)*

**Electronic Signature in Global and National Commerce Act (E-Sign)** is a federal statute that prescribes a method whereby an "electronic signature" may be used for purposes of validating contracts in cyberspace, which contracts are binding in the same manner as they would be if entered into through traditional means.

**Employee stock option plan (ESOP)** is a plan established by a business entity using the company's stock for purposes of funding an employee retirement plan.

**Equity** is the current market value of an asset minus any loan or liability.

**Estate** is all of the assets and debts left behind by an individual when that person dies.

**Estate taxes** are all federal or state taxes on the value of the assets left at death. Also called *inheritance taxes* or *death taxes.*

**Executor** is the person or institution named in a will to carry out its instructions. A female executor can be called an executrix. Also called a *personal representative*.

**Exordium clause** is the first clause in a will that usually declares that this is the "Last Will and Testament" of the testator and often states where the person lived when the will was made

**Express warranty** is a statement of fact or representation by a seller with the respect to quality or other attributes of particular goods to be sold. See also *implied warranty*.

# F

**Fair use** is a copyright concept developed by case law and codified in the Copyright Revision Act of 1976, as amended, to provide a defense for one who copies the protected work of another when the copying satisfies the guidelines set forth in the statute. See the Copyright Revision Act of 1976, as amended.

**Federal estate tax exemption** is the amount of an individual's estate that is exempt from federal estate taxes.

**Federal Trade Commission (FTC)** is the federal agency charged by Congress with responsibility for policing interstate commerce and trade within the United States and at its borders. It has also assumed responsibility for policing activities on the World Wide Web when those activities affect commerce in the United States.

**Fiduciary** is a person that has a legal duty to act primarily for another's benefit. The scope of that duty varies from relationship to relationship, and has been more carefully defined in the myriad of cases dealing with individuals who owe or are owed the duty. Classic examples of fiduciary relationships are the agency relationship (where both parties owe a fiduciary duty to each other) and the trust relationship (where the trustee is held to owe a fiduciary duty to beneficiaries). Administrators, executors, personal representatives, guardians, and conservators are all fiduciaries.

**First sale doctrine** is a copyright concept whereby the copyright owner may control the first sale of a copyrighted work. Resales of that work, absent an agreement to the contrary, may be made without involving the copyright owner. For example, a book publisher may, by virtue of the copyright in the book, control the first sale of that book but, absent some agreement to the contrary, a purchaser may resell the book without involving the publisher in the resale.

**Foreign corporation**. See *corporation*.

**Franchising** is a process whereby a successful business pattern is licensed by the originator (franchisor) so that a licensee (franchisee) can create comparable businesses. In order for a franchising arrangement to be legal, the franchisor must comply with federal and state requirements and provide potential franchisees with the disclosures, known as a franchising disclosure document, required by those laws. Classic examples of successful franchises include McDonald's, Burger King, KFC, and other purveyors of fine foods.

**Full disclosure** is the concept of providing all relevant and pertinent information when securities are offered for sale or sold. It was first discussed by the US Congress, later by state legislatures, and the securities laws require "full and fair disclosure of all material facts" relevant to the transactions involved.

**Funding** is the process of transferring assets into a trust.

# G

**Gain** is the positive difference between what you receive for an asset when it is sold and what you paid for it. This amount is used to determine the amount of capital gains taxes are due. When the amount is negative, it is called a *loss*.

**General partner** is the person or entity who has full personal liability in a partnership. A general partner can be one of the parties involved in a general partnership, which is defined as two or more persons who are co-owners engaged in a business for profit, or the person or entity who runs a limited partnership and has full personal liability for the acts, contracts, or omissions of that business entity. See also *limited partner*.

**Gift** is a transfer of something valuable from one person to another without any compensation.

**Gift tax** is a federal or state tax on gifts made while you are alive. The person giving the gift pays the gift tax, not the recipient.

**Goodwill** is an intangible, which has been defined in cases as the propensity of customers to return to a business. It has also been defined as including the business' reputation, marketability, and success.

**Grantor** is the person who sets up or creates a trust. Also called *creator, settlor, trustor, donor,* or *trustmaker.*

**Gray market** is the market that develops when a legally licensed product is introduced into a market other than the one in which it is licensed. For example, a trademark owner in the United States may license the use of its mark in Canada, since the owner has captured the US market. If the Canadian licensee begins selling the Canadian-licensed products in the United States, those sales of otherwise legally licensed merchandise in the restricted market of the United States would be gray market sales.

**Gross estate** is the value of an estate before the debts are paid.

**Guardianship** occurs when a guardian is appointed to be responsible for the care of another individual. Also called a *conservatorship.*

# H

**Health-care proxy** is a legal document giving another person the authority to make health-care decisions for you if you are unable to make them for yourself. Also called *durable power of attorney for health care* or *medical power of attorney.*

**Heir** is a person who is entitled by law to receive part of the estate.

**Holographic will** is a will that does not comply with the laws for a classic will. Typically, it is handwritten, signed by the person writing it, and not properly witnessed.

**Homestead exemption** is the portion of your residence (your home and surrounding land) that cannot be sold to satisfy a creditor's claim.

# I

**Implied contract** is a contract created by the law for the purpose of preventing injustice. It is a contract that the parties may or may not have expressly agreed to. For example, when a merchant sells a product without an appropriate disclaimer, the law implies a contract whereby the purchaser may expect the product to be "merchantable," even though merchantability was never specifically bargained for. See also *contract.*

**Implied warranty** is a warranty implied by law and exists whether or not the parties have negotiated for it. Classic implied warranties are the implied warranty of merchantability, the implied warranty of fitness for a particular purpose, the implied warranty of title, and the implied warranty that the item is not infringing the intellectual property rights of another. Implied warranties may, if the party against whom it is enforceable complies with the statute, be disclaimed. See also *express warranty.*

**Incapacitated** or **incompetent** is being unable to manage one's own affairs— permanently or temporarily. An *incapacitated* or *incompetent* person has no legal power.

**Independent administration** is a form of probate available in many states that simplifies the probate process by requiring fewer court appearances and less court supervision.

**Independent contractor** is a person who engages in his or her own independent business and provides goods or services to another. An independent contractor must be distinguished from an employee, who is employed by another for purpose of providing goods or services. The legal distinction between these two categories is that an employer has the right of control over the conduct of an employee's activities, whereas the employer does not have a right of control over the conduct of an independent contractor's activities; rather, the employer contracts for the results. For example, an in-house bookkeeper who provides bookkeeping services for only the employer and is subject to the employer's direction and control is an employee, whereas a bookkeeper who provides similar services for several businesses and is not subject to the employer's control is likely an independent contractor.

**Individual Retirement Account (IRA)** is a form of pension account created by Congress by individuals.

**Inheritance** is the assets received from someone who has died.

**Intellectual property** is the body of law that deals with "products of the mind." It includes patent law, copyright law, trademark law, trade secret law, and other forms of protection for creative works. See *copyright, patent, trade dress, trademark.*

**Internet Service Provider (ISP)** is a business that provides access to the Internet/World Wide Web, usually for a fee. Examples of ISPs include Xfinity and Spectrum (formerly known as Time Warner Cable).

**Inter vivos trust** is a trust created by one during his or her lifetime.

**Intestate** is the legal term defining a person who dies without a will.

**Irrevocable Trust** is a trust that cannot be changed, revoked, or canceled once it is set up. The opposite of a revocable trust.

# J

**Joint and several** is the term used to define the liability of two or more individuals who are each liable for the entire amount of any damages awarded, or a pro rata share of those damages, depending on the wishes of the person in whose favor the damages are awarded.

**Joint ownership** is a form of ownership in which two or more people own the same asset together. Types of joint ownership include *joint tenants with the right of survivorship, tenants in common,* and *tenants by the entirety.*

**Joint tenants with the right of survivorship** is a form of joint ownership in which when one of the joint tenants dies, that person's share automatically and immediately transfers to the surviving joint tenant(s).

**Joint venture** is an arrangement between two or more persons to accomplish a specific task. It is distinguishable from a partnership, in that a partnership is established for the purpose of conducting an ongoing business, whereas a joint venture is created for the purpose of achieving a specific goal. Thus, if two or more persons get together for the purpose of building an apartment complex, it would be a joint venture; if the agreement goes on to say that they will continue to manage it on an ongoing basis, it would be a partnership. A joint venture can be expressed, when the parties work out their terms, or implied, when the parties merely perform the identified task.

**Joint work** is the term defined by Section 101 of the Copyright Revision Act of 1976, as amended, as a work created by two or more persons contributing their creative elements and intending that those elements be combined into a unitary whole. Cases have established that the contributions of each must be independently copyrightable. A classic example of a joint work is an illustrated text, where one creates the illustrations and the other prepares the text.

**Judgment creditor** is a person or entity in whose favor a court has rendered a money judgment.

**Judgment debtor** is a person or entity against whom a court has awarded a money judgment.

**Jurisdiction** is the word used to define a place where a lawsuit may be properly filed, a corporation may be created, a building may be erected, or the like. It is a geographic area that has been defined by statute or case law for specific purposes. In the context of litigation, "jurisdiction" refers to the court system within which a case may be filed; for example, the US District Court will accept jurisdiction of only those cases that deal with federal questions or involve citizens of different states or foreign countries, and amounts in excess of $75,000; state and local courts, on the other hand, have different jurisdictional requirements. See also *venue*.

# K

**Key-person insurance** is a type of insurance procured on the life of a person key to a business. It is typically obtained by the business entity to compensate it for the loss it will sustain when the key person dies.

# L

**Land trust** is often used for privacy because the title to the land is transferred to a corporate trustee or corporation but the owner retains control over how the property is managed. Also called a *title holding trust*.

**Lawyer**. See *attorney, attorney-in-fact*.

**License** is a permitted use. In business, licensing is typically used to permit one to use the intellectual property of another. For example, a copyright owner may license the use of a copyrighted work. Licensing may also refer to other permitted uses; for example, states issue driver's licenses and municipalities issue business licenses.

**Life insurance trust** is a form of trust created for the purpose of owning a life insurance policy and distributing the proceeds of that policy when the insured party dies.

**Limited liability company (LLC)** is a business form that allows those who conduct business through it to enjoy the benefits of limited personal liability while electing the method by which the entity is to be treated for tax purposes. It was created to overcome the restrictions imposed on small business that could qualify for so-called "S-corporation" status.

**Limited liability partnership (LLP)** is similar to a limited liability company except that it was created for the purpose of allowing partners in partnerships to have a personal liability shield similar to those who conduct business through corporations.

**Limited partner** is a person or entity who owns an interest in a limited partnership but who is a passive investor and who enjoys limited liability.

**Limited partnership** is a partnership having one or more general partners with full personal liability and one or more limited partners who may enjoy limited liability but may not play an active role in conducting the business of the limited partnership. It is created by statute and the partnership must comply with the limited partnership statute of the jurisdiction in which it is created.

**Liquid assets** are cash and other assets like stocks that can be easily converted into cash.

**Liquidation** is the process of converting assets to cash and distributing the cash. It should be distinguished from "dissolution," which refers merely to the legal relationship between those who are conducting the business. For example, when a general partner in a general partnership dies, there is a dissolution by virtue of the death of a partner. The remaining partners may, if their agreement permits, continue the partnership or, if the agreement does not or they do not wish to, they may then liquidate the partnership by converting its assets to cash and properly distributing the cash.

**Litigation** is the term used to describe filing and prosecuting a lawsuit.

**Living probate** is a court-supervised process of managing the assets of someone who is incapacitated.

**Living trust** is a written document that creates a trust to which you can transfer ownership of your assets. The trust document will contain instructions for managing the transferred assets during your lifetime and their distribution upon your incapacity or death. A living trust can avoid probate at death and court control of your assets upon incapacity. Also called a *revocable inter vivos trust.*

**Living will** is a written document that states your wishes about medical care when you are terminally ill or injured.

# M

**Marital deduction** is a deduction on the federal estate tax return that lets the first spouse to die leave an unlimited amount of assets to the surviving spouse free of estate taxes.

**Marital trust** is a trust set up for the benefit of a surviving spouse and the married couple's heirs.

**Medicaid** is a federally funded health-care program for low-income families and individuals.

**Medicare** is a federally funded health-care program primarily for individuals who are sixty-five years of age and older.

**Merger and acquisition** are the terms used to define corporate and other business entity arrangements whereby two or more entities are formally combined, or one entity is acquired by another. A merger is a situation where two or more business entities are combined together and the combined entity emerges as a single entity. Acquisitions are when one business entity acquires another business entity or only the assets of another entity. Both mergers and acquisitions are regulated by statute. That is, the business organization statutes regulate the process and the federal, as well as state, securities laws also impose requirements on entities covered by them.

**Minor** is a person who is under the legal age for an adult, which varies by state but is usually age eighteen or twenty-one.

**Minutes.** State statutes governing corporations, LLCs, and other business entities typically require those entities to have annual meetings and permit those entities to have periodic meetings. Written records of these meetings are known as "minutes" and are customarily kept in the organization's "minute book."

**Money order** is a financial instrument purchased from an authorized seller, which includes banks, post offices, and many retailers. See also *cashier's check, certified check.*

**Multilevel marketing (MLM)** is a form of doing business whereby a product or service is distributed through a multi-tiered structure. The structure is referred to as a "down line" and, customarily, each person in the line receives some compensation for "down line" sales. It is referred to "multilevelmarketing," since each person is able to both sell product or service and enlist "down line" distributors, who can establish their own sales and distribution networks as well. The consumer who pays for the product or service is actually providing a revenue stream that flows up through all distribution levels. Classic examples of successful multilevel marketing are Amway and Mary Kay Cosmetics.

# N

**Net estate** is the value of an estate after all the debts have been paid. Federal estate taxes are based on the net value of an estate.

**Net value** is the current market value of an asset minus any loan or debt.

**Nuncupative will** is an oral will—a will not written down but just told to another witness.

# O

**Offer** is an element of contract whereby one party, known as the "offeror," presents an opportunity, known as the "offer," to another party, known as the "offeree." If the offer is accepted, a contract is made. See *contract, counteroffer.*

**Operating agreement** is the document that defines the internal workings of a limited liability company. By statute, the agreement can be extremely flexible, and the law provides the parties creating the agreement the ability to determine whether the organization will be run by its owners, a panel of owners, or a single manager; whether the organization will be taxed as an "entity" or not. In fact, the law makes it clear that the drafters have extraordinary flexibility in creating the organizational arrangement they desire, so long as the limited legal requirements of the law are adhered to. This document is not filed with any governmental agency, but is kept in the organization's minute book.

# P

**Partner.** See *general partner, limited partnership, limited liability partnership.*

**Partnership.** See *general partner, limited partnership, limited liability partnership, partnership.*

**Partnership agreement** is the agreement between two or more persons who desire to conduct business in a partnership form. A partnership agreement can be expressed, when the parties work out the arrangements between themselves; implied, when they merely conduct their business as a partnership; oral or written. When the parties do not work out the details of a formal partnership agreement, the law imposes certain terms on the relationship.

**Patent** or **letters patent** is legal document issued by the government to those who comply with the strict and technical requirements of the patent law. It is a form of intellectual property.

**Payable-on-death account (POD)** is a bank account that transfers to the person who was named when the account was established when the account holder dies. Also called a *transfer on death* ("TOD"), *in trust for* ("ITF"), *as trustee for* ("ATF"), or *Totten trust* account.

**Pension plan** is a plan adopted for the purpose of providing a pension for individuals who retire so they can augment the Social Security payments obtained from the government.

**Per capita** is a way of distributing an estate so that all the surviving descendants share equally, regardless of their generation.

**Per stirpes** is a way of distributing an estate so that all of the surviving descendants will receive only what their immediate ancestor would have received if that person had been living at the time of death.

**Personal property** is movable property. It is the opposite of real property, which is non-movable (like land and buildings). It includes cash, stocks, furniture, jewelry, automobiles, and equipment.

**Personal property designation** or **personal property memorandum** is a list of items that you want people to inherit. To make the designation legally binding, you must sign it and refer to it in your will. Not all states recognize a personal property designation.

**Personal representative** is another name for an executor or administrator.

**Pour-over will** is a short will often used with a living trust. It states that any assets left out of your living trust will become part of (pour over into) your living trust upon your death.

**Power of attorney** is a legal document giving someone legal authority to sign your name on your behalf. It is valid during incapacity but ends at death.

**Preferred stock** is a form of stock that contains some form of preference. The preference can be in the payment of a dividend; that is, the holders of this type of stock must receive a dividend payment before any dividends may be paid to holders of common stock. The preference may also be in the form of a liquidation payment; that is, when the entity is dissolved and liquidated, holders of preferred stock with liquidation preferences must be paid the preference before holders of common stock will receive any payment on account of their interest in the liquidated company. Preferred stock can have either or both of these forms of preference.

**Principal** is the term used to define the person on whose behalf an agent acts and who controls or has the right to control the conduct of the agent. This term also refers, in a financial context, to the amount upon which interest is calculated.

**Probate** is the legal process of validating a will, paying debts, and distributing assets after death.

**Probate estate** are the assets that go through probate after a person dies. The probate estate usually does not include jointly owned assets, payable-on-death accounts, insurance, and other assets with beneficiary designations and assets in trust.

**Probate fees** are the legal, executor, and appraisal fees and court costs when an estate goes through probate. Probate fees are paid from assets in the estate before the assets are fully distributed to the heirs.

**Product liability** is the legal doctrine that applies to situations where a defective product results in injury to person or property. The defect can be a design defect or a manufacturing defect.

**Profit-sharing plans** are plans whereby business owners agree to share business profits with participants in the plan. These plans are very technical and require specialists to assist in their formation and administration.

# Q

**Qualified domestic trust (QDOT)** is a trust that allows a noncitizen spouse to qualify for the marital deduction.

**Qualified plan** refers to a pension or other plan that qualifies for special tax treatment under the Internal Revenue Code and state taxing statutes.

**Qualified terminable interest property (QTIP)** is a trust that delays estate taxes until your surviving spouse dies so more income will be available to provide for your spouse during his or her lifetime. You can also keep control over who will receive these assets after your spouse dies.

**Qualifying Subchapter S trust (QSST)** is a trust that meets certain IRS qualifications and is allowed to own Subchapter S stock.

**Quitclaim deed** is a document that allows you to transfer title to real estate. With a quitclaim deed, the person transferring the title makes no guarantees but transfers all of the interest that person owns in the property.

# R

**Real property** is land and other property that is permanently attached to the land (like a building or a house).

**Receiver** is a person who is appointed on an interim basis to administer a business for the benefit of creditors or others. A receiver is typically appointed by court order and reports to the court.

**Recorded deed** is a deed that has been filed with the county land records. This creates a public record of all changes in ownership of property in the state.

**Reorganization** is the process whereby a business may be restructured for the purpose of satisfying its creditors when it is unable to pay them in the regular course of business. Reorganizations can involve use of the business entity's stock or ownership interest as vehicles for payment. Non-insolvency reorganizations can occur when businesses are restructured for the purpose of accomplishing other goals; for example, a business may reorganize in order to change its business form, add or delete new product lines, or the like.

**Required Beginning Date (RBD)** is the date you must begin taking required minimum distributions from your tax-deferred plans. Usually, it is April 1 of the calendar year following the calendar year in which you turn age 70½. If your money is in a company-sponsored plan, you may be able to delay your RBD beyond this date if you continue working (providing you are not a 5 percent or greater owner of the company).

**Required Minimum Distribution (RMD)** is the amount you are required to withdraw each year from your tax-deferred plan after you reach your Required Beginning Date (RBD). This amount is determined by dividing the year-end value of your tax-deferred account by a life-expectancy divisor found on a chart provided by the IRS.

**Residuary provision** is the provision of the will that acts as a "catchall" and distributes any property not already distributed by other provisions of the will.

**Revocable trust** is a trust in which the person setting it up retains the power to change (revoke) or cancel the trust during that person's lifetime. It is the opposite of an irrevocable trust.

**Right of survivorship** is a status for real property owners that automatically transfers the deceased owner's shares in the property to the survivor without probate.

**Royalties** are periodic distributions paid pursuant to a licensing agreement.

# S

**S-corporations** are corporations that comply with the requirements set forth in the Internal Revenue Code and elect to be treated, for tax purposes, as if they were still run as sole proprietorships or partnerships.

**Securities and Exchange Commission (SEC)** is a federal agency, charged by Congress with responsibility for policing the securities market.

**Securities exemption** is the term used to define specific and technical requirements necessary to avoid having to register securities with either the federal Securities and Exchange Commission or the state securities agency (in every state in which the security is to be sold). The two most common federal exemptions are the so-called "intrastate offering exception" for securities that are offered for sale and sole only within the boundaries of one state, and the exemption available for those potential purchasers of the security who are deemed "sophisticated" or wealthy enough not to need the protection of the securities laws.

**Security interest** is the interest created by statute in favor of a party, known as the "secured party," in the assets of another for the purpose of protecting an obligation owed the secured party by the other party. A security interest may be "perfected" by having the proper document filed with the appropriate governmental agency.

**Separate property** is, generally, all assets you acquire prior to marriage and assets acquired by gift or inheritance during marriage.

**Separate trust** is a trust established by one person. A married couple has separate trusts if each spouse has his or her own trust with its own assets. In contrast, see *common trust*.

**Service mark** is a trademark used to identify a particular service with its provider. Service marks may be registered with the federal trademark office and appropriate state offices, as well. Classic examples of service marks for airlines providing travel services are Western Airlines' slogan "The only way to fly" and Braniff's "We move our tail for you."

**Settling an estate** is the process of handling the final affairs (valuing the assets, paying all debts and taxes, distributing the assets) after someone dies.

**Settlor**, see *grantor*.

**Shareholder** is the person or entity owning stock in a corporation.

**Shareholder meeting** or **annual meeting** is the meeting required by the state corporation code for every corporation. It must be held at least once a year for the purpose, among other things, of electing the corporation's board of directors.

**Shareholders' agreement** is the agreement between a corporation's shareholders and the corporation governing certain rights and restrictions of the owners with respect to their stock.

**Shareholder's derivative action** is a cause of action provided the owner of stock in a corporation to vindicate a right or redress a wrong to the corporation. A shareholder's derivative action may be brought by the holder of even one share of stock in a corporation, though certain procedural restrictions are imposed when the ownership interest is small.

**Simplified Employee Pension Plan (SEPP)** is a type of pension plan permitted by statute for employees.

**Sole proprietorship** is the term used to define a business owned by a single individual.

**Special gifts** are a separate listing of special assets that will go to specific individuals or organizations after your incapacity or death. Also called *special bequests.*

**Special needs trust** allows you to provide for a disabled loved one without interfering with government benefits.

**Spendthrift clause** is a clause in a trust that protects assets in that trust from the beneficiary's creditors.

**Spouse** is a husband or wife.

**Statute of frauds** is a law that was first enacted in England for the purpose of preventing fraud and perjury. It recognized the fact that certain transactions are so touched with the public interest that they should not be permitted enforcement over the objection of a party unless they were evidenced by a writing signed by that party, though parties could voluntarily perform the transactions if they wished. Since the English feudal system was a governmental process based on land ownership, one of the first transactions covered by the law was real estate transfers. The law was later extended to cover transactions in goods in excess of a certain value. The law also prohibited oral wills, since it would be too easy for unscrupulous individuals to misstate the wishes of a dead person. These laws have been refined and adopted in the United States.

**Stepped-up basis** or **stepped-up value** occurs when assets are given a new basis when transferred by inheritance (through a will or trust) and are revalued as of the date of the owner's death. If an asset has appreciated above its basis (what the owner paid for it), the new basis is called a stepped-up basis. A stepped-up basis can save a considerable amount in capital gains tax when an asset is later sold by the new owner. Also see *basis.*

**Stock** refers to the ownership interest in a corporation and, traditionally, was evidenced by a stock or share certificate. The stock can be common or preferred. In addition, both common and preferred stock may be issued in different "classes," typically identified by alphabetical designations.

**Stock** or **share certificate** is the document used to evidence stock ownership in a corporation. Historically, it was a steel-engraved form, though some companies created unique and distinctive versions of their certificates. For example, Playboy Enterprises used stock certificates with "playmates" depicted on them. Today, many stock transactions are electronic, and no physical certificates are issued.

**Stock option** is a method by which an individual or business may acquire the right to obtain corporate stock at a defined price for a limited period. Options themselves are tradable and, in fact, there is an option exchange. Those who deal in options are said to "trade on equity," since their exchanges are for the appreciation in the value of the underlying stock, rather than trading in the stock itself.

**Stockholder** or **shareholder** is the individual or entity owning stock in a corporation.

**Subchapter S corporation stock** is stock in a corporation that has chosen to be subject to the rules of Subchapter S of the Internal Revenue Code.

**Successor trustee** is the person or institution named in the trust document who will take over should the first trustee die, resign, or otherwise become unable to act.

**Surviving spouse** is the spouse who is still living after one spouse has died.

**Survivor's trust**, see *A trust*.


**T**

**Tax** is the term used to define a government's right to extract payment from its citizens. In the United States, the federal income tax was initially declared unconstitutional, as "confiscatory," and voided. Unfortunately for the taxpayer, the Constitution was amended to permit an income tax.

**Tax-deferred plan** is a retirement savings plan, such as an IRA, 401(k), or a pension, that qualifies for special income tax treatment. The contributions made to the plan and subsequent appreciation of the assets are not taxed until they are withdrawn at a later time—ideally, at retirement, when your income and tax rate are lower.

**Taxable gift** is, generally, a gift to someone other than your spouse that exceeds the federal gift tax exemption. After you have used up your exemption, additional gifts will be taxed, usually at the highest estate tax rate in effect.

**Tenants-by-the-entirety** is a form of joint ownership in some states between husband and wife. When one spouse dies, his/her share of the asset automatically transfers to the surviving spouse.

**Tenants-in-common** or **tenancy in common** is a form of joint ownership in which two or more persons own the same property. At the death of a tenant-in-common, his/her share transfers to his/her heirs.

**Testamentary capacity** is the mental capacity required of the person making a will in order for the will to be valid. In order to have testamentary capacity, the person must know the nature and extent of the property, know who the people are who would inherit the estate if there was no will, and understand the distribution plan created under the will.

**Testamentary trust** is a trust created by a will and can only go into effect at death. A testamentary trust does not avoid probate.

**Testate** is when a person dies with a valid will.

**Testator** is the legal term for the person who made a will.

**Title** is a document proving ownership of an asset.

**Totten trust** is a *pay-on-death* account, a bank account that will transfer to the beneficiary who was named when the account was established.

**Trade dress** is a form of intellectual property law that was initially developed through cases for the purpose of protecting the unique and nonfunctional characteristics of product packaging. It was later extended, by case law, to cover everything from product design to the "look and feel" of businesses. It has even been used to protect the distinctive characteristics or "look and feel" of an artist's distinctive style.

**Trademark** is any words, phrases, name, symbol, logo, or combination of them, when used to identify a product or service. When used in connection with services, they are referred to as "service marks."

**Transfer tax** is the tax on assets when they are transferred to another. The estate tax, gift tax, and generation skipping transfer tax are all transfer taxes.

**Trust** is a legal arrangement whereby a person, referred to as the "settlor," "trustor," or "creator," conveys property to another, referred to as the "trustee," for the benefit of one or more persons or entities, known as "beneficiaries." The trustee is a fiduciary, owing a duty to the beneficiaries.

**Trust company** is an institution that specializes in managing trusts. Also called a corporate trustee.

**Trustee** is the person or institution who manages and distributes another's assets according to the instructions in the trust document. See *trust*.

**Trustor**, see *grantor*.

**Truth-in-Lending Act** is a federal statute requiring certain lenders (usually institutional lenders) to comply with its requirements when loans are made.

# U

**Unfunded** is when a trust does not have assets transferred into it.

**Unified credit** is the amount each person is allowed to deduct from federal estate taxes owed after death.

**Uniform Commercial Code (UCC)** is a body of commercial law, adopted in every state of the United States, though its periodic modifications may not have been universally accepted.

**Uniform Offering Circular** is the document required by statute to be used when franchises are offered for sale.

**Uniform Transfer to Minors Act (UTMA)** is a law enacted in many states that lets you leave assets to a minor by appointing a custodian. In most states, the minor receives the assets at legal age.

**Unincorporated association** is an association of two or more persons who have not adopted a legal business form. Since the individuals are conducting business without having the benefit of a liability shield, such as through corporations, LLCs, or the like, they are legally partners and, thus, have full personal liability for the debts and other obligations of the business.

# V

**Venture capital** is funding obtained from business speculators who provide money in exchange for ownership interest, control, and other defined benefits of the business. Since venture capitalists frequently provide large sums of money in a single block, they are customarily in a position to extract more rewards than individuals or businesses that invest modest amounts. Many venture capitalists were "burned" by the so-called "technology meltdown" and, thus, the availability of venture capital today is limited.

**Venue** is the legal requirement imposed in litigation defining the specific court where a case must be filed and tried.

**Vesting** is the process whereby an individual's interest in a retirement or pension plan is secured. For example, many pension plans provide that plan participants are "vested" 20 percent per year for five years; thus, an employee who leaves the company after three years will be 60 percent vested and entitled to receive only 60 percent of the amount that would otherwise have been available to a fully vested participant.

**Voting trust** is an arrangement whereby shareholders or owners of interests in other business entities pool those interests and agree to have them voted in a particular way. These are typically formal arrangements embodied in technical documents that comply with the business code of the state in which the entity is created.

# W

**Warranty** is a form of guarantee that is either expressed or implied by law and provides protection to the purchaser when the characteristics warranted are not present.

**Warranty deed** is a document that allows you to transfer title to real estate. With a warranty deed, the person guarantees that the title being transferred is clear (free of any encumbrances). If the title is defective, the person making the transfer is liable. Compare to *quitclaim deed.*

**Waste** is the abuse, destruction, or permanent change to property by someone who is merely in possession of that property. This means that the trustee cannot allow the property to fall into disrepair, make permanent changes to the property, or otherwise destroy the property in the trust.

**Will** is a written document with instructions for disposing of assets after death. A will can only be enforced through the probate court.

**Winding up** is the process whereby a business completes its activities and prepares to end its operations. This can be a technical dissolution and liquidation.

**Works made for hire** is the copyright term used to define works created by employees within the scope of their employment, or by independent contractors whose work is specially ordered or commissioned and the arrangement is embodied through a written contract, which arrangement falls into one or more of the categories enumerated in the statute.

**World Intellectual Property Organization (WIPO)** is a multinational organization created for the purpose of administering the interface of copyright laws between its member nations.

# XYZ

**Zoning** is the government's designation of limitations on the use of land and structures. Classic examples of zoning laws are those that prohibit commercial activities in residential areas and those that prohibit individuals from living in commercial structures.

# About the Authors

**Leonard D. DuBoff**, founder of the law firm the DuBoff Law Group, PC, graduated magna cum laude from Hofstra University with a degree in engineering, and summa cum laude from Brooklyn Law School, where he was the research editor of the *Brooklyn Law Review*. He was a professor of law for almost a quarter of a century, first teaching at Stanford Law School, then at Lewis & Clark Law School in Portland, Oregon. He also taught at the Hastings College of Civil Advocacy and lectured for the AAA of the Hague Academy of International Law. He is the founder and past chairperson of the Art Law Section of the Association of American Law Schools; the founder and past president of the Oregon Volunteer Lawyers for the Arts; the former president of the Tigard, Tualatin, and Sherwood Arts Commission; past member of the board of the Oregon Committee for the Humanities; former Special Projects Coordinator for the National Endowment for the Arts; and a recipient of the governor of Oregon's prestigious Arts Award in 1990. DuBoff has testified in Congress in support of many laws, including the Visual Artists Rights Act of 1990. In fact, he assisted in drafting that law as well. He is also responsible for drafting and testifying in support of numerous states' art laws and is a practicing attorney specializing in the field of art law, business law, and publishing law. DuBoff was on the task force that drafted the Oregon Corporation Code, Oregon Nonprofit Corporation Code, and began work on the Oregon LLC statute. He has represented numerous prominent businesses as well. His scholarly articles and books are frequently cited by courts and commentators. DuBoff is a pioneer of the field of art law and remains one of its most important and influential scholars in that field. He is a prolific author of law review articles and other publications as well and has written numerous books on art law, business law, and other related subjects. For more information about his writing, you can consult Amazon.

**Amanda-Ann Bryan** graduated from Brigham Young University with a degree in music and received her master's degree in writing with an emphasis in book publishing from Portland State University. She graduated magna cum laude from Lewis & Clark Law School with a certificate in intellectual property law. Amanda was the National Jurist Law Student of the Year for Oregon and was the recipient of numerous academic scholarships and awards. She was the ghostwriter for a book on entertainment law while in law school and edited a case book on copyright law. She is a practicing lawyer, representing clients from all over the world, specializing in intellectual property including copyright, trademark, and related subjects. Amanda ran a digital publishing services company for many years, has taught digital publishing, ebook production, and legal publishing at Portland State University, and has presented continuing legal education programs for attorneys.

# Index

# Books from Allworth Press

To see our complete catalog or to order online, please visit *www.allworth.com*.